A TAPESTRY of RED & BLUE

OLE MISS SPORTS 1945-1970
AN ORAL HISTORY

Introduction by Robert Khayat

AL POVALL

For information contact Nautilus Publishing, 426 South Lamar Blvd., Suite 16, Oxford, MS 38655.

ISBN: 978-1-936-946-64-8

The Nautilus Publishing Company
426 South Lamar Blvd., Suite 16
Oxford, Mississippi 38655
Tel: 662-513-0159
www.nautiluspublishing.com

First Edition

Front cover design by Le'Herman Payton. Interior design by Wil Oakes.

Library of Congress Cataloging-in-Publication Data has been applied for.

Printed in The United States of America

10   9   8   7   6   5   4   3   2   1

To Janet, always,

and to my siblings,
Patricia Povall Lewis, Amanda Povall Tailyour, and John Kirkham Povall,
who distinguished themselves, each in their own way, at Ole Miss,

and to my mother, Mary Elizabeth Povall Staub,
and my father, Allie Stuart Povall (1912-1967)
to whom I am grateful for sending all of us to Ole Miss.

To Jimmy Lear, Lyman Hellums, Cosmo Lloyd, and Farley Salmon,
great Rebels who graciously interviewed for this book
but did not live to see its publication.

I am grateful to Langston Rogers and Michael Thompson of the Ole Miss Athletics
Department for most of the photographs that appear in this book.

And finally, to
George Harrison Butler (1917-1998)
and
Lawrence Joseph Franck (1931-2014),
my friends and mentors from whom I learned so much
and whom I miss every day.

INTRODUCTION
ROBERT KHAYAT

I sat on the Baton Rouge ferry listening to the melancholy sound of its foghorn as the ferry made its way back and forth across the Mississippi River. The 1959 LSU-Ole Miss football game had ended several hours earlier, but for me, the game had not ended — would never end. As I rode the ferry, I tried to get my head around what just happened the night before — Halloween night — to my teammates and me in the confines of Tiger Stadium. During my 21 years, I had experienced personal failure, loss, pain, and grief, but nothing could have prepared me for what I saw when I looked at the Tiger Stadium scoreboard.

LSU beat Ole Miss, 7-3. Our world was turned upside down.

What would become one of the classic football games of all times, one that would live in glory if you were an LSU fan, or in infamy for Ole Miss fans, had its beginnings a year earlier, when LSU beat Ole Miss 14-0 in Tiger Stadium. In fairness, I must say that the '58 national championship LSU team was simply the better team that year. I must also admit that in the aftermath of that game, those of us who would be coming back the next year vowed that what had happened that dreary night in Baton Rouge would not happen again. So from that point forward, we were focused on Halloween night, 1959, when our chance for redemption would come.

The road to reclaiming our rightful place actually started on August 29, 1959, when we reported to campus for fall practice and the dreaded "two-a-days," which for the next three weeks would prepare us for the 1959 season. We had moved into the new athletics dorm — Miller Hall — which included an apartment for the freshman football coach, Wobble Davidson, his wife Sara, and their two children. Along with the Davidsons, we took our meals in the private dining room there: all you could eat, all of the time, with T-bone steaks available on demand. The days took on a routine that caused each day to blur into the next: sleep, breakfast, morning practice, lunch, team meeting, another practice, position meeting, dinner, sleep, get up, do it all over again. Finally, it was time to play football.

Our team rolled through the first six opponents that fall, outscoring them 189-7. That lone touchdown was scored by Tulane following a fumble on our own five-yard line. It was now time for LSU. For revenge. We attended our Sunday afternoon meeting at Coach Vaught's office riding the crest of a victorious wave. Both teams would enter the Halloween game ranked in the top three nationally. We were ready. Retribution was at hand.

The coaches practiced us in shells — no pads, no helmets, no physical contact — all week, which allowed us to rest our legs and work on details: timing, offensive and defensive game plans, punting, kickoffs, extra points, and field goals. In the shells, we felt light and fast. We got our legs back. We were ready.

Ole Miss football players and coaches represented not only the University when we travelled; we represented the entire state. So we dressed — coats and ties — and boarded the twin-engine airplane that would take us to Baton Rouge. Team buses were waiting for us at the Baton Rouge Airport and took us to the stadium for our first look at that historic venue. Tiger Stadium loomed large, right in the heart of the LSU campus, which was alive with signs and banners, with cheers and boos, with electricity. The stadium seemed as large as the Roman Coliseum, and the analogy of Christians versus lions was not lost on us as we changed into shells and took the field for a "loosening up" practice — light running, exercises, throwing, kicking, and a short talk from Coach Vaught.

It was a long night and an even longer day as we awaited the 7:30 kickoff. Then 5:30 finally came, and it was time to go to the stadium for the traditional team "walk around." We left our jackets and ties in the locker room and walked onto the field. Our first surprise came at the moment we stepped onto the field: the stadium was almost full, and a guttural roar unlike anything any of us had ever heard swept over us like thunder. Our second surprise came a moment later. There had been no rain that day, but the field was wet . Wet fields negate speed, and Coach Vaught's teams — and success — were built on speed.

Two things became apparent: any speed advantage we had over LSU would not be a factor, and we would move on hand signals rather than voice commands .

We returned to the dressing room and then went back onto the field for warm-ups. The roar had intensified to the point that it sounded like a hurricane. It would continue that way, unabated, until late in the game.

Wes "Doc" Knight was our trainer, our supporter, our nurturer, and our physical and emotional healer. Doc came to Ole Miss when Coach Vaught became head coach in 1947, and two generations of athletes would come to know and love Doc Knight. Leader of the pregame prayer, Doc would conclude his prayer with "Amen, now let's go beat the hell out of them." This night was no different, and we took the field as the stadium shook with that incomparable roar.

The game was a defensive struggle from the outset. We kicked one field goal in four, first half approaches to their goal line then settled into a war of attrition punctuated by punts. In fact, Ole Miss punted eight times (three times on first down). Coach Vaught believed that no one could drive the ball on his defense and score. He was correct. No one, including LSU, could. But LSU had given up only seven points all season too, so after the first quarter and a half, we had trouble driving the ball on them. The two defenses ruled the day, and the game slowly ground toward its conclusion, with Ole Miss holding what increasingly looked like an insurmountable lead.

With 10:59 remaining in the game, our quarterback, Jake Gibbs, punted. The ball landed on the LSU ten-yard-line and bounced ninety degrees sideways right into the arms of a surprised Billy Cannon, LSU's All-American halfback. Coach Dietzel had instructed Cannon not to field the wet ball, but when the ball kicked right into his hands, Cannon instinctively headed up field, hugging the sideline. Eight — eight! — Ole Miss Rebels hit him. Eight Ole Miss Rebels bounced off of him like tennis balls. Eighty-nine yards later, Cannon crossed the Ole Miss goal line into immortality, and we found ourselves down 7-3 with ten minutes to play.

The rest of the game is draped in the lore and legend of that far-distant Halloween night. Doug Elmore and the "Blue" team took the field and drove the ball down to the LSU seven where they had it first down, goal to go. Coach Vaught had the "Red" Team fresh and ready to go against a weary LSU defense. We waited for him to substitute wholesale, waited for him to put that group of All-SEC and All-Americans into the game to cover the last seven yards. He didn't

Two plays took us to the two. Hoss Anderson, our fullback, was stopped for no gain. It was fourth down, still from the two. Doug Elmore, our third team quarterback, called "roll out left," a quarterback sweep around left end. One of our linemen missed his block, and an LSU defender grabbed Doug's leg as he started left. Doug broke the tackle, but that aborted tackle had cost him precious momentum, and the LSU defense swarmed over him before he could cross the goal. It was over. The impossible had happened. Again.

There were many lessons to take home to Oxford from "the game." Foremost among them was that life is not always fair, that unjust things can happen to you over which you have no control, and even when you do have control (or think you do). In times like that, you learn that in spite of your best efforts, you will not always prevail — in football or in life. Those were bitter lessons for young men then, but lessons like those are always bitter. We learn them. We move on.

· · ·

This is one poignant memory of my magical time at Ole Miss. This book contains many such memories, told by the people — in their own words — who lived them, who made those memories in that golden age between 1945 and 1970. I hope that you enjoy this book as much as I have, which is far more than I enjoyed the 1959 Ole Miss - LSU game.

PRELUDE:

The War Years

WILLIAM WINTER

1940-1943

I went to all of the football games. That was a big time. We would have all of 7000 people for the Ole Miss-Mississippi State game. Harry Mehre was the coach then. I was sports editor of the *Mississippian* and I got to know him very well. He was a delightful man and was an old Notre Dame football player who had played on the 1920s George Gipp teams at Notre Dame. Coach Mehre had a droll sense of humor and one of the finest football minds of anybody in coaching. Ole Miss had not fared very well in the SEC so we hired him away from Georgia in 1938. The first game was down in Baton Rouge that fall—September of 1938, two years before I got to Ole Miss—and LSU had been the perennial champions of the SEC. Well, we went down there and won. Coach Mehre won four straight from LSU, his first four years. He had some outstanding players: Parker Hall was an All-American back. Then Merle Hapes and Junie Hovius. And in 1941 for the first and only time in the history of the SEC, Ole Miss and Mississippi State played for the SEC championship in Hemingway Stadium. Ole Miss was a heavy favorite but State won six to nothing in a game that broke my heart.

Bill Schneller was the quarterback on one of those Mehre teams, maybe the 1938 team. He made a famous interception return against Arkansas in Crump Stadium. Schneller intercepted an Arkansas pass and ran for the touchdown that beat them. As he went down the sideline, just before he crossed the goal line, he turned and thumbed his nose at the Arkansas team, and that set off one of the all-time big riots in Crump Stadium history. As Harry

Mehre was walking off with his team, he said this big burly fellow with an Arkansas pin on came up to him and said, "Hey fellow, where're you from?" And Mehre said "Arkadelphia." All Arkansas had to do was run the clock out but they passed inside their own twenty yard line and Schneller intercepted and ran it in for the winning touchdown. A member of the Arkansas Legislature introduced a bill to prohibit the University of Arkansas football team from passing inside its own twenty yard line.

I went to all of the games in Memphis, which is where we played most of our home games. In 1942 we played four SEC games in Memphis. In 1946 we played two or three. We just didn't play many in Oxford. Transportation made it hard to get to Oxford. We always went to the Peabody and had pep rallies there. Most of the games were afternoon games, and we'd gather at the Peabody for a pep rally then go out to Crump Stadium.

Before the war, Colonel Rebel was not a great symbol. Blind Jim was really the mascot at football games. He would come out with the team and would lead the cheers. He was almost a caricature figure who was beloved by the students and was treated well. He could go wherever they went: to the lobby of the Peabody, to various stadiums, wherever. The fact that he was black made no difference.

Author's Note: *Jim Ivey began attending Ole Miss sporting events in the late 1800s.*

LILA LEE NOSSER MCWRIGHT

1942-1947

My sophomore year (1943) there was no football anywhere but we had it my junior year. Then, my senior year, everyone started coming back. We had a football game in Memphis that year. I can remember as a cheerleader, we had not even had a chance to practice so we got up on the roof of the Peabody Hotel before the game and practiced. The game was at Crump Stadium and I can remember the soldiers in wheelchairs around the field. After the game everybody went back to the Peabody.

The boys started coming back to school that fall. That's when Bill McWright—who was to be my husband—Buddy Bowen, Roach Conerly and all of them came back. So that year was better: every time we turned around someone was coming back.

Ole Miss had a strike over Coach Harry. The team went to Florida and he didn't get to the game because he was drunk. When he came back the administration wanted to fire him but some of the boys didn't want him fired. Instead, they wanted Chancellor Butts fired. That's when this group wanted all of the students to go to Fulton Chapel and not go to classes the next day. It was right after football season and The Commercial Appeal came down and wrote an article on it. I didn't go to Fulton Chapel. Two of my friends went and they said "You've got to join with us," and I said, "I'm not going to do that." And they said you've got to come with us because we are going to strike and you need to be with us. I was running for Miss Ole Miss and I said, "I'm not going to do it. Bill McWright's mother is an educator in Columbus and she told me if we did that we might stand a chance of not being accredited as a university. It might hurt our standing." I didn't know whether it would or wouldn't but I didn't want to take a chance so I didn't do it. They said, "If you don't do this we're not going to vote for you," and I said, "Well, I can't help that. I'm not going to do it." So I barely won. You know young people will go and be a part of something and they don't even know what they're doing. They went to Fulton Chapel and I stayed in my dorm room. My dad would have shot me.

They fired Coach Harry after the 1945 season and Coach Drew came in that spring. Johnny Vaught was one of his assistants. I met the new coaches who came with Coach Drew in the spring of my senior year—in 1946. There was an assistant named Coach Whatley and there was one named Farley Johnson and one was a Coach Stone. I was crazy about all of them but I didn't know Coach Vaught. That spring we had a pep rally to welcome the new coaches. I was married and I was jumping up and down and doing a flip and I said, "I'm married. I ought not to be doing this. I can't believe I'm doing this," but I think I had just gotten married. Coach Drew and that group coached that football season of 1946 and then they left and Coach Vaught became head coach in 1947. I was a cheerleader the last time for the 1945 season.

My senior year is when I got married. Bill McWright was from Columbus Lee High. He and I were the same age. Bill had gone into the Air Force when he graduated from High School. I met him after the first Ole Miss football game in 1945. He was on that team and I was a cheerleader. Bill was a good athlete but he was slow. He played halfback but Coach Harry told him he couldn't beat a herd of turtles in a race. We liked Coach Harry but I kind was scared of him. I don't know why I was scared of him. But I tell you something about him. The paperboy told me—his name was Jerry Leavell— went to collect for the newspaper from Coach Harry and Jerry said, "I've come to collect for the paper." Coach Harry said, "Are you the one who delivers my paper every morning?" The paperboy said, "Oh yes."

So Coach Mehre left the door and went back to his room and came back to the front door and said, "Are you sure you're the paperboy before I pay you?" and the boy said, "Yessuh" so Coach Harry took the money and threw it all over the front yard and said, "Now you look for that money like I have to look for that paper every day."

I knew Robert Khayat's father, Eddie. He came up here my sophomore year as a coach and helped with the intramural sports because we had no varsity sports that year. He was very nice. Because Ole Miss had no football team that year, the Army troops played each other. We also had the Murder Bowl between the med school and the law school.

Blind Jim was an institution there. They called him the "Honorary Dean of the Freshman Class." Every football game he'd be out there and people would pass the hat and give him money. He always had on a new suit and he made up yells for every team we played. We would let him lead the crowd. The only one I can remember is the one he did for Arkansas: "With a hack saw; with a circular saw; go to hell Arkansas." He'd pause after each line, and everyone would repeat the words behind him.

I can remember putting Blind Jim on a bus in Oxford to go to Nashville to the Vanderbilt game. In Nashville, we went and got him off the bus and took him to the game. Someone else took him back and put him on the bus to take him back to Oxford. And someone met him in Oxford and got him off. Everyone took care of him. He would sit with the students at the games but usually he was standing up.

My sisters married football players: Betty—everyone called her "Boop"—married Crawford Mims and Nina married Kayo Dottley. Nina and Boop were cheerleaders three or four years between them. Crawford was an All-American and one time he asked me where my Hall of Fame certificate was. I told him it was in a drawer and he said, "Lila, you know that honor meant more to me than all of the All-American things I got. I put mine up before any of the All-American stuff." So I went and put mine up. I was really proud of it. That wasn't why I hadn't put it up. I just felt funny about showing it.

LEO BOOLOS

1941-1942; 1946-1947

Harry Mehre was the coach in 1941-1942. Charlie Conerly was on that team. He was from Clarksdale and we had played ball together in the summer. My cousin was Bill Sam, for whom the dorm is named. Bill got hurt playing football. He had a bad leg as a result of the injury and never got over it. Bill was from Vicksburg and was President of the Student Body. He was very well known and very popular at Ole Miss. Bill was killed by his own men on Saipan.

When the veterans came back from the war, the size of the University swelled. One of the main impacts was that we went from two to three in a room. The athletes had a special dorm. I think it was either Barr or Vardaman. The football players ate downstairs in the cafeteria at special tables. They gave them $15 a month laundry money.

You know, Harry Mehre went to Florida with the football team but he was drunk and we lost the game so there was a lot of flack about it. Then, there was more criticism about his ability but he got sober and we won games we weren't supposed to win.

THE GOLDEN
ERA BEGINS

WILLIAM WINTER

1946-1949

Law School

I still went to the football games when I came back to law school after the war. We didn't let law school stop us. In 1946 we had the Red Drew team, which was not a very good team. Then John Vaught, who had been one of Drew's assistants, came in 1947 when Red Drew went back to his alma mater Alabama after one year at Ole Miss. Nobody knew much about Vaught and then he proceeded to win the SEC title his first season with pretty much the same players Drew had in 1946. Of course, Charlie Conerly came into his own that year and we had Barney Poole who had been at West Point for three years, so that passing combination of Conerly to Poole made Ole Miss a very formidable opponent. The 1948 team was the Farley Salmon team and we lost one game and didn't go to a bowl. I remember they put in the T-formation that year. Clark Shaughnessy had introduced the T-formation with his undefeated Stanford team in 1940 and then after the war it was picked up by many universities, including Ole Miss. Interestingly enough, Harry Mehre in 1942 was unable to do very much with an inexperienced team so he switched to the T-formation in mid-season. He made a T quarterback out of a freshman from Memphis named Sonny Boy Shelby. Vaught stayed with the double wing his first year, however, and then Farley Salmon became the first T quarterback at Ole Miss in 1948.

MOOCH MARCUS

1943-1948

As far as I know, I am the only cheerleader ever to get a letter from the M Club. You see, I knew Coach Tad Smith and I knew different ones and the coaches from just hanging around and they thought, "Well, let's make him an honorary M Club member," so I was initiated. Ray Poole put me through the initiation. It was rough. I went through like the regular athletes. Man, they came with the paddling. We went down a line with one of them on one side and then one of them on the other and they would beat you. And then they'd take you out in the country with nothing but a towel around you and put you out. It'd take us about three hours to get back. I was a cheerleader first when they had the ASTP (Army Specialized Training Program) boys here and we didn't have football, but they had two companies, A and B, who played each other. Then, when I came back in 1944, I was a cheerleader in 1945, 1946, and 1947. You know, Dean Guess was the Dean of Men at that time and he pushed the Jewish students. Mose Wander from Charleston, Mississippi was Jewish and in the mid-thirties he was president of the student body.

Ole Miss didn't have football one year during the war. I think they restored it in 1944 and Harry Mehre was coach. One time we were playing State over there and I asked Coach Harry if I could borrow the athletic car. He said, "What do you want it for?" and I said, "Well, we got to go out here and get a plane. We're going to drop leaflets on State." He said, "Yeah, go ahead and take it." So he let me have the car and we bombarded State with it and a couple of nights later, we went over there in a car to try and paint the campus up, but some of the State boys found our car. So they said, "What we ought to do is go hide this car." The others thought that was a good idea. One of them said, "What we're gonna do, we'll start pushing and then we will just drive over here in the dark part of campus." Well it was about five of us that were from Ole Miss watching them, and I kind of whispered to them. I said, "Okay, when they start pushing, one of y'all jump in and start it up and the rest of us will get in and then we'll go back to school. So we did and they chased us all the way back to Houston, Mississippi.

Another thing was when Chancellor Butts fired Coach Harry. There were a lot of us on the campus who weren't very happy about that, so we were having a meeting in the old armory and what we were gonna do is we were gonna boycott the school and not go to classes the next day. What we didn't realize was if we had done that, we could have been kicked out of school. Coach Harry had been in Jackson and he drove back and came in and said, "Boys I appreciate what y'all are doing for me, but this is not the way to do it. Let's just let it run its course and y'all go back to school." So we did the next day and of course, they let him go. Then Chancellor Butts left and Chancellor Williams came in. The day after the Coach Harry Mehre thing I was walking around the campus and Dean Guess passed me by in his car and stopped and said, "Get in." I got in his car and he said, "I'm not going to ask where you're headed. I want to know what part you played in this." You know, he didn't have any children, and he loved the students. It was the same way when Chancellor Williams came. Dean Guess was always right there with the students. He would fight for you. If you did something wrong and you wanted to rectify it, he was the one to help you rectify it. He was a big Sigma Chi man, but he didn't show any favorites to the fraternity at all. When we reorganized Phi Ep, he gave us a room up at the Med School building to use as a fraternity room.

After they fired Coach Harry, Red Drew came in for one year with Happy Campbell. Johnny Cain was the backfield coach and the rest of them were Junie Hovius and Wobble Davidson and then John Vaught who came in as the offensive line coach. That was the best thing that ever happened to Ole Miss. During Red Drew's one season, a team completely annihilated us and the newspaper said whoever scheduled the game ought to have had to play half of it. Walking across from the cafeteria, one of the freshman told some of their fans, "You may have won the game but we haven't ever lost a party." When Alabama called Red Drew back over to Alabama, Johnny Vaught became head coach.

At one point in there during the war, we had Eddie Khayat as the intramural coach, a guy named Stone was a coach, Tad Smith was the athletic director and Jeff Hamm was the business manager. I will never forget. We played Alabama down in Mobile (1944). That's when Harry Gillmer was playing for Alabama and Jeff Hamm made me pay my way as a cheerleader to get to the game. He said, "That's the only way to do it." Back in those days, the only thing the cheerleaders got was the emblem to put on the sweater. If you got to the games, you got there yourself.

Lila Lee Nosser was a cheerleader with me. She married Bill McWright who was a football player. She lives in Greenville now. She was just a great girl, I'm telling you. A sweetheart. The funny thing is, a few years ago they had a cheerleaders' reunion and Friday night, they had a dinner party and we went to it. Lila Lee was there with her brother-in-law, Kayo Dottley, who was married to Nina Nosser. Nina was also a cheerleader and she was a pretty girl. Lila Lee was a beautiful girl. I think she may have been Most Beautiful one year and I know she was Miss Ole Miss and Hall of Fame. Another one of our cheerleaders was Sara Davidson, Wobble's wife. We had Ann Powell from Batesville, Mike Louis from Clarksdale and Bill Smith from Houston. He married one of the Hardy girls from Columbus.

We went with the team on the road but when we went, like I said, it was at our own expense. I was somewhat of a conniver so one year I went to a little store out in the country and told him that I needed some free gas. He asked what I needed it for and said, "Well, we're playing in Atlanta and I've got to get to Atlanta." So he gave me some gas and we went to Atlanta. Went on Highway 6. It took us about seven hours to get over there. We were playing Georgia Tech (1946). The quarterback from Ole Miss was Buddy Bowen from Greenville and the Tech quarterback was Dickie Bowen, Buddy's younger brother.

I played against Charlie Conerly when I was in high school at Jonestown. He played at Clarksdale and they didn't like to play us because we were country boys. They called him Roach and he was by far the most complete athlete I have ever saw: football, baseball and basketball. He could do it all. Once, the M Club decided to go to Memphis and have a big party at the Peabody. Well, the brewing company in Memphis was giving us the beer and we were going to buy the whiskey but the Peabody didn't want us to bring our own whiskey. They wanted to charge us for their whiskey, so I called over to the old Gayoso Hotel, which was right next door to Goldsmith's on Main Street, and I asked them if we could come over there. They said, "Yeah and we will even give you a party room." I said okay, and we went over there. Later, we were running out of booze so Roach said, "All right, I'll go ahead and buy the booze if y'all will vote the money out of the M Club to pay me back when we get back to school?" They all said, "Yeah, that's right. We'll do it." But I said, "Roach, don't do that. You know I'm secretary and treasurer of the club right now so as Treasurer, I can pay me my money back without a vote but if you give them your money, we'll have to have a vote to pay you back and they may not vote to pay you back so you'll just be out what you pay today." Needless to say, he didn't do it. The next morning there was glass about two inches in that hospitality room. I paid the bill for the rooms and all and I told them, "Okay boys, we're through with it. From now on, it's yours."

You know, Memphis was like home to us because we played more games in Memphis than we did in Oxford. We played Tennessee there and Coach Neyland thought he was above everybody and that Ole Miss was just a practice team for him. I will never forget, one time on a punt, they like to have had a fight there because Farley Salmon went over to catch the ball, went to signal a fair catch and they plowed into him, nearly knocking him out. The teams came on to the field and I did too. That's the same season when we were down at LSU when Conerly was playing tailback and Buddy Bowen was playing quarterback. Ole Miss kicked to LSU and Y. A. Tittle got the ball. Buddy Alliston grabbed Tittle and his belt broke. So he was running with one hand holding up his pants and the other holding the ball. He said, "If my belt hadn't broke, I would have scored a touchdown." Buddy Alliston said, "No, if your belt hadn't broke, you'd have been down where I caught you."

Well, the last play of the game, a fight broke out, and the cheerleaders had run out on the field to congratulate the players. I was out there and some guy from LSU turned me around and bopped me, so I took one of the helmets and wrapped the strap around my hand. I saw one of the LSU players and took that helmet and bopped him and then ran behind Ray Poole. He was the biggest man on the field.

We had pep rallies on campus with bonfires and in Memphis at the Peabody. The cheerleaders would stand on that fountain. In fact, they used to have a picture of us in the lobby there. We did Hotty Toddy and O,O,O,L,E. M,M, M,I, S, S. The band played "Forward Rebels" and "Dixie." "Dixie" was kind of our theme song. We took the train to New Orleans and had a parade up Canal street and then we played Tulane in the old Sugar Bowl stadium. That's when Tulane was in the Southeastern Conference. Well, Tulane had an All-American center there by the name of Bernie Smith. We had Joe Johnson at one end and a fellow named Hopper at the other end. Our two tackles were Mann and Lambert, and we had Paul Davis at center. He was from Tennessee and coached under Mehre. Paul Davis later became the head coach at Mississippi State and then was the assistant head coach at Auburn.

During that time, we had this adopted mascot, Blind Jim. He was the responsibility of the freshmen boys. They had to make sure that he got to the games. It's amazing how many games he went to. You know, in 1949, they went up to Boston to play Boston College, and when they got to the hotel, Blind Jim was there. He always said he never saw Ole Miss lose a game. He hung out on campus and it was amazing how he could tell your voice. I mean, he knew everybody by their voice.

WILL LEWIS, JR.

Boyhood

The first football game I really remember was in November of 1941: Ole Miss versus State for the SEC championship. We were favored but they had a good team. Ole Miss had not lost in the conference; maybe State had. We lost, 6-0, on what was described as a sleeper play but it was actually State running off the single wing. The blocking back took the ball, turned around with his back to the line and just sat there while all of the movement went one way and then he went the other way. His name was James Mote and he was from Greenville. It is embedded in my mind because there was such a big buildup for the game. I had been looking at the photographs of the Mississippi State team before the game and I knew at an early age not to like State. I thought they wore black uniforms because that's the way they came out in the black-and-white photographs in the newspaper, but of course they were maroon.

Pearl Harbor was about two weeks later. State did not go to a bowl that year; they had gone to the Orange Bowl the year before. Allyn McKeen was the State coach and to this day has far and away the best record of any coach that State ever had. But he ran the single wing when Ole Miss went to the T and everyone else did, too. Even though he was running some T plays they got rid of him because he didn't run the T exclusively. McKeen was a Bob Neyland disciple. After the game my father said I was crying as we walked across the bridge and he told me to quit crying. Among the players, Junie Hovius and Merle Hapes were the stars. And a guy named Rex Pierce ran the ball down the sidelines and scored but they ruled him out of bounds so it came back. And that was the big thing: people argued about whether he was out of bounds. Wobble Davidson was the captain of the Ole Miss team and was an end on that team. I asked him about the game once or twice but he didn't want to talk about it much even though it was forty or fifty years later.

I didn't miss any State games from that game until the time I went in the Army in 1958. I missed a couple there and actually I've missed a couple since that were on television. Until I went into the Army I saw them all. I remember this: after that 1941 game State beat us bad in 1942. We were sitting on wooden stands across from the press box down in Starkville and I remember the traffic jam coming back from that game with my father. We were ten or eleven o'clock getting back. My mother was very worried. The roads were primitive then. We didn't play football 1943. The 1944 and 1945 State games were great games. We won here in 1944 and in 1945 in Starkville and really shouldn't have won that game. Those weren't very good teams. State had Shorty McWilliams for the 1945 game. I'm pretty sure he had come back from West Point but he was hurt and we won 7-6 in Starkville—Harry Mehre's last game. In 1946 Red Drew won two games. Conerly was back and Ray Poole was here. People were coming back from the war and showed up here in October to play. Jerry Tiblier did that. We played State here and thought we were improving and would be a good match but State won 20-0. They scored all of their points in the first half. State had Harper Davis and Spook Murphy, who later coached at Memphis State. Spook was the captain of State's team, and Harper Davis was the star. State had another tailback named Eagle Mattalich and I remember this: he made the most exquisite run after intercepting a pass. He ran sixty yards for a touchdown through the Ole Miss team and he was cutting back at the right time. It was a pass from Conerly.

They fired Harry Mehre after the 1945 season. My family was friends with Dr. Butts who was the Chancellor. He got credit for firing him and he gave himself credit for firing him. One of the things frequently cited was that Mehre went down to Florida in 1944 and got drunk and couldn't go to the game, which Ole Miss lost 26-13. It was said that the assistant coaches locked him up in his room because he was drunk. Mehre did have bouts with the bottle. That much was known. But they didn't fire him then; he stayed on through 1945 so it wasn't just the Florida game. It must have been a cumulative thing. Mehre was a raconteur. He wrote a column for the Atlanta paper after he left here. It was really a pretty funny piece. He was a center on the four-horsemen Notre Dame team and had that Gaelic humor to him. He had been the coach at Georgia and came over here. I think they were in the process of getting rid of him over there because Wally Butts was given credit for pushing him out. Mehre had been fairly successful there and he was successful here. He came in 1938 and after we had not had good teams he had winning teams in 1938, 1939, 1940 and 1941 and he was particularly adept at beating LSU. He went down to Baton Rouge a couple of times and beat them. Mehre was here in 1943 and coached the Army Special Training Program guys. In 1943 nobody in the SEC had a team but Georgia Tech and Tulane. The Army program had guys who were non combatants. They would come through here and train to be company clerks. We called them the ASTP guys. They would stay nine or twelve weeks or something and Mehre would get up a football team. Eddie Khayat Senior was one of his assistants and Goat Hale was here. Eddie Khayat was a coach on the coast and he was a known quantity and of course he taught his sons to play football. When he left here I don't think he ever went back to coaching.

Mehre brought the Catholic boys down here. Hapes was from California but his brother had played here in the mid-thirties Schneller was from up in the Midwest.

Most of the vets didn't get back for the 1945 season but were back for the 1946 season. One thing about the war years, you could walk around town and there was nothing going on, but there was particularly nothing going on on campus so we just had the campus as our playground: the YMCA, the gym, the field house. Then, when the veterans came back and started playing football—we were all athletically persuaded—we'd hang out at the field house. When things first got started they didn't have any trainers to pick up stuff on the field. There was a black guy named Luke who seemed to do everything and he'd ride a tractor around with a trailer behind it. We'd pick up the equipment and throw it in there. But you could walk in the field house and talk to these people who were willing to talk to a kid, so that cemented my interest in and fascination with the Ole Miss football team.

After the war they not only listed your height, your weight, and what position you played on the game program, but also the branch of service you had served in. That was important. In 1947 we had 53 men listed on the program and 35 were veterans of the Marines, the Army, the Air Force or the Navy. In 1948, 52 were on the roster and 27 had served. Billy

Gates once put out a brochure about the 1948 team telling exactly what some of these players did in the service and the ones that stick out are like Bobby Oswalt. He flew the maximum number of missions in the Army Air Force and was a third string quarterback who kicked extra points. He was highly decorated. Buddy Bowen flew Corsairs off of carriers in the Pacific, flew fifty missions, and then was back here playing football. Dixie Howell, they called him Sarge. He had been a sergeant in the Marines and had seen extremely difficult combat out there according to Wobble Davidson, who was also out there. Dixie Howell was right in the middle of it and came back and played football. Having had that experience, if Oswalt was kicking extra points and missed one, well it wasn't the worst thing that ever happened to him by a long shot. He had seen a lot of life.

In the 1947 roster, they give the ages of the players and it ranges, from Babe Pearson from Clarksdale who was 17 to Bill Erickson who was 26 years old, nine years difference. Erickson had been in the Marines. Wobble was also in the Marines. He called himself the Dean Guess of the South Pacific. Dean Guess was the man in the YMCA who kept up with everyone when they graduated. Wobble had a mission of contacting these veterans of the war out there. Billy Sam was a Marine. He was President of the Student Body, a halfback, who was killed on Saipan. He was Lebanese, from Vicksburg. Wobble was on the same island and knew about it when it happened. Wobble was an officer and Sam was an officer. Dixie Howell was enlisted. Buck Buchanan was 25 and he was in the Marines and had a distinguished career.

Barney Poole was on the 1948 team and that was his seventh year of college football, a national record. He had played three at Ole Miss, one at North Carolina and three at Army. He played on the undefeated Army teams with Blanchard and Davis and played for the national championship. His last year up there was in 1946 because he came back here and played in 1947 and 1948. Wobble said Barney made a big mistake because if Barney had gone on to the pros after West Point, which he had a chance to do, he could have made a living playing pro football. After two more years in college, he didn't play pro football and I don't know whether he even tried out.

Wobble was very resentful of any guys who stayed in the States and played for these service football teams and therefore didn't get into combat like Wobble did. He said some of them had crawled across Europe on their stomachs getting shot at all the time and these other people stayed home and played football. And that was the rule. For example, Shorty McWilliams went to Army and Arkansas's star, Clyde "Smackover" Scott, went to the Naval Academy and was an All-American, then came back and played for Arkansas. That time in the academies didn't count against your eligibility. Smackover was plenty good and was also a medalist in the 110 meter hurdles in the London Olympics in 1948. He got the name from his home town, Smackover, Arkansas.

Coach Vaught was an officer in the Navy. Wobble didn't like Vaught at all—Wobble was probably the only coach Vaught fired here or maybe it was a mutual parting—and, according to Wobble, Vaught was coaching somewhere and got wind that you could get these commissions if you knew the right people. So he went to North Carolina Pre-Flight and when the war was over, Red Drew got the job here. Someone who knew Vaught recommended him to Drew as the line coach so when Red Drew decided to take the job at Alabama, of course, Vaught was named head coach here. Wobble greatly resented the fact that Vaught was coaching in the States while these other boys were getting shot at and killed overseas. I think Vaught learned the T at North Carolina under Jim Tatum and Bear Woolf. He went on to Corpus Christi and maybe was a head coach there or up at Providence.

When the veterans came back we would go out there for practice. Grade school didn't start until late September and the football players would come in early, so we just went out there and hung around. They really pushed them to get into shape. There was one—Hunter Gates, a guard from Jackson—who had been a POW in Germany and he played on the 1946 team. He was in the Army Air Force. And another one got shot down and avoided capture. He went underground and finally made his way back and then came back here and played football. And you know, if they lost a game, it certainly was not the worst thing that ever happened to them.

With Drew they ran the Notre Dame Box and the single wing and he went two and six so everyone was glad to see him go. We got beat by Mississippi State in 1946. That year, we had Conerly and Barney Poole, and some of the young ones like Farley Salmon were coming on. Buddy Bowen flew those fifty missions in the South Pacific during the war and here he is playing football in 1946, 1947 and 1948. He was married to Mary Ann and lived in a house on University Avenue, two or three houses toward town from where the museum is now. Right there where that two-story condominium development is now. The story is that Buddy kind of took it easy. He was late coming out to campus to catch the bus for one game so they pulled the bus up to his house on the way to Memphis. Vaught went in the house and got Buddy and put him on the bus and they went to Memphis and played the game. Buddy also had a launderette at that time and he and Mary Ann ran it. Buddy won the Jacobs Trophy as the best blocker in the SEC in 1947. He was 25 years old. The next year they went to the T and he was still on the team but of course they had no blocking back. Buddy was kind of slow so he didn't fit and didn't get to play a lot.

I was out there the day that Barney Poole set the record for passes caught in a season against Chattanooga. Scrappy Moore was a big buddy of Vaught's; they turkey-hunted together, as did Vaught and Spook Murphy. It was a breather before State and whatever number Barney needed to break the record, Conerly just threw these little short passes to him to break the record. The papers picked up on it and Walter Stewart or maybe David Bloom were critical of the way that Poole broke the record. The next year with Farley Salmon at quarterback out of the T, Barney caught maybe fifteen or so passes because they didn't throw and Farley was so small he couldn't see over the line. Maybe that's why the pros didn't go after him.

Vaught ran the Notre Dame Box in 1947. They'd line up in a T and one of the halfbacks would shift down the line behind one of the ends and the fullback would be back. Conerly was the left half, but the right halfback would cross in front of him and it was innovation because Conerly was always back to pass. Conerly was always going to receive the snap. The right halfs were Jerry Tiblier and Farley Salmon. John "Honey Boy" Shelby was a right half along with Cecil Dickerson and John Bruce, who had been the hero when we beat State in 1945. Tiblier and Farley Salmon were the right halfs and weren't blocking backs. So the way it was: the QBs were Buck Buchanan and Buddy Bowen and they would shift away from under center and the snap would go straight to Conerly. They would run counters and Conerly would throw. They threw from the beginning. His ends were Barney Poole and the Stribling brothers. They had a guy named Everette "Hairline" Harper, called Hairline because he was very thin. He had been in the Army Air Force during the war. He graduated from Law School in 1947 and was playing football while he was in Law School. Bobby Jabour was a sophomore quarterback and he was in med school while he was playing. He was 26 years old and had served in the Navy.

We beat State over in Starkville bad in 1947 and we beat Tennessee for the first time ever. That game was in Memphis. Bob Neyland said Conerly was the best tailback he'd ever seen and he was glad he was graduating. I went to Memphis in 1946 and saw us beat Arkansas, one of the two games we won. Clyde Scott played for them. We won that game 9-7 on a safety. The next year, 1947, we lost to Arkansas in Memphis before a sellout. Tennessee was a sellout and we lost our other game to Vanderbilt. That was the year that we had a pass from Conerly that bounced off one receiver to another receiver who ran it in for a touchdown but it was against the rules then and that beat us. I didn't go to the Delta Bowl. It was very cold and it was on the radio and during the day you could listen to the games out of Memphis but you couldn't get those stations at night so you'd go to the Square where they would have speakers set up. Everyone would honk their horns when we scored.

COSMO LLOYD
(JANUARY 25, 1927 - MAY 30, 2015)

1944-1949

We had some great train trips to football games, and I made all of them. One of the things I remember very closely is that we played Vanderbilt at Vanderbilt Memorial Stadium in 1947. We won the SEC, and it was one of two games we lost. The score was 10-6 and we also lost to Arkansas, but that was a non-conference game. The stadium was full at Vanderbilt but Coach Vaught made them put some folding chairs down on the track at field level for Ole Miss students, and that's where I sat for that game. They called an Ole Miss touchdown back because of a rule that has since changed. The rule then was that two offensive players couldn't touch the ball on a pass and have it complete. Now, today, ten offensive players can touch it and it's still a valid completion. Roach threw the ball to Joe Johnson and Joe scored, but an Ole Miss offensive player had tipped the pass and then it had bounced into Joe Johnson's hands. Joe scored but they called it back. It was right within the rules then. Now it would have been okay. That cost us the game. We won the SEC anyway, but 10-6 was that score and it was the only SEC game we lost that year.

When I got there in 1944, my friend Jerry Tiblier who was on our high school football team here in Jackson, was an excellent football player. That great big guy, Harry Mehre had a little rain hat that he wore in practice and I remember one day, Jerry broke loose in practice and ran and got out in the open field and tripped and fell. Harry Mehre took that hat off and threw it down and started jumping up on top of it. He weighed about 240. Oh, yeah, he was big. And he jumped up and down and smashed that hat, then he put it on his head and he said, "Wait just a minute," and he ran down there where Jerry fell. Coach Mehre picked up a blade of grass and dropped it on his shoe and acted like he had tripped. Then he said, "NOW RUN IT AGAIN!" I thought that was the funniest thing I had ever seen. Coach Mehre was a riot. He was a big joker. He had some good teams but kind of tailed off there at the end. Well, I don't remember exactly where he went, what he did, but I remember we beat State 13-8 that year in 1944, and Jerry intercepted a pass on the last play in the end zone to save the game.

And then Vaught came. I saw most of the games. One year, I saw thirteen games in one season and my roommate saw fourteen. We had Conerly in 1947 running the single wing and then Vaught went to the "T" with Farley Salmon. And Dixie Howell. I don't know what his first name was, but everybody called him Dixie. We also had Killer Erickson. Bill Erickson was a Yankee from New York, and he was a really good football player. He played tackle.

JACK YATES

1945-1946; 1948-1951

Blind Jim came to all of the ballgames. People thought the world of him and all he'd do was kind of stand there and wave. The students loved him and treated him well. I don't remember seeing him during the week and rarely saw him around campus. I saw him just at football games and someone would always get him there. We had pep rallies every Friday night. That was a lot of fun. They had a big bonfire and the students would gather round and have a big time, cheering and carrying on. Buddy Bowen had been the best blocking back in the SEC the prior year but when Johnny Vaught went to the T in 1948, Buddy was no longer a starter because he didn't fit the new offense. Buddy was a good friend and fraternity brother of mine. He had been in the Navy and then came back. Great guy. Those guys who were in World War II had been in terrific battles and within a year they were back in a classroom or playing football. What a change. They were three or four years older than most of the students and had to make a big adjustment.

HARTER WILLIAMS CRUTCHER

1952-1956

My father was J. D. Williams, Chancellor of the University from 1946 to 1968. The administration when we came was Chuck Trotter, who was a main one. Jeff Hamm was the business manager of the Athletic Department. Johnny Vaught became the football coach the year after we came. Tad Smith was the Athletic Director and was our first guest who ever came to see us. He took my family all over the stadium.

Coach Vaught took over Daddy's second year. I was part of that conversation but I was just listening. You see, I was an only child. Mother and Daddy had been married ten years when I came along so they were well into their lifestyle and they didn't want it upset. The fact that I was an only child meant that all I had to learn was how to go along to get along. And so often I was just on the sidelines listening. I remember that conversation well. We weren't doing real well with the coach who had been there and Daddy said, "This is a time of great change for the University because we have all of these returning veterans and we've got to have housing for the military. We have to have a really first rate faculty to get this place on the map and to do that we need a lot of money." Well, we were a poor state so Daddy thought we needed a good football program. Daddy had started out being a basketball coach as well as principal and he knew the power of athletics so at that time he said, "We're going to find the best coach we can and we're going to pay him whatever it takes to get here because that's the way we're going to build the program. Then people will start noticing us and then they'll start giving us money." And it worked.

Coach Vaught came in with a bang. He didn't waste any time. He understood what he was supposed to do and he did it. Daddy had a good relationship with Tad Smith and he had a good working relationship with the faculty. That was one of the things that was really important to him. And with the student body. He was real close to the student body and a lot of the dinners we had were for different members of the student body. We entertained a lot.

Daddy and Mama and I went to the away football games. Daddy loved sports and went to the baseball, basketball and football games. He thought it was real important to have a presence at all of those events. Daddy was big on personal presence. Mrs. Carrier would sit with Daddy at football games. She would show up just before kickoff down on the track around the field in her big Lincoln Continental. People would comment on that and wouldn't like it and Daddy would say, "Well, you know what, if you will give us a building..."—the Carriers had given Carrier Hall—"we will let you come on the football field."

LAUCH MACGRUDER

1946-1950

My first football team was the Red Drew-coached team of 1946. It wasn't a very good team but I went to every game I could get to because I loved football. I went to Memphis for the games there, the big deal of the semester. Sometimes I hitchhiked and sometimes I'd be lucky and catch rides and sometimes they had special buses. When we played Tulane, we had a train that picked us up right there on the campus and took us to New Orleans and back again. There wasn't that much drinking on the train. I was real naïve. I knew about drinking because my parents would have a cocktail most evenings but it didn't mean much to me.

I was a cheerleader and for cheers, we did Hotty Toddy and we'd spell Ole Miss and Rebels and "Go Rebels Go" but Hotty Toddy was prevalent. It had been around since the 1920s, I understand. I liked football so well and I figured that was a good way to stay close to the game so I went out for cheerleader. There were judges who whittled down the number of people trying out and then there was an election. That was the fall of 1946 and I did it again 1947. 1947 was the year that Coach Vaught and I together won the SEC. I used to kid Johnny about that and say, "Don't ever forget you and I did it together."

The 1947 team opened with Kentucky and won 14-7 and went on. We weren't anticipating anything like the success we had. Vaught took the same players Drew had the year before and won the SEC. A lot of them were veterans, including Charlie Conerly. I knew a number of them. I knew Charlie and Barney and Ray Poole and Bernard Blackwell and some of them from the dorm because they lived in the regular dorms that year. I knew Buddy Bowen well. We courted the same lady for a while—Sabin Blankenship, a beautiful girl from Tuscumbia, Alabama. She stayed just one year. I would kid Buddy, see him in the Grill and I'd walk up to him and say you're dating my girlfriend and you better just back off. My friends thought I was nuts the first time I did it but we were we good friends. Then he took up with Mary Ann. She was our speech teacher. The players took their meals in the cafeteria with everyone else. I had some interaction with Coach Vaught. I hung around the football team and then as a cheerleader I saw him a good bit.

The 1947 season, I remember the Tennessee game in Memphis. On a kickoff Vaught ran a reverse and either Jerry Tiblier, Helen Henry's first husband, or Dixie Howell got the handoff and ran all the way back for a touchdown. I was looking across the field and when he crossed the goal line, General Robert Neyland kicked this blackboard thing they had on a stand about ten feet. That was exciting. At that time, Tennessee was a predominant team in the South and the country. Conerly had a career day and I tell you, Charlie was a tough monkey. He had been a Marine in combat and he wasn't all that big, certainly not heavy, but he could take whatever they gave him. In fact, I used to say that if he hadn't been the toughest guy on the earth he wouldn't have made it with the Giants because the first three years their only play was snap the ball to Conerly and kill him. They had no offense and he took a beating every Sunday. Conerly punted, did everything. He was also a heck of a baseball player. Buddy Bowen was the blocking back. He'd played some in the service. He was another tough one. You couldn't stop him if he had his mind on what he was going to do. He was stocky and strong and one heck of a blocker. Buddy made All-SEC.

PERIAN CONERLY

CHARLIE CONERLY

I met Charlie when I was lifeguarding at the Clarksdale pool. It was the summer of 1947, the summer before his senior year. Farley Salmon introduced us, and we went out that night with Farley and his date. I had never known Charlie. He was five years older than I was, and our paths had just never crossed, but I had gone to church with his sisters. We didn't know where his nickname—Roach—came from. He got it as a child. He played for a baseball team that everyone called the "Roaches," because when they were asked who they played for, they would say "I play for Roach's team."

In 1946 most of them had come back from the war and had done pretty much whatever they wanted. In 1947 they came back from the summer and got together and said, "We're going to do better." Coach Vaught took over at that time from Coach Drew. Coach Drew was pretty relaxed and he let them do pretty much whatever they wanted. They could go in and out of the game on their own. And then under Coach Vaught they won the SEC in 1947.

Charlie had a great experience at Ole Miss and made friends with guys he stayed in contact with. Ray and Barney Poole and Farley Salmon and really all the other guys he played with. Ray and Barney both played with him at the Giants. Jimmy Patton came along but he was a little younger. He was a wonderful player.

Charlie was a really good baseball player. I think he batted either .427 or .447 his senior year. He also punted for the football team and did it two years with the Giants. At Ole Miss he had to play two ways some and he played defensive back. He didn't like punting with the Giants. Charlie always said there was no one to blame if you messed up unless the center snapped it over your head. Tom Landry took it over when he came to the Giants from the New York Yankees old American Football League football team, which broke up when that league went under.

Landry was a defensive back and was like a coach on the field, and then be became the defensive assistant. Vince Lombardi was the offensive coach. He and Wellington Mara were good friends, and Vince had head coach written all over him. Jim Lee Howell was the head coach at the time and kept threatening to quit but wouldn't, so Lombardi left to go to the Packers the year before Jim Lee quit or he would have been head coach of the Giants.

Charlie had a great time at Ole Miss.

STELLA CONNELL SALMON AND FARLEY SALMON
(APRIL 20, 1926 - JUNE 7, 2015)

1945-1951

Farley: I grew up out about sixteen miles from Clarksdale and played football at Coahoma High School. The reason I came to Ole Miss was because, growing up, they were willing to play smaller guys. Junie Hovius and Ray "Little" Hapes were both small. I graduated in an accelerated class from high school in February of 1945 with several good friends who were going in the service but I came over to Ole Miss and stayed until April. Then I went in the service and six months later, I came back. It was in

November of 1945. I was on campus one week and they put me in the Ole Miss-Tennessee game. Tennessee beat us 34-0 and the next week we played State. There were twelve guys from Clarksdale on the two teams. State was highly favored, but we beat them 7 6. That was Harry Mehre's last game. I loved Harry Mehre. He was a great guy, a big, heavyset guy. He came to Clarksdale once and some alumnus had him out to his house and Coach Harry had too much to drink. It hurt his recruiting because a lot of the Clarksdale mamas didn't want their sons playing for him. I heard that he had gotten drunk before the Florida game but I never heard that he fell off the bench.

I played for Red Drew in 1946 and Coach Vaught was the line coach on that team. We always looked up to Vaught. He was the rock even though he was an assistant. Vaught was an unusually good man. When he took over in 1947, number one, he was the boss. There wasn't any fooling around on the players' part. All of that stopped. Coach Vaught—I loved the man—was very fair. I was prejudiced because he didn't care what size you were. As long as you could run and play and do what he wanted you to do, you were okay. In 1947 he ran the single or double wing with Conerly and I played halfback. Buddy Bowen was the block-ing back. That was the year we went to the Delta Bowl. It was freezing cold. Seven degrees. We beat TCU in a close game.

Vaught's practices were harder than Red Drew's. We did a lot of hitting. Coach Vaught was a firm believer in hitting. If you could knock the other guy down you were in good shape. And he expected you to play through pain. He didn't believe in being hurt. Next to my own father, I was closer to Coach Vaught than anyone I've ever known. He was a great guy. Wobble was the guy we were scared of. I never had him as a coach because I was a sophomore when he got there. But he was a terror for the freshmen. We lived in the athletic dorm, Heddleston, and Wobble and Sara lived on the first floor.

I was the first T-formation quarterback in Ole Miss history and I think in the SEC. I played both football and basketball and lettered in both. I don't know how Coach Vaught learned the T formation. He coached the quarterbacks and could teach technique. Coach Vaught was well-informed man and he knew how to motivate kids. In the split T, I would take the ball, turn to one side or the other and either handoff or fake and then keep and run. We didn't throw much; threw just enough to keep them honest. The year before, Roach had thrown a lot.

In 1948, when I was the quarterback, Barney Poole was still playing. Dottley was there. He was a good ballplayer. Mustin was there. He was a character. Mustin talked constantly.

Sometimes I thought he was crazy. They put him in the same room with Charlie Conerly. I don't think Mustin had ever been out of Canton until he came up to school. We went to some function where we had to wear a tie and he didn't own one so I loaned him one. When I tied it for him and began to pull up the knot, he hollered because he thought I was choking him. Charlie was a very quiet man. Roach and I could spend a week together and not talk. Charlie said, "I'm going to Coach Vaught about Mustin." He said he couldn't take it. So we went to Coach Vaught's office and Roach said, "Coach, you got to get Mustin out of here." Coach Vaught said, "Oh, all of these guys are back from the war and there isn't any room and I don't know where I'd put him." Charlie said, "It's me or him." And he grabbed me by the arm and turned around and walked out. Well, Mustin was out of the room before we got back.

The equipment was primitive but at the time I thought it was great. We had leather helmets. No protection for the face. I never got hurt that much. My mother said when you get hit, jump up so I'll know you're not terribly injured. And I always did that. I wanted to be sure I wasn't dead. But quarterbacks never got hurt. The linemen got hurt. And the blocking backs. Doc Knight was the trainer. What a great guy. He would give the most devout prayer and then say, "Now go out there and beat the hell out them!"

After I got out, I scouted the 1952 Maryland team for Coach Vaught. He just asked me to do it, and I was so close to Coach Vaught, I'd walk to hell for him. I've forgotten how many Maryland games I scouted but there were quite a few. I was living down here so we just travelled up there for the games. I remember going to the North Carolina game. Maryland had a big tackle named Dick Modzelewski and I picked up on the way they did their spacing on defense. On offense I saw that the quarterback, Scarbath, always looked the opposite way from which he was going to go. If he looked left he was going right. It was just a habit he had and luckily, I picked up on it. In our game with them, we were ahead and at the end of the game they passed from their own end zone and completed it. Coach Vaught called up to me in the coaches' box and said, "You told me they would never pass that far back. You told me they weren't going to do that. What in the world?" He jumped all over me. But the reason was that in all of the games I'd seen, they were never behind so they never had to pass down in their own end zone. But against Ole Miss they were desperate. He jumped on me on that phone. I mean it.

I introduced Perian and Charlie Conerly. She was Perian Collier and was lifeguard at the local pool across the street from where Charlie and I were working out. He looked over there and saw her sitting on the tower and said, "Who is that?" and I told him. He said, "Come on. You're going to introduce me." I took him across the street and introduced them. It was love at first sight. And that was it for both of them. She was younger and Roach had been in the service so they didn't know each other.

Stella: When Perian wrote her book, Farley told her to put a picture of herself on the cover in a negligee and call it "My Twelve Years as a Pro." Perian went to MSCW and Farley would go down to Columbus with Roach to see Perian. When I think back about Ole Miss I think of the people throughout the state and the friendships we made that have lasted a lifetime, people we've met and kept up with all of these years.

Farley: For me, it was a maturing thing, my first time away from home. I looked up to the upper-classmen. There was no hazing when I was a freshman. I didn't get into it. We lived together and ate together. We were close. I made life-long friends with football and basketball players. I was also a KA with Cosmo Lloyd and all of those guys, but I didn't have time for the fraternity. With me it was all sports.

WILL LEWIS, JR.

Boyhood

The 1948 team beat Tennessee in Memphis when they were really good. Mustin and Tiblier were back in dual safeties for the kickoff and Mustin handed off to Tiblier who ran it for eighty years to win the game. That was a Vaught innovation. The big thing was the University was 100 years old and the homecoming game was Vanderbilt. We had parades for the 100th birthday and there was a big crowd here. They were tough. We were behind the whole game. The stadium seated about 25,000, and we were behind 7-6 when Farley made a beautiful run. We went up 13-7 and then we scored again late on an interception to win it. They carried Farley off the field. The only game we lost that year was to Tulane and we didn't get a bowl bid. The reason was we just didn't have the ticket base and they wanted someone who could draw in the Sugar Bowl. And then we had bad years and didn't go anywhere. 1949, 1950, and 1951 were rough years and in 1952 we began coming out of it a little bit. Vaught said in his book that he was going to be fired all those years if he didn't beat State but he did beat them all of those years. We didn't lose to State from 1946 to 1964.

BUBBER BLACKWELL

1946-1951

I grew up in Memphis and graduated from high school there. In 1942 they dropped the draft age to eighteen so I was drafted in December of 1942 and went into the Army. I served in Europe beginning right after D-Day and got back from the service Christmas Eve of 1945. On January 3, 1946, I went down to Ole Miss. Wobble Davidson took me in to see Red Drew and said, "Bubber's here and we need him as a trainer and manager at the field house." Red said, "I see you're red-headed like I am so all we need is for Tad to say the same thing." I went right in to see Tad Smith and Tad said, "Oh yeah, you start right now." So I started to work as a manager in January of 1946. It was my second stint as a manager because I had worked there first back in 1941. I ended up staying there the second stint for five years. I had known Wobble in Memphis. We went to the same high school. He was about three or four years older than I was, but we had been good friends from having gone to Southside High School.

Harry Mehre was a showman. In other words, he would put on some kind of an act to get his point across. I learned later that they had some problems with Mehre before he had resigned. At the Florida football game down there he didn't show up until the half. He was still at the hotel and he showed up at the half looking for the team. Let's just say he was under the influence.

The 1946 football team was not very good. The only game that stands out from the 1946 season is the Arkansas game. They had promised Red Drew the head coaching job over there and he didn't get it even though he had gone over there to sign up, so he really prepared for them. Arkansas had a good running back at that time named Kenny Holland, who had played at Central High School in Memphis. Coach Drew got fired up at the team talk before the ball game and raised his voice beyond normal. We won when Conerly hit Hairline Harper in the end zone with one of those long stretch-out catches. Hairline was from Pascagoula or Moss Point. That win was the year for Coach Drew. It meant so much to defeat the team that turned him down.

The 1947 team was practically the same as the 1946 team. Dave Bridgers was the center,

Blackwell and Crawford were the guards, and Erickson and Roland Dale were at the tackles. Hairline Harper was one end and Barney Poole at the other. The backfield was Conerly, Buddy Bowen at blocking back, and so forth. The big difference was that John Vaught was the head coach. The main difference between Coach Vaught and Coach Drew was that we really didn't know Coach Drew. He was an older gentleman but Vaught was just a few years older than I was, so there wasn't a big age difference like there was with Coach Drew. Coach Vaught was well accepted because he came in the dormitory the night he got the job and said, "Now look, I'm committed and I want all of you to be committed, too." That was up at Heddleston "B."

Before going out on the field, and at the halftime, Vaught was more or less the one to go around and talk to the individuals as they were working on the blackboard. Vaught was interested in the people at the half. Drew was just a different man.

There were a lot of veterans on both of those teams. With the veterans you had always had a captain or someone was in charge of you in the service and you did what you were told to do whether you liked it or not. And you accepted that. There were a few on the team who had never been in the service but those who did come back were able to accept discipline, or at least get around it.

Charlie Conerly was his own man. He was one of the greatest athletes I've ever been around. We lived in the same dormitory together. Charlie made up his mind to try hard for his last year at Ole Miss and he really put out. He had been in some rough combat during his service in the Pacific. But his last year he was more of a leader than just an individual player. It was a combination of Charlie making up his own mind and Coach Vaught asking him to be a leader. I played baseball with Charlie. He and Bobby Wilson were two of the outfielders. Ray Poole was on that team. Ray was a pitcher and called me his standup catcher. I was so short that I could stand up and catch him. Ray could throw a hard baseball and on one play he hit the Auburn quarterback who was also on their baseball team and dropped him right there at the plate. They were trying to get him up and as he did rise up, Ray said, "You got to stay loose. You got to stay loose." Ray went on and pitched professionally. He signed straight out of Ole Miss with the Cubs. They put him in the minor leagues at that time with Meridian and he ended up playing down there in Meridian.

Like I said, Conerly was one of the greatest athletes I ever saw and the best I saw while I was at Ole Miss He was a great hitter in baseball. Aww man, he could hit it. Left field ran all the way to the wall at the football stadium back then, and Conerly and Bobby Wilson could hit it over that wall. Conerly was just a natural athlete. Football or baseball, he could do it all. Buddy Bowen was something else. He was the blocking back his first year at Ole Miss in 1946 and in 1947, he was all SEC and won the Jacobs Trophy as the best blocker in the conference.

Farley Salmon, we called Fish. He was great, a good man. He came at the right time with the right people. He and Conerly were very close in their relationship. Fish was a communicator. He could get along with everyone. Could talk to them. Conerly was the opposite. Conerly was not outgoing like Fish. Farley was a small guy. He couldn't see over the line. He was about five-seven but he could run the T formation and that was what was needed at that time. We needed someone who could handle the ball back there and hand it off either to Dixie Howell or Bobby Wilson or Red Jenkins, who was the fullback in there.

There was a guy Vaught had up in the press box named Mike Brumbelow. He was one of the greatest coaches I've ever been around and when he would explain a play or talk to players, he knew everything about that player: his good parts and bad parts. He could see everything on each play. And I remember when he did leave, he was on the airplane going back to Texas when Ole Miss played State. The play that he set up for them to run on the opening kickoff, they scored a touchdown on and that was just because Mike had found this one weakness in State's kickoff coverage and set up a play to take advantage of it. He was Vaught's close personal friend and after he left, he ran a sporting goods store out at Texas. Vaught wanted him to quit the sporting goods business and come on as an assistant coach but he turned him down and said he had come that one year just to help Vaught get things going.

Buster Poole had arrived on campus and they hired him. They brought Johnny Cain in—he was an Alabama guy—and he replaced Happy Campbell as the backfield coach. Wobble was still here. Junie Hovius was here. And Ed Stone. We had Tad as the Athletic Director and Jeff Hamm was the finance man. He was tough on the money. They couldn't buy anything unless they got approval and he might tell them that they didn't need it. Expenses were tough back then. The head coach was making only ten or twelve thousand a year.

Bruiser was not back then. That conversation went on in the dressing room at the Arkansas game in Memphis during the 1947 season. Bruiser came in the dressing room and met Tad Smith in the training room where we were taping ankles. Tad told him, "Looks like everything's all lined up for you so whenever you're ready, we're ready for you to come back." So Bruiser came on in 1948.

There was a situation where you had three or four Yankee boys like Bill Erickson. He was one of the best tackles Ole Miss ever had. One of them came out of Ohio—I'm not going to call his name—but Wobble was the disciplinarian, no two ways about it. He had the Marine deal out there in the service and was keeping up with it. We found someone was messing around with the lockers. We think now it was this guy from Ohio because they later found that he was stealing typewriters on campus and hocking them in Memphis. He didn't stay around very long. Wobble used to check on the restrooms and he put a big sign up on the urinal where there was a button you pressed, "Press like hell to remove the smell." But he wanted everything cleaned up. When Wobble got on the bus the first thing he'd do when he got on that bus was to tell them, "You're playing for the University of Mississippi. You represent the University of Mississippi and your character on this trip will be what the University will be judged by. And not just the football team, the whole school." He had that military style, which was tough for some of the younger guys coming on, but the older guys—the veterans—knew how to accept it. That's just the way things were.

We were good in 1947 and 1948 and then we slipped. Coach Vaught realized he was going to have to change over to the new type of players coming in. These weren't military boys and you couldn't address them the same way. I heard him say one time he only assisted in getting one player and that was Dottley. Dottley got everything he ever needed. Vaught was very proud of Kayo. He said he had personally recruited him.

Sloppy Horner and Joe Gary worked with me. Sloppy was the equipment manager. Joe was from Byram and had hurt his knee so he came to work as one of the two equipment managers. I was the manager under Doc Knight, the trainer. We three were the oldest ones down there. Jimmy Crawford was one of the young men when they had all the veterans in there and he kept a bee hive out in the woods. He could handle bees that made honey. He and Bob Fuerst roomed together and every time they got ready to have a little freshmen initiation, Bob and Jimmy would go out the window and get the bee hive and put it in the window so no one would try to come in on them. Jimmy played the whole four years. He and Bernard Blackwell—no relation to me—played together. Bernie was from Saucier, and they were our two best guards. Jimmy played the whole time except he got a kidney injury down at LSU and had to stay out two or three weeks. Doc Knight had found it and held him out. Jimmy was pretty wild at first but he became a good Christian man and set a fine example in his later life.

Bernard Blackwell used to tell the story that during baseball season he'd go home and they'd say, "Well we see where you played baseball this week," and I'd tell him I used to do the same thing up at Memphis and they'd say, "We see where you had a good game in football," but it wasn't me, it was Bernard. People just got our names confused: me, Bubber, playing baseball, and him, Bernie, playing football. He was later real active in high school athletics and they named a stadium for him in Gulfport. I think the trophy for the state championship in high school football is named for him, also, and he ended up head of the Mississippi high school coaches. We were close friends.

Kayo came in there later. He played as a freshman on the varsity right off the bat. Kayo was good from the outset. He was very sociable. One time Kayo came on campus with a new car. He said that he had won the car in a contest but no one believed him. If he won it in a contest, he was the only one in the contest. I knew his wife, Nina, knew those Nosser girls. The first one was Lila and she married Bill McWright. He was an end who graduated up there in 1945. Nina married Kayo and then Betty married Crawford Mims. They called her 'Boop.'

The dressing room was down there where the Manning Room is now. Both dressing rooms were there. The Ole Miss teams dressed on the south side of it and the visiting team on the north side. The visiting team dressing room was used by the freshmen during the week but on game weekends, they had to move their stuff out so the visiting team could use it. That was in the old field house.

My jobs were student manager, trainer and baseball player. I also travelled with the basketball team. In fact, I travelled with every team they had down there. I was a handyman. Quaker Oats offered me a job as a salesman. I met with my friend at Quaker Oats in Chicago for three days so they had me lined up to go to work in Jackson, Mississippi. I got back on campus and one of the staff said, "Vaught's been looking for you." So I went over there to see Vaught and he said, "I was counting on you to stay here and get your master's degree and work with Doc Knight another year and also be freshman baseball coach." I said, "Fine, that's what I want to do," and so that's how they kept me down there my fifth year. I got my master's and I was the freshman baseball coach and worked with Doc Knight in the training room. I also travelled with the basketball team, with Bonnie Lee Graham when he was breaking in. I did everything they wanted me to do.

That's when the marriage thing happened with Coach Vaught. Dynamite Harper came in there one day and said something about his wife Jane having their first baby. And Vaught laid a couple of dollars out on the table and said "Get you a package of rubbers. That's what you need. You don't need any help with your baby. You need help on not having babies."

That was the old military way, of course. Dynamite went home and told Jane "Pack your bags, we're going home." So Tom Swayze caught up with him down at Pascagoula and brought him back. They made some kind of living arrangement for him and then Vaught put the rule in: no more marriage.

They never had anyone like Tom Swayze, because man, he was the best recruiter. Tom had been an end on the Ole Miss football team back in the early 1930s and when he recruited, he didn't start at the high school football field; he started at the principal's office. Tom wanted to see what their academic records were and if they could do the academic work. If they signed someone who couldn't pass the work, then Tom Swayze was a failure, so he wanted to know about the whole boy. Tom was able to get out and recruit. I don't think any of the other schools had anyone to recruit full time like Tom Swayze.

Showboat Boykin scored more touchdowns against Mississippi State than anyone in college football ever scored. He was a real fine player and we beat them about 49-7 in 1951. Showboat scored seven times on the same play. It was a trap play and State never did figure it out and never did stop it. Showboat was a very fine man.

Country Graham did some football scouting, too. When he came to Ole Miss, he had been coaching basketball on a junior college team. I went with him and the team down to New Orleans and he took me aside and said, "What you are doing scheduling us meals in the hotel? Who's gonna pay for it?" I said, "The University is going to pay for it." And he told me that when the junior college basketball team traveled, they always ate at the other school's cafeteria. I said, "You're in the big leagues now. You're gonna have hotel rooms and hotel food, so you've got to get away from that junior college stuff."

The GI bill paid my tuition and gave me a stipend each month. Ole Miss gave me my food and books so I was in good shape. We made some great trips: we flew to Boston to play Boston College. We went to Miami, Nashville, LSU, and New Orleans for the Sugar Bowl. When we went to New Orleans, we'd fly into the Navy Base down there. We also travelled on the train. The train would come to Oxford and we'd catch the train and go up through Holly Springs and on down through Birmingham. It'd take a day and a half to get down to Florida, but we'd fly to Knoxville and Nashville and we flew out to Fort Worth to play TCU.

My last team was in 1950 and I graduated in June of 1951. By that time Vaught's staff was pretty much in place: Bruiser, Buster, Junie Hovius, Johnny Cain, Ray Poole, and Tom Swayze of course was doing the recruiting. He worked directly for Vaught as well as for Tad when he coached baseball. And don't ever forget Doc Knight because next to Tom Swayze, he was the best thing that ever happened to Ole Miss. Doc Knight could fill in as a father, as a doctor, as a coach, as a teacher, any way that you needed help, and you could talk to him about things you couldn't talk to some of the other coaches about. He was a father figure to the boys. There is a picture of the training staff in either the 1949 or 1950 annual. Butch Lambert was on the staff, and me and Ed Horner. Joe Gary is in it. Maybe a couple of more. Doc had trained at Fordham and he and Vaught had been together in the Navy so Vaught brought him down there when he was getting started. When they first introduced me to him he thought my name was Bubbles instead of Bubber and he called me that from then on. He was a great friend and you couldn't find a better trainer.

What comes to mind when I look back at my time at Ole Miss is that I found the best thing that ever happened to me. I got my wife, Jeanine Pelham, down there. We've been married 67 years. Her father had the seafood business in Pascagoula where I met Dynamite Harper. I knew Ken Farragut and Rocky Bird and all of the Pascagoula bunch. That's what comes to my mind. Ole Miss gave me my wife.

MARY ANN BOWEN

1945-1950

BUDDY BOWEN

The men started coming back right after Christmas in 1945, so many that we had to hire another speech teacher, so I got a friend of mine to come to Ole Miss and teach here with me, which was fun. Buddy (Bowen) was in my class. In fact he had already made a speech. I have a little piece of newspaper that I wrote his assessment on that day. I gave him a B+. Buddy was a Navy pilot. He loved flying and was in the Pacific in World War II. Then we were recalled to Korea, after we left Oxford.

I lived in an apartment off campus but then moved in with Jim and Dutch Silver—in one of the rooms they rented out—because I got tired of riding my bicycle to campus. They lived in faculty housing, maybe number 27, one of the ones they moved off campus to the new place a few years ago. So I moved in there. The friend from Wisconsin came and shared my room and we had a hoot of a time. Then, so I could date him, they put Buddy in my friend's class, or I couldn't have dated him, because we weren't allowed to date students. Jim and Dutch were talking about how many of the Delta boys and the big guys, Roach and some of them, were coming over to play football at Ole Miss. I was chaperoning a dance and the football players came in, so I said to Buddy, "I heard something about you today." I mean what a line! "Well what was it?" Buddy asked. So at that point somebody else cut in and he couldn't dance with me for the rest of that song, but he came back at the next one. I was just mad about him. It was love at first sight.

We started dating hot and heavy, I think our first date was just after the Spring Game when he had broken his nose. That was the end of March and we married June 28 of 1946 in Ohio.

A lot of the guys on the football team had served during the war and were more mature, or at least they were supposed to be. Bernie Blackwell, Red Galey, Lester Williamson, Everette Harper, Ray Poole, and Charlie Conerly, for example. It was great fun with the returning veterans. Three of us who had married football players got pregnant at the same time. Both Bernie's wife and Red Galey's wife, Ruby, had boys just two weeks before I was due. We knew there would be no chance for three boys in a row but it happened, all of us over at the small hospital on Van Buren. Jimmy Faulkner was one of Bernie's friends then, too, and he couldn't drink at his wife Dolly's house, so he would bring his bottle over to our apartment. We were in the basement apartment over there. We were double dating when I went into labor. An ice storm came and we could hardly get up the driveway. So Bo was born in 1948, after we had been married for a couple of years. That's how it all began.

When Coach Vaught took over from Red Drew, Roach was playing tailback and Buddy was playing quarterback. Buddy didn't pass then. Roach did the passing from the tailback position. I remember one of the games we played in the old Memphis Crump Stadium. It was pouring rain and Buddy's daddy was with me that day. It was so wet that we took the empty whiskey bottles that were in the stadium and put our feet on them to keep our feet out of the water.

The school paid our rent back then. This was before the NCAA started. Buddy would get a stipend for the rent and a food allowance and laundry every month. We all were on the GI Bill, and I was teaching so we were living high on the hog. I just felt like we always had lots of money but in Oxford there wasn't much to do for our age group. We ate and drank and we would go to Grundy's, which was just off the square. We would also go to the Hard Road near Sardis, and take our bottles and brown bags and stay until it was gone. The place was a honky tonk. They had music and we would dance and drink and then drive home. We had mostly football players in our group: Ray Poole and Wanda weren't married yet, and neither was Roach but we would go with them and other players and their wives. We had great fun on those trips.

NORMAN "BUDDY" SHAW

1946-1950

Vaught came in with Red Drew as the line coach and Red Drew won two and lost seven in 1946. Then he went back to Alabama and Vaught stayed and became the head coach. Vaught took that same bunch of boys and won the conference. We went to the Delta Bowl that year. I was a cheerleader at that time and we damn near froze to death at that Delta Bowl. It was in old Crump stadium and I remember I got so cold there was an appliance store next door and it was open so I would run out there and get warm and then come back. All they gave us were cotton shirts, cotton pants and cotton sweaters. I don't know why we didn't freeze to death. I saw recently in the Ole Miss alumni magazine where Nina Nosser, who was one of my fellow cheerleaders and married Kayo Dottley, had died. Betty "Boop" Nosser, I knew, and Lila was the most attractive in the whole family. They were all good-looking. I remember seeing Kayo one time at a football game and I always stuck my hand out and said my name and he said "Hell Buddy, I know you. I see you every day." I guess Nina had a picture up on the wall of the cheerleaders. I was a cheerleader with Nina my sophomore and junior years. Boop married Crawford Mims. That was a really good family. They were great people. Lila is still a lovely woman and always has been.

HAM BISHOP

1947-1951

My real name is Clarke Daniel Bishop. I was the last of six children, and Mama liked some of these famous people so she was going to name me Hamilton. But my siblings said people would call me Ham so she said, "Then I'll name him Clarke." But everyone called me Ham anyway. Hell, I went to school four or five years before I knew I had a real name. My report card even said Ham Bishop.

Tom Swayze appeared there at Drew where I grew up and recruited me in the spring of 1947 for Coach Vaught. My dad was a plantation manager out east of Drew for most of his life. I grew up out in the country and started school in the first grade at Drew then graduated in May of 1947. I was over there (at Drew) in school but somebody came in there and got me out of class and said Tom Swayze wants to speak to you. I'd already tried out over at Mississippi State and I didn't make it over there so Coach Swayze invited me up to a tryout about a week from then. I went on over there to Oxford to try out. Wobble Davidson was single, living in that old gymnasium, and they had a bunch of bunks in there. Coach Vaught was out of town but he came back the next day. There was another guy from Tennessee in there with me. So the next day we worked out—it was on a Friday—and they told me later on I had made it. They said I had a four-year scholarship. I was elated because that's the only way I could've gone to school, so I came home and told my parents and they were elated too. It didn't work out quite that way but that was the deal. At least that's what I thought the deal was.

So we went back up there June 1 and we went through six weeks of training—really they were just more tryouts—and they picked six of us to start playing varsity ball that fall. Kayo Dottley was one of them and about four or five more. Ken Farragut from Moss Point was a center. Babe Pearson from Clarksdale was one. There were maybe three more. One old boy from Memphis, he never did play and left a year or two after that. That was the last year freshmen could play varsity ball. There were about thirty-something of us and I was there from June 1 to about the middle of July then came home. Then I went back up there September 1. I was a freshman the first year Johnny Vaught was head coach and we won the SEC that year. He had been there the year before as line coach. Red Drew left and went to Alabama and they promoted John Vaught. He and Charlie Conerly were there, with Barney Poole and some more people. We lost two games—Arkansas and Vanderbilt.

I went to Ole Miss as a running back but I was a little too slow for them and so they put me at defensive end. Wobble and Junie Hovius were the freshmen coaches and the B team coaches. We played two or three freshmen games and one or two B team games. It was pretty informal back then. That's just the way they did it. I don't think there was any limitation on the number of scholarships you could give. And they could just run you off. Just like that. We called it breaking your plate. What we got was a place to live, meals, books, and I think we got free dry cleaning and laundry and maybe 28 dollars a month. I don't know how many they had on scholarship but it was a bunch and if you messed up a little bit, you'd be gone. They didn't have any qualms about it. You can't do all that stuff now that they did back then.

They had an athletic dorm—Heddleston—Garland was on one side and Mayes was on the other. At first, some coach lived there with the players so they could have a ten o'clock curfew at night and kind of keep everybody on the straight. All of the baseball, basketball and football players were living up there together. There was a scout guy from Texas and Wobble had him up there in the dorm. He was doing all of the scouting for the games and all of that and then there was someone else the next year. We were up there three years, and by this time Wobble had gotten married and had children so they went down into Garland and took over three rooms then put an outside entrance to it. Wobble and his family moved in there permanently. Before he was married, like I said, he lived in the back of that old gym. Wobble stayed in Garland with his family and rode hard on everybody the whole year. It was unlimited substitution that year—1947—and later they had a deal where you couldn't substitute but once a quarter but that was after I left. In 1947, they just ran us in and out of there. I got redshirted the next year and then I played my junior year, in 1949. In high school, we had run the single wing and the first year at Ole Miss Charlie Conerly was up there and they ran the single wing or something like the single wing. Charlie was the tail-back.

They started the freshmen off in 1947 in the split-T and the varsity went to the split-T the next year. Vaught got that from that coach up there at Missouri. And instead of lining everybody up there on the line foot to foot, they'd split, so you could take the man out and open up a hole quicker. In 1947 there would be three lined up in a T and then they'd shift into a Notre Dame Box. Vaught wanted Charlie at tailback all the time so they didn't shift him. The others would line up in the T and then shift. Charlie punted and passed and ran and hell whatever a player could do, he did it. They'd shift right and have a fullback, a block-ing back and a wingback. Farley Salmon was a small guy but he could play and the next year we had the competition in spring practice when they decided to switch everyone over to the split-T. Farley Salmon got the job of being the T quarterback. We lost one game that year, to Tulane. They were in the SEC then so we didn't win the conference. We were eight and one and didn't get a bowl bid. There were only two head coaches who won the SEC their first year and Johnny Vaught was one of them.

That first team went to the Delta Bowl. We had been up there the summer of 1947 working out and doing all of that stuff and sometime during that summer these people got the Delta Bowl together. They didn't think Ole Miss was going to be that good and I guess the Ole Miss guys didn't either so they went on and signed a contract that summer to play up there. Well, it turned out that we won the conference and got offered the Sugar Bowl—they didn't have but four or five bowls back then—so the Ole Miss people said, "Naw, we can't break the contract." They lived up to it and played TCU up there in the Delta Bowl on one of the coldest days I have ever been in. It was in Crump Stadium. We won, though, in a close game.

We had a training table but it wasn't in the dorm. That was later on. We just went down to the cafeteria. We had a food card and we let them punch that tag. Then, that fall, they had a basement down there under the cafeteria so they put us down there and we ate together. They built two or three classrooms out of that old military stuff. They had so many people who had come home from the war that they had to expand to take care of them so they built right down east of Heddleston, right down the slope. That was the athletic cafeteria. That's where we ate the rest of the time I was up there until they built Miller Hall.

There were a whole bunch of veterans on that 1947 team. I enjoyed being with them. They were older and more mature and you could just listen to them. They were about three or four years ahead of you in life and living and they had grown up a little faster but they got in shape that year and kept the training rules. After the season was over you'd see them smoking and they'd be going out to the beer joints. They had a place in Panola County about halfway to Batesville that they called the Post Office Box, but they didn't do that much. Some of them were married. They lived in Vet Village on the west side of the campus. The school administration took some more of those old barracks and made apartments out of them and that way if you were married you could get in Vet Village and have your wife and your family with you.

We had two or three of them married but still living in the dorms. One time Vaught forbade married football players but he lost some good guys doing that so they changed the rule. Charlie Conerly was about 26 when he graduated and he didn't get married until he graduated. But there were some older ones up there. Some of the basketball and baseball players were married, too.

Well, on that 1947 team Jimmy Crawford was a guard and he was a standout. Buddy Bowen was the blocking back and he won the Jacobs trophy that year. Bob Fuerst was a guard. He was from North Little Rock, Arkansas. Jimmy Clark was a tackle, Barney Poole was one of the ends. Hairline Harper and Jack Odom were also ends. Farley Salmon was on that team, as was Will Glover who was from Alabama. Dixie Howell was a back. Bobby Hemphill was playing. The center, Ken Farragut, was from Moss Point. Ed Jenkins was a fullback. Bernard Blackwell was also on that team. He was first string guard.

I wasn't on the 1948 team because I was in the Air Force at that time, but I made the 1949 team and played enough to get a letter. Ole Miss football was the hardest manual work I've ever done but I wouldn't take anything for it. I was so glad to get that letter, because there were so many who came up there and didn't make it, couldn't hang on. A lot of them would wind up over at Delta State.

The 1949 team was not as good as the 1948 team. We just didn't have the material. We won four or five games but weren't nearly as good as those other two teams I was up there with. I left in 1951 and the next year, 1952, they beat Maryland. After I left they started getting a little better. They had Jimmy Lear at quarterback and after they got him they started having all of those quarterbacks up there. In 1952 is when they really it going. I think 1951 was okay but in 1952 we got pretty good.

We had to scrimmage against the varsity when I was a freshman. They were better but didn't hit any harder than we'd already been hit. Back then, of course, they weren't nearly as big as they are now. Our biggest player was Jimmy Clark and he was about 240 pounds. We had a guy from New York (Bill Erickson) who was real good at the other tackle. He played in the Delta Bowl and then left and we never saw him again. He was about 220 pounds and the guards weighed about 210. We didn't have facemasks so you were just open to getting hit. People used their forearms a lot and they could split your face open. They showed a guy who was gonna catch a punt and didn't fair catch—he was from Drake—so someone forearmed him in the nose. That blew it up and they changed the rules so that you couldn't forearm anyone in the face. Then they came in with facemasks and that put an end to it but forearming was pretty prevalent when I was up there.

We mixed with the students pretty much. Of course we had classes and we got to know a lot of people. We were dating so we'd get out on the campus after spring practice. Back then spring practice went six weeks straight through and after that, we had a little time to have some fun. And that's what I majored in.

Even after the six weeks of spring practice, they had us down there working out on our own. They were supposed to be looking out the window at us and that lasted about a week, then they came out there with us. We wouldn't be in pads but would be in shorts and running plays and it's hard to keep from running into somebody, I don't care if you got pads on our not. We did that three or four weeks and we called it working out on our own. They didn't want us fooling with weights. The theory was that if you got to pumping weights you'd tie up your body where you couldn't move fast. They learned later on how to do that and that's how they get all muscled up now. But they didn't want us fooling with weights. Some of them had weights in their rooms up there but nobody really got after it.

Buster Poole was my position coach. We had a banquet down in Jackson and they bought in Bruiser Kinard as the offensive line coach and Buster Poole as the defensive line coach. They hired John "Hurri-Cain" to coach backs. Vaught coached the quarterbacks by himself even though he had been a lineman in college, but he was a smart guy. He would get up there and show them. He was real exact and he'd get the ball and say this is the way you do it and when you turn to the right you put your right foot here and right here meant right there, not two inches back. He'd tell them where to throw the ball. He wouldn't teach them how to throw it but he wanted it where he wanted it. In the spring you had Wobble Davidson and Junie Hovius working with the backs. Wobble was a character. I liked him. A lot of them didn't. He was tough as hell and you didn't mess with him. He was pretty funny sometimes. He was a Marine and they say he killed a guy somewhere—not in the war—but he was a good guy. You just didn't mess around with him. If he told you something that's what he meant.

When I was a freshman hazing was pretty regular. Jimmy Crawford and some of those upper-classmen were up there that first summer. We'd be up there asleep at eleven or twelve at night and they'd come down that hall bam bam bam on your door, make you bend over and give you two or three licks. But during the season there wasn't much of that. They cut our hair when I was a freshman. What they wouldn't do is mess with anybody who had come back from the service. They just didn't mess with them. When I made M Club I was so glad to make it. And then we had M Club initiation. You undressed and they'd give you a towel and that's all you had. Then they blindfolded you with the towel and put you through all that stuff. They asked you all those stupid questions that you couldn't answer right and you'd get a paddle across your butt. They'd put a raw egg dipped in acid and then you had to swallow it and that was pretty bad. They had stale cigars that they'd make you smoke and hit you across the butt and you'd sit there drawing that smoke in and you'd get sick. At the end they get plaster of Paris and they made you take a big blob and put in your pubic hair and then up under each arm. Then they'd make you clamp your arms down and close your feet together and make you sit that way until it hardened. They had blue and red paint and they'd paint all over you. Then, finally, you got through. Finally, they said, "You can take your blindfold off," so we'd go on up to the room and get some gasoline and everything else around there to get that damn stuff off. You had to take a razor blade and pull that stuff up and cut the hair to get it off of there. We were probably up there an hour or an hour-and-a-half. They told us you ain't gonna like it but you'll be glad you got through it. They were right about that.

The first year we were up there the M Club was on probation. I asked what the hell they were on probation for. They said when they'd had M Club initiation the last spring, they took the guys getting initiated out on a truck out there at the golf course and let them out on the road somewhere. Well, all they had was a towel and they came up sorority row. That bunch of idiots started taking their towels off and waving and hollering and waking up the sororities over there. Well, the girls were looking out the window and they were out there buck nekkid so that's what got them on probation. Bob Burt and Jimmy Crawford were up there then and they did all that stuff.

We didn't want to join fraternities because we felt we had the best group on campus so there weren't many of us then that joined fraternities. But after about two years some of them started joining fraternities again. The M Club was about the strongest group on campus for a couple of years.

The games I remember best: we beat Tennessee in Memphis in 1947, 43-13. That was the first time Ole Miss had beaten Tennessee. And we beat the heck out of them. Conerly was throwing that ball anywhere he wanted and he was burning them up. I was a freshman and we played Kentucky up there that year (1947) and beat them 14-7. That was kind of an upset. It was the first game of the year.

In 1949, Bear Bryant was at Kentucky and he brought them down to Oxford. We worked and worked because Coach Vaught thought Bear Bryant was a big rival and wanted to beat him. We had had beat Memphis State and Auburn both 40-7 and we were about two touchdowns favored over Kentucky. Well, they beat us 47-0. Kentucky knew everything we were gonna do. What happened was, we had a guy who lived up in the athletic dorm. We called him a Scabini: he wasn't gonna play but worked out with the B team. I know that guy was there as a mole and he was feeding them information. We had twelve skull meetings the week before we played Kentucky. We'd meet after lunch and then we'd go over there after supper and work on the plan. We had one where they got up there and if our linebacker got up too close Vaught would give them a signal and the linebacker on the other side would drop back. Well, they knew all of that and they beat the hell out of us.

After that we went up to Vanderbilt and they beat us by one point, like 28-27. And the next week we went to Boston College. We flew a DC 6, four engine prop and that was my first airplane ride. We flew down to Montgomery to play Auburn. The plane would hold 44 people which was the coaching staff and the team. We played TCU in Fort Worth and they beat us three or four points (33-27). We beat State at the end, 26 to nothing. Some of the alumni were grumbling about Coach Vaught and he gave us a talk over there in the mess hall and he said "I'm not planning on you getting me fired," but he was under some pressure. And the next year he started getting some players. In 1950 we weren't doing that good (5-5) but then he got some good players and Mississippi State had some bad coaches over there during that time so we didn't have much competition to get good players.

Vaught had a good season in 1951 (6-3-1) but really got it going in 1952. He started recruiting some guys who could really run and that turned it around. He finally got where he could get anybody he wanted and of course there weren't any limits on scholarships. They had all kinds of guys. "Why are you recruiting all these quarterbacks?" people asked, and he would say, "They normally are the best athletes on the high school team." He'd move them around. He'd recruit fullbacks and make linemen out of them. Bear Bryant was the same way: he wanted agile players who could run. That stopped when Alabama was playing Notre Dame and Notre Dame put in those big backs and linemen and just overpowered them. After that everyone started getting the bigger guys. They needed meat. Warner Alford was captain of the 1960 team and I don't think he weighed 200 pounds but he played on the line.

Doc Knight ran the training room. He did all of the wrapping. Bubber Blackwell was a baseball player and he helped Doc Knight wrap ankles. He had been in the service during World War II. The equipment guy was great. He would do all the packing into the big boxes and when you went into the locker room in Fort Worth it was all laid out for you. All you had to do was put it on. Ed Horner was his name. He lives in Germantown now. He was one hell of an equipment guy.

When I think about my time at Ole Miss, I had a lot of fun up there—too much fun probably—and I'm sorry I didn't graduate. I was anxious to get to work and start making a living after the Air Force. I met my wife in the Air Force and then after I got out, I went up to Ole Miss for another semester. But I quit after only one semester and got married, then went to work. If I had worked a little more I could have graduated. I wasn't the only one. I'm just proud of being an Ole Miss Rebel and I'm proud of being in the M Club.

WANDA ENGLAND POOLE

1947-1951

RAY POOLE

I grew up in a little place called Boot Creek down in Calhoun County. My brother-in-law Bob Church and my sister Juanita married right after the war. He had come back from France, so when they came to Ole Miss, I came, too. I met Ray Poole in the Grill my sophomore year. Barney was also here and I knew him and of course, Buster was coaching but I had never heard anything about Ray, never even heard anyone mention him. Everybody gathered at the Grill, which was where the post office was then, and just crowded around a table and drank coffee. Ray was there and so somehow or another he asked me to go out. I had never heard of him and I thought I'm not going out with him so I got home—I stayed with brother-in-law Bob and sister Juanita in Vet Village the first year I was here—and I asked Bob and he said "Oh, he's a Poole brother and its okay." In Vet Village we had one telephone and it was in a little booth down on the corner. I was down there making a call. Well, up drives Ray and tapes me in the booth with duct tape. So that was my first experience with Ray Poole, and I should have known right there that he was a jokester. Then he asked me again to go out. He kept going back and forth to New York while he played professionally after Ole Miss and I finished in three years and we got married then. But what a grand time I had at Ole Miss

Vet Village was right across from where the law school is now and it ran along that street that backs up to the Chancellor's House. It had those two story buildings that came from the barracks or something. I stayed upstairs with Bob and Juanita. The Lucketts were across the hall—Bill Luckett, Jr.—he was a little bitty baby. I have a picture of me holding him. It was a lot of fun. There were a lot of people, all back from the service. There were veterans all over the place. I got here just as they started coming back from the war.

Buster was the oldest Poole boy and then Ray and then fourteen months later came Barney. Their daddy died when Ray was four so Mama Poole raised them on that little red clay farm down there. Ole Miss got them out of there and it's no wonder they loved it so. The Poole women were big women. My daughter Patty used to cry and say, "Daddy, I am a big old Poole woman." The men were big-boned men and so were the women. Three Poole brothers married three Berryhill sisters, so there were tons of double first cousins. Ray and Buster and Barney were bigger than their cousins for some reason. I don't know whether it was the fact that they had to work so hard because they didn't have a daddy or what. That whole family was close-knit, like a Poole clan. But it was really amazing. They lived out in the middle of the Homochitto National Forest. I think there are 28 or 29 M Club members who came directly from that family. They were all athletic-minded.

The other two Poole brothers who married Berryhill sisters were Phillip and Flemon. Ray's daddy had a ruptured appendix and lived for three months with gangrene so the three boys and sisters stayed with Phillip and Flemon. The cousins, they just never got as big. Ray was the tallest. He looked just like pictures of his dad. Barney and Buster looked like the Berryhills. But they had more fun living out in that community with fifteen or twenty cousins. And the sisters also produced athletes. Sister Hilda had Paige Cothren who was an All-American here. Then sister Willodene had Robbie Robertson but he never got to play a lot because he was here when we had so many big old athletes. But the Robertsons were kind of a shorter group and I think Robbie got some of that. Then the cousins like Reggie Robertson, their mothers were Pooles but not sisters of Buster, Barney and Ray. It's a clan.

The three brothers played other sports as well. Barney was a pitcher in baseball and Ray was captain of the basketball team and permanent captain of the football team. He also played baseball. He was a pitcher and he played pro baseball for the Chicago Cubs while he was playing pro football for the New York Giants. He would pitch for them in their season and then he'd go play for the Giants. We don't have people like that anymore. They never lifted weights. They just grew from throwing bales of hay and all of that work they did growing up.

Ray had an uncle who was a wild man—they could have made a TV movie out of him—and he hauled them around in the summers. They played on baseball teams that were all Pooles and would take on anybody. This uncle would pick them up in the back of a truck and haul them anywhere to get a game. Buster came up here and then here came Ray. I never saw Buster play and I never saw Ray play college ball but I did see him play pro. Barney was at the end of his career when I saw him. I think he had played college so long and every year he'd gain a little weight and his mother would say Barney looks so peaked. But Ray would work out down there in a rubber suit and I'd hold the ball in the pasture for him to kick.

After that first year in Vet Village I moved into Somerville dormitory. I didn't go through Rush because I couldn't afford it. We had a really, really good independent group of boys and girls. There were about thirty of us. And at that time the Syrian girls from Vicksburg were not allowed in sororities. So we had Nina Nosser, who married Kayo Dottley, and her sister Boop, who married Crawford Mims, and Lila Lee, who married Bill McWright. None of them were allowed to join a sorority—that was in the day—so they were all my friends and we had a great group and we did everything they did. We just didn't have to go to study hall like the sorority girls did.

When I was in school, we dressed up and wore hats and gloves for the games. It might be burning up but we'd have wool clothes on. Everything back then was about the way you looked. I finished in three years and graduated in 1950 with a degree in education. Then I taught at the University in the PE department.

You know those people came back after the war after serving on Saipan and all those places. And they had been through stuff so they didn't take to a lot of rules. Miss Hefley liked Ray. He was Colonel Rebel and he was good when he was in school here. Miss Hefley would let me go out with him and we could go two miles off the campus. She was tough. She had rules, and she held us to them. But the school was little and you knew everyone and I just don't remember anything bad until the later years when we had the riots and all of that.

MOOSE RAMSEY

1947-1952

The big thing with the Memphis football games was the Creel Room at the Peabody Hotel, right off the lobby. There was a liquor store inside the hotel but we usually stopped at the Allenberg Liquor Store, just south on Second Street. I think then that James E. Pepper, a popular bourbon, was $3.50 a fifth. Setups and beer in the Creel Room were cheap and everybody gathered there waiting for the pep rally to be held around the fountain in the lobby. The Ole Miss band and the cheerleaders would be there. Depending on the game time, we ate at Fortune's on Union, which was walking distance to Crump Stadium. Some guys got together and rented a room at the hotel next door, perhaps the Claridge. After the game we usually went to the College Inn. It was too expensive to go up on the Plantation Roof of the Peabody. Some maybe stopped at the Gulf Trail Lodge in Sardis on the way back.

PIGGY CALDWELL

1948-1952

I was born and raised in Tupelo, graduated from Tupelo High School and went to Ole Miss on a combination baseball and football scholarship in 1948. I was a freshman on the Farley Salmon T-formation team in the fall of 1948. I played freshman football that year and hurt my knee in the Vanderbilt game, which we played up there. My freshman coaches were Junie Hovius and Wobble Davidson. We played four freshman games, and we scrimmaged the varsity every day. Coach Vaught later told me that was the last year he ever did that because lot of the freshmen got hurt. So many of those varsity boys had been in the war and had come home and they were older. Barney Poole had come back and in those days they assigned a freshman to a varsity player, and you did everything he needed done so I had to sell his football tickets for him. They got six tickets for every game. Barney was the mildest guy you've ever seen. He would say, "Piggy I need for you to sell my tickets this week." So my daddy and his buddies got six 45-yard line tickets every week for $6 apiece. Barney was at least 26. He and Shorty McWilliams of State played more college football than anyone. He first went to North Carolina Pre-Flight and played a year and then he played three or four years at Army and then came down here and finished his career at Ole Miss. He probably played seven years. I was eighteen and I think he said he was 26, so there was a lot of difference.

If we were playing Tennessee, Coach Wobble and Coach Junie would get the freshmen out and we would learn the Tennessee plays. On Sunday afternoon we had to go watch a film, and we would learn their plays and then run those plays against the varsity every week. Now later on, about 1950, they used what we called the Scabini Squad. The Scabini's ended up running those plays because they were older and more mature than a bunch of eighteen-year-old freshmen. No one wanted to be on the Scabini Squad, which was made up of the guys who were being redshirted, or maybe some third stringers who weren't going to get to play. But they would line up and run the Tennessee offense or some of the defense of Mississippi State. It worked pretty good for Vaught but at that particular time, until those veterans graduated, there was too big of an age difference to have the varsity scrimmage the freshmen.

Wobble and Junie were great. I really respected Wobble. Both were young enough at that time that I could remember when they played football at Ole Miss and I used to come see them as a little boy. I asked Wobble one time how he got that name but after I saw him run down the field I knew why. He just wobbled his legs when he ran. They were very good coaches and they were fair. Wobble was tough but all he asked was for you to give your best. He and I got along fine. We were friends later on.

We had an athletic dorm—Heddleston Hall up towards the hospital and the laundry—and Wobble and his family lived downstairs. It was about the last one on the right and the Davidsons lived in the bottom right apartment. I can assure you that dorm was run pretty tight. Lea Paslay and I played together and one night Lea was calling his future wife on the phone. Wobble hollered and said, "Get off that phone. It's ten o'clock." Well Lea didn't get off the phone and Wobble went up to the third floor and jerked the phone off the wall and threw it on the floor and said, "Now go to bed." He could be tough and he wanted it done his way. But he was fair. Wobble was responsible for us having a pretty good team. They had very few discipline problems around Ole Miss in those days.

Wobble and Junie taught us fundamentals. I had a good coach in high school but I learned more that freshman year—the little intricacies of how you blocked and how you tackled. They were excellent coaches. I guarantee you we were all better by the time we got through freshman football.

They got us up in Heddleston on the fourth floor and they cut our hair with electric razors. We had to pay them a dollar for cutting our hair. We had two veterans who were freshmen and had been in the service and they didn't cut their hair, but they cut ours. I didn't see any hazing. I was never struck by anyone when I was playing. Now one thing I saw Wobble do and Coach Vaught did this later on: if you did something wrong you had to run the steps of the stadium. You had to go over there and run up and down the steps. Of course, it wasn't but about forty rows high then. But you run up there in your football gear and down and you feel it. If you got too slow, one of the coaches might pop you on the rear end with a paddle.

I played end. That's why I was assigned to Barney. Unfortunately for me at Vanderbilt I had my knee pretty well torn up and that ended my career. I had to have all my cartilage taken out. I really went over there to play baseball primarily. Coach Swayze was the baseball coach and he recruited me. And when they told me I couldn't play football I said, "Well I can play baseball can't I?" And they said, "No, we had to take out the cartilage and if you were to slide into second base and that knee went out all we could do would be to put a steel plate in there." So they pretty well convinced me I needed to be a civilian. But that was probably the best thing that happened to me. I probably would have turned out to be a bum and instead I ended up with a good wife and a good family. So it was the best thing the Lord ever wanted me to do.

Jimmy Lear played baseball a little bit. However back in those days I don't think they gave scholarships to any player other than a pitcher or a catcher. The rest of the team was pretty much made up of football players. They gave plenty of scholarships for football. I think there were probably close to fifty on my freshman team. Now the year before I got there they had a good baseball team. Charlie Conerly played outfield and Bobby Wilson did, too. Wilson was going to graduate and Coach Swayze told me he needed a left fielder, and that's what he wanted me to do, so he gave me a football scholarship. I promised Coach Vaught I'd play football and was supposed to be Coach Swayze's left fielder but the knee ended that. Conerly hit over .400 his senior year. The left field didn't have a fence. You were facing the football stadium. I saw Conerly hit a ball that bounced twice before it hit the football stadium. That ball had to have gone 500 feet. He could really hit it. Bobby Wilson was that good, too. Conerly played centerfield and Bobby played left field. Bobby was a safety on the football team. Big tall guy, West Point I think. We've had a few good players but Conerly was as good as anyone we ever had.

Getting hurt at Vanderbilt was a freak thing. Rocky Bird threw me a pass over the middle and I jumped up and caught it. Well, one guy on one side hit me and the one on the left just hit me and popped that knee out. It just separated it. I was watching that football game the other night. We played in the old Vanderbilt Stadium and their dressing room wasn't any better than a high school. They were pretty good back then. The only conference loss we had in 1947 was to them. Ole Miss was recruiting me in 1947 and I got to go to all of the games and stand on the sidelines when Conerly was playing. The loss to Vanderbilt that year was on a disputed call. In those days two offensive men couldn't touch the ball, so if an offensive man touched it and another offensive player caught it they called it incomplete. A buddy of mine played linebacker for Vanderbilt and they threw the ball and I think Hairline Harper caught the ball and Daylight Fletcher said he touched it in the middle but so did Tommy Patterson so that's the game we lost. And that's when we won the SEC the first time.

We were joking about Crump Stadium. You know I went to all of the games. Even after I got hurt, I got to go with the team. We would go to Crump Stadium and Vaught told us we went to make money because they held 30,000 and Oxford only held 28,000. We always played Arkansas and Tennessee in Memphis. Back in the old days Tennessee wouldn't play us until we agreed to play them in Memphis.

After I got hurt they were very nice. I kept my scholarship. It was a five year deal. Five to play four. I helped Doc Knight for a while and they were very nice about it and didn't take away my scholarship. There were several of us there who had injuries like that: Pat Massey and two or three on the freshmen squad who never got to play varsity because of those early injuries.

We would help with taping ankles. We got to make some wonderful trips all over the U.S. flying with the team. Doc Knight was just super. We've never had anyone like him since then and we never will. He loved football and loved Ole Miss but he really knew the intricacies of an injury and he'd tell Vaught someone couldn't play today. If Coach Vaught said, "Well, what about taping him up?" Doc would say "No, he can't play today." He was one of the biggest fans Ole Miss ever had. He'd be on the sidelines and jump up and cheer. He was a little guy. Doc coached track and they had some pretty good runners when he was coaching. Wes was his first name and when we got to know him a lot of us called him Wes but he didn't like that. He wanted to be called Doc. He would say a prayer before the game and then he'd say "Now go beat the hell out of them." He was a good Christian man.

Al Borgia was one of the top athletic guys at that time. He came to see me and said, "We want you to go be an assistant coach at the University High School. If you do you won't have to take any PE classes and you'll get credit for it like a class." So I went out there in my junior year. The coach was Bert Carpenter and they won the Little Ten that year. I was the line coach and coached the defense. They called me the next summer and said they hadn't signed anyone else and wanted me to come back. So I was able to coach them two years. I happened to be there the night that Bobby Holcomb was killed. He was tackling Kiger Adams out of Amory. I had a deal with Bert Carpenter that when someone was hurt I ran out there with a wet towel. Bobby looked up in my eyes and said, "Coach, I'm hurt," and he closed his eyes and I really believe he died right then because he never regained any consciousness. Well, anyway I got that experience. Every time I go to a baseball game I look out there where Oxford-University High School used to play football. Except for losing Bobby, it was a good time.

My freshman year we did a heck of a lot of running. Wobble had been a drill sergeant in the Marine Corps and we would run 100-yard sprints. You took your shoulder pads off and he would separate you by position and they'd time you on the first two and then the rest of them were to wear you out. But one thing Wobble did do—he was quite a physical specimen—you'd reach your arms all the way out and twirl your arms around without letting them down and of course by about five minutes we were worn out but he could do it for fifteen minutes. That was about the only maniacal thing he ever did because he loved to show out.

I had to run the stadium steps one time but some of my buddies ran quite a bit. Kline Gilbert was on my freshman team and he later made All-American. When Kline got to Ole Miss he was a good football player but I think Wobble made him into a great football player by just staying after him. Kline didn't like to put out too much and he wasn't going to give it his all but by the time he got to the varsity he was a pretty good player. Then Bruiser took over and made him a great player. But Wobble and Junie were good freshmen coaches. They prepared everyone just right.

We ran the single wing with Conerly in 1947 but Vaught did it a little different from Tennessee. If you shifted right, Conerly would be the tailback and when you shifted left, he would reverse and come around that guy shifting so he'd always be at tailback. It was a pretty thing to watch and see him the way he could shift around back there. He ran defenses crazy. But when Farley was there, he went with Vaught to Missouri and they saw Coach Farout and that's how Vaught and Farley learned the intricacies of the quarterback position. That was the year Vaught went to the T. And the rest is history. You had a wingback out on the wing and you had your fullback and tailback and blocking back still there and it wasn't spread out. Usually the quarterback would roll out where the man in motion went and that gave you three receivers going out with the quarterback rolling that way, so he could either run or throw to the three. It was almost impossible to stop.

Coach Vaught always said, "I never want the opposing quarterback to beat us." He would have the defensive end go to the quarterback when the quarterback rolled out and that would make him throw the ball. That takes the quarterback out of the equation. If you tackle him that leaves the other players to take care of the rest.

Coach Vaught was real picky about what you wore on a trip. We wore sport coats and ties when we travelled. Even when I was helping Doc Knight, we all had to wear sport coats and ties on the planes or the buses, however we went. Coach Vaught always had that coat and tie and that hat and all of the coaches dressed up like that.

Barney Poole and I got to be good friends. He was head of Memorial Stadium in Jackson and we always laughed about one game in particular. We got down to Tulane in 1948 and

Barney got hit in the jaw and I'm not so sure it didn't break it. He was really hurt. And his brother Buster went out there on the field and he said, "Get up Barney. Mama's in the stands and she'll think you're dead." So he jumped up and went to the sidelines and played later in the game. That was a big game that year—we lost 20-7, our only loss—but Tulane was good. And losing Barney early in the game hurt us. He was one fine football player.

When Vaught took over, the only coach he changed was to get a guy he asked for: Mike Brumbelow. John Cain, Buster, Bruiser, Junie, Wobble, and Hurri-Cain were here. And Ray came pretty soon. At halftime, Brumbelow would be in there when the team came in and he'd be writing on the board. Brumbelow could write on the board better than anyone we ever saw. He and Vaught would decide what needed to be done. You very rarely saw an Ole Miss team that Vaught coached get beat in the second half. Brumbelow was a big part of that. I never saw him do any on-field coaching. He probably stayed until the mid-fifties.

The players really respected the coaches because they had been great players themselves. Vaught was a quiet man and didn't associate with the players on a personal basis very much but he was fair and the players really respected him. You never heard much rah rah from Vaught. His deal was preparation. Doc was the hollering guy. Vaught would say we are prepared better than that team out there and it's just a matter of whether you want to give your best and if you do we're going to win the game. He never ranted and raved and jumped on tables. If someone had made a particularly good play at the end of the game he'd go over and give them a pat on the back.

Coach Swayze was the baseball coach and he was A-1. He was the contact man for recruiting. Country Graham, the basketball coach, would scout the team we were going to play. Coach Graham was a quiet, fine man. I was crazy about him. He took someone with him to scout and never saw a game on campus. He'd come back and tell you what the other team was going to do.

We played Boston College in Boston and I remember going up there. Boston's such a big town and we stayed in a big hotel downtown. We never played anyone else like that. We played TCU out in Texas and we played Florida in Gainesville so I got to make a lot of trips that ordinarily I wouldn't have gotten to make. Our opponents treated us very nice. No hard feelings back then from the other team. Kayo was really something. Hardest man to tackle I ever saw. I don't think we've ever had a running back any better than Kayo Dottley. Showboat was a lot like Dottley. He ran with reckless abandon and wasn't going to let anyone bring him down. He played a lot with injuries. Teddy Millette was behind us two years.

Teddy was about 195 and could really run. He got hurt and never got to play on the varsity. He would have written a lot of records. He was a pretty thing to watch. Just so smart. So intelligent. Teddy was going to make the right move every time. He scored a TD in practice and turned around to go back to the bench and twisted his knee and ankle. Of course in those days the doctors didn't know what they know today. There was a doctor in Memphis, Dr. Allen Spude, who operated on me. I had trouble years later and went up there. He said, "If we'd known back then what we know today you'd have been playing baseball in three months and football in six." Now they can repair cartilage. I tore the medial ligament and the cartilage.

We had good teams in 1947 and 1948 but we ended up in 1949 and 1950 with not quite the kind of players Vaught thought he had recruited. We just weren't very good until 1952, when he really came back. He recruited and got some better players in there and turned it around. Kayo was pretty much all we had before 1952.

When they recruited us, Coach Vaught sent us a letter and said he wanted us to get in the National Guard. They were beginning to draft some people, so we all got in the National Guard in our local units. I was in the 31st Division in Tupelo and enjoyed it. We went to Fort Benning twice, so when I got to Ole Miss every player on the freshman team was in the National Guard wherever they lived. The only National Guard unit in Oxford was the band and you should have seen that old bunch of football players going down there and playing in the band. It was something. When they called up the 31st for the Korean War I said, "I want to go with them," so when the Army got me for the physical they took my knee and moved it round and round. That doc said, "Who sent you down here?" I said, "I want to go with my buddies." The doctor said, "You're not going anywhere." And I still have the card and he wrote on it, "Permanently 4F: Don't send this candidate back for a physical."

Right south of Heddleston there was one of these old wartime temporary buildings. They made one of them the athletic cafeteria and it was something. We could eat anything we wanted. They didn't care but there was a big sign, if you put it on your plate, you've got to eat it. They let you have all you wanted but if you took it you had to eat it. You'd see the players mixing and mingling with the students down at the Grill. Most of them dated girls right there. Heddleston had all the athletes in it and we were pretty close together. There weren't but about 2500 students then and everybody spoke.

ALTON COBB

1948-1951

When you took a girl to a football game in those days you bought her a mum, which she wore to the game. That was a requirement then, and the girls dressed up for the games. The boys dressed up, too. I remember the game with Kentucky, when Babe Parilli came to town. Ole Miss was picked to win and they beat us pretty bad (47-0). The players I remember from that era are Rocky Bird and Billy Mustin. Farley Salmon was great. He played quarterback and they called him Fish. We beat Maryland the fall after I left, with Jimmy Lear. The next year we went up there and they beat the stew out of us.

HENRY PARIS

1948-1952

I was in the band my first year so I went to most of the games. The band had ninety pieces and we had a Confederate flag that covered the entire band. We would come out and play Dixie and then go down the field with the Rebel Flag over us. We would go to LSU and spell out R-E-B-E-L-S. We had little lights on our caps, but they forgot to tell us to turn on the lights, so nobody in the stands knew what we were doing, because no one in the band turned the lights on.

I became a cheerleader my last three years at Ole Miss. Why I became a cheerleader is beyond me. Mooch Marcus was a cheerleader. He had been influenced by a guy named Bruce Labens to become a cheerleader. Mooch was ahead of me. I never dreamed of being a cheerleader. I really wanted to play football but I lacked the size. For cheerleader, we ran in an election. It was not on any ability. You had to pass certain committees, which was not hard, and then it was a campus-wide election. It certainly was not what it's like now. They are gymnasts now. During my campaign, I went to every fraternity and sorority house and spoke.

When I was the Head Cheerleader, I had to plan the pep rallies before each game. So we would go and get one of the outstanding players from the week before to speak and then the coaches would speak. Coach Vaught was very reluctant to speak, however, so it was hard to get him. He was very nice; he just didn't like to speak. We would have big pep rallies in Fulton Chapel. We'd be up on the stage and sometimes, Coach Vaught would give a speech, but he didn't like that limelight. We did a lot of Hotty Toddies, did them over and over. We had six yells, but the students didn't know any of the others and didn't care. Dean Malcolm Guess said, "That's not a good yell; there's cussing in it. We need to get rid of it," and I said, "If the cheerleaders don't lead it, the students will do it anyway and there is nothing we can do about it." And that was true. I don't know when Hotty Toddy started but I suspect it was back in the twenties or thirties.

Dorm life was fun. You were just wide open. There wasn't any privacy, but that was okay. The athletes had their own dorm, but with me, talk about closest friends, most of them were football players. I mean, they were students, too. Like Jimmy Lear and Rogers Brashier. He played guard at Ole Miss. They were just great dear friends. Some of the people were somewhat reluctant to go to the athletic dorm. But I wasn't. In fact, when I ran in all my elections, I went to every room in the athletic dorm. I never saw them bully anyone. I'm sure some of it went on, but I never saw it. They were a great group of guys. When I was a freshman a guy named Jack Odom, who played end, said, "Bend over, freshman. I'm fixin' to whip your tail." I said, "Okay, Mr. Odom." He said, "How did you know me," and I said, "You're the greatest defensive end that has ever played for the Rebels," so that's how I got out of it.

Coach Vaught was very nice, extremely nice to me as a cheerleader, and I have a book that he autographed and wrote something personal in there. Coach Vaught was a wonderful executive. He ran his staff like a business, and he would have been successful in anything he did. Coach Vaught delegated authority and responsibility to his assistants. He didn't like the limelight. Coach Vaught was a private person and I don't think he ever got intimate with any of his players. He liked them and loved them, but he kept that certain distance. For instance, my friend Rogers Brashier, who played, lettered three years, so about five years after he got out of college, he smoked but he didn't want Coach Vaught to see him smoke. He had that kind of respect for him. I could go see Coach Vaught at any time about a pep rally or something like that. He was very nice, very businesslike, and very formal. He was certainly a guy you didn't want to cross, and his players really respected him.

The cheerleaders got zero money to travel with the football team to away games. When we went to Vanderbilt, for example, we would have to get somebody's car and pay for the gas and our rooms, or we stayed with someone because we got absolutely nothing in expense money. I never went to a bowl game. The bowl games were after my time. We went to the Memphis games, went to Vanderbilt and Auburn but not Miami or Georgia. We had our pep rallies in Memphis at the Peabody and stood on the fountain. I was a great cheerleader, but I stepped into the fountain. We were playing Memphis State and we were running out onto the field. They had a cable going to the PA system or something. Well, I tripped over it and went down and said "Arggh, ooooh" and there I was, lying on the ground. So that game stood out. We had multiple uniforms. One of them had red satin shirts and white pants with stripes and when it got cold, we had white sweaters with the big M on the chest and blue pants. We sang: "From Peabody's Lobby to Whitey's Saloon, we'll do the town tonight. The faculty will not interfere, they know we're in the right."

You know, one time before the State game, some guy from Ole Miss—I was not involved in it—got the State bulldog and brought him back to Ole Miss the week of the game. We had that big Rebel flag that would cover the band and State got it and took it back to Starkville. So the President of the Student Body down there called the President of our Student Body, Jack Geary, and said, "Look, this has got to stop. We want to send some people up there and you send some over here and let's get this thing handled." So Jack asked me and a couple of other guys to go and we went over and met with them. They were great. They were leaders and we gave them the bulldog back and we got the Rebel flag back. Later, the State people burned a big M on the grass in Hemingway Stadium. But we never lost to them. I was down in Starkville on the field when Showboat Boykin scored those seven touchdowns. Jimmy Lear kicked seven extra points. Showboat went on to be a career military guy and came out a full Colonel. I think the play was 48 trap, the four back through the eight hole.

FROM LEFT: GENE BISHOP, MISSISSIPPI STATE STUDENT BODY PRESIDENT TOMMY CROOK, JACK GEARY, AND HENRY PARIS

MARTHA ANN MCMULLAN AASEN

1949-1951

I made some road trips to football games. I went to LSU at least once. We drove down there and when it was time to come home it turned out that the people who had taken us in their car were not to be found. They had had too much to drink and no one knew where they were when it was time to come home. We spent the night and they still didn't show up the next day. I think eventually I ran into somebody else I knew and two of us crowded into their car. There was an enormous amount of drinking at Ole Miss Oh my God. An absolutely enormous amount. They got their booze at some little town and it was very plentiful on campus.

JOHN MURRELL MCRAE

1948-1953

I was a cheerleader my second year. The Phi Delts had me run for cheerleader and I got elected. The Sigma Chis put up Wade Strickland and he got elected along with Allen Thompson, the son of the Jackson mayor, and Henry Paris. We had a wonderful time. That was the 1949 season when Kayo Dottley led the nation in rushing. I was also a cheerleader my junior year. That was when we went to Baltimore for the Maryland game. We drove up with four of us in one car. I think we drove straight through. Our uniforms were white pants and some kind of jersey with Ole Miss on the front. We had pep rallies in the Peabody and did cheers standing on that fountain with the ducks in it. It was fun.

Jimmy Lear was from Greenwood and Teddy Millette was from Greenville. They were the two prime football players in the state and both signed with Ole Miss. Jimmy became a Phi Delt with me. Marvin Trauth played and later on he owned a nightclub in Gretna. I'd go to see him very two or three years. He could be his own bouncer. I loved being a cheerleader. In high school I played football at Lexington. Allie Povall, Sr. coached football one year. And then Bill Schneller came. He was a quarterback at Ole Miss and had made All SEC. He talked me into going out for football at Ole Miss, so I went out for three weeks before classes started. I just didn't have a lot of confidence. I was there with Rocky Bird and Jimmy Patton and when school started and lab started. I dropped out, but I wish I had stayed with it. I probably could have gotten a letter. I was a running back on that Murder Bowl team and we—the med students—beat the attorneys pretty good. Sterling Tighe was their big gun. Tommy Addison had played tackle at Jones Junior College so we had some players. I played intramural football and basketball and ran intramural track: me, Rusty Field and Bill Chatham.

I had a lot of interaction with the athletes, especially the football players. We had a dormitory that a lot of the medical students stayed in that was close to the athletic dorm for the football players. I got to be friends with several of the athletes. In the offseason we were kind of drinking buddies. Once up in West Memphis after a Memphis State game I was wising off and someone was just getting ready to take my head off. Our All-SEC tackle Marvin Trauth saved me. He said to that guy, "Don't touch him," and he didn't. Jimmy Patton and I got to be a hunting buddies. He went on and played with the Giants. We hunted ducks out on the Natchez Trace and got on each side of an old dead river run. I had a bottle of whiskey. It was cold so every few minutes Jimmy would walk all the way around this dead river run to get a slug of my whiskey. We saw a something coming down the run. It scared us to death. We didn't know it was but it turned out to be a beaver.

I had known Jimmy Lear in high school because he was from Greenwood and that was part of my playground. Wissy Dillard was another friend. He was from Itta Bena. Teddy Millette, from Greenville, hurt one of his knees. When he was a freshman he was great. And Showboat Boykin ran for seven touchdowns in the 1951 game against State. My freshman year was when Vaught switched to the T from the single wing of Charlie Conerly. Farley Salmon was quarterback of that first T team.

JACK "BOUNCER" ROBERTSON

1949-1953

The way I got in the M Club was I had run track in high school but I wasn't going to go out for track at Ole Miss. So they had an intramural track meet and I won the quarter mile, the half mile and the long jump. I set a new intramural record in the half mile, and Doc Knight was out there watching. He had put one of his half-milers in behind me and the guy kept trying to pass me. I thought it was just another guy in the meet, so I was running my guts out and the guy never did pass me. I don't know if he just didn't want to or couldn't, but anyway, Doc Knight after it was over said, "Son, you've got to come out for track." So that's how I went out for track. I wasn't planning on it but I did and lettered.

Lettering, of course, put me into M Club initiation. They told to come over behind the football stadium. So we got over there and they blindfolded us and made us take off everything but our pants. They tied our clothes in knots and threw them into a big pile and then they beat the stew out of us. They painted us red and blue and I then I mean they really beat us. It was rough. All of the former members, big old football players came down there and beat on you. Our rear-ends looked like hamburger meat. Marvin Trauth and I were big buddies and he was a great big old tackle who was really good. He beat on me some, but you were blindfolded so you really never knew who was beating on you but it was really bad. We were naked all of the time so they poured plaster of Paris on our heads and crotches. When it was over they said that our clothes were over there in that pile and we could put them on and go. But I said to heck with the clothes and I ran all the way back to Sam (Hall). I guess I was the original streaker. After I was initiated I never went back to an initiation. I thought it was cruel.

I played intramural football several years, and Coach Vaught tried to get me to come out for football but I was running track and that was enough. I got to know Coach Vaught and later he was on the board of my company, Gulf Guaranty. We remained friends through the years. When he became head coach we had that Charlie Conerly team in 1947 and went eight and two and won the SEC. The next year, we went eight and one. We had little Farley "Fish" Salmon at quarterback. Coach got everyone together after Charlie left. He knew he was going to have to run something besides the single wing so he tried them out in the T and decided on Farley. He brought Farley up there that summer and worked with him all summer long to get him ready for the season. Farley was a little, bitty guy but he could run that T offense. I think Coach learned that system in the service from Jim Tatum, who later became the coach at Maryland. Coach always said that beating Maryland and Tatum was Number One. He hated General Neyland at Tennessee, though, and loved to beat him. He didn't like Paul Dietzel but he liked Charlie McLendon. He couldn't stand Frank Broyles but he loved Spook Murphy and Bear Bryant. Broyles was kind of snooty and arrogant and Dietzel was the same way. And Neyland thought he was such hot stuff. He looked down on everyone else. Coach Vaught beat Bear Bryant more when Bryant was at Kentucky than Bear beat him, but Bear beat him more when he was at Alabama. The thing is, though, that Alabama wouldn't play Coach during his glory years.

One year we were playing Memphis State and Archie was the quarterback. Well, Coach Vaught told me Spook and I had played so much that he knew my offense as good as I did so we couldn't move the ball against him at all. So finally I said, "Archie, I'm going to run everyone to the right, but I want you to fake a handoff and run an option left." Well, those defensive guys keyed on certain things and when nobody went over there with Archie, they didn't think Archie had the ball. They thought it had gone the other way, so he just walked in for a touchdown and that won the game for us. So after the game, Coach said Spook came over there to see him. They had become good friends through the years but Spook started screaming and yelling and said, "You can't run an option without someone to pitch to," and Coach said, "But I did, didn't I?" Coach said he had to call Buster Poole over there to get Spook off of him.

Coach had a great instinct for calling plays. One time a guy I think whose name was Ross—he was an ex-player—came to see Coach Vaught. Ross had become a computer expert and he said, "Why don't you let me put your opponents on the computer and I'll be able to program it so you know what they are likely to run in any given situation: third and five from the 25 and so forth?" So they did. Well, our coaches thought it would be a good idea if we put our own tendencies on the computer but none of them wanted to bring it up with him. Eddie Crawford was the youngest coach so they got him to do it. He suggested it and said it would help them to know what they were likely to do in certain situations so they could do something else. Coach said, "I don't need that, Eddie." And then he took the game they had played the week before and ticked off every play they had run in every situation, where they were on the field when they had run it, and how the play had done, did it for the whole game. Eddie walked out and said to the other coaches, "I don't believe we need to put it on the computer."

Another story about Coach Vaught concerns Possum Price. You know, Coach Vaught said Possum was the best linebacker he ever coached. Well, Coach had an absolute rule against smoking and if you smoked and got caught, he would kick you off the team. So Wobble went to Coach Vaught and said he thought Possum was smoking again and he asked Coach, "If I catch him again, what are we going to do? We'll have to punish him." And Coach said, "Well, Wobble, just don't catch him."

Crawford Mims from Vicksburg was an All-American lineman and he went up to Ole Miss and tried out. Coach wasn't sure he wanted to sign him so Coach had him put on pads. Then Coach went out there with no pads or helmet and went one-on-one with Crawford. This was early in Vaught's career and he tore him up. So I asked him about it and he said, "Bouncer, I was a man and they were still boys." I think he did that with a lot of players. He would try them out and I think they said he whipped them all. Of course, he was an All-American at TCU. Coach probably had the greatest physical body of anybody I have ever known. You know, he was in his nineties and he would go on these trips with us. He never let you carry his bag, never complained. He was going to do everything that you did.

I think Coach wanted to retire after the 1970 season, but then he came back in 1973 when they fired Billy Kinard as coach and Bruiser as Athletic Director. So Porter Fortune, the Chancellor, came to Coach and asked him if he would come back as Athletic Director and head football coach, and Coach said, "Yes, but you have got to get rid of Bruiser. I'm not coming back if Bruiser is still there." So Coach went back over there and went into his office. Well, in comes Bruiser, still over there in the athletic offices, and Bruiser asks if he can stay on in some position. Coach said he got on the phone immediately to Porter Fortune and said, "Porter, Bruiser is still over here and you told me that he was going to be gone. Well, one of us is leaving. Either me or Bruiser." So Porter went over there and personally escorted Bruiser out of there.

JIMMY LEAR
(MAY 14, 1931 - JANUARY 12, 2015)

1949 - 1953

I was from Greenwood and went to Ole Miss because I had a sister seven years older than I who had gone to Ole Miss during the war, so I was oriented in that direction all along. My father loved football games and we didn't miss Ole Miss games. We would even go to Memphis to see them play. I was just a Rebel all the way and knew I would end up there.

I played high school ball in Greenwood in 1947 and 1948. They would broadcast our game against Greenville. I played there in Greenville twice. My junior year we played there.

That was the first time we had played them in the last six years because we had played them in Greenwood one year and they beat us 102 to nothing. The reason for that was Shorty McWilliams from Meridian and Buddy Bowen from Greenville were each trying to score more points than the other, so Greenville just ran the score up. We were playing ninth and tenth graders because a lot of our boys were in the service.

The Ole Miss scout, Tom Swayze, got in touch with me. There was another fellow from State who contacted me. I also had a chance to go to UCLA but I didn't know where that was. I was just a boy from Greenwood and I was going to California? So I just told them no. In fact they came by my house to pick me up and I told them I just couldn't go.

We ran a single wing in Greenwood. Then Coach Maddox came and we ran a formation that was close to a Split-T. The quarterback always reversed out and we'd open up and go down the line of scrimmage. You just turned around and you'd either fake to a back or give it to him. The T was relatively new then. Coach Maddox had been at West Point and they ran it there. They had Blanchard and Davis. Mr. Inside and Mr. Outside. He brought that with him. Coach Vaught had it installed by the time I came along at Ole Miss. Roach Conerly had run the Notre Dame box and then the next year, Farley Salmon was the quarterback and they ran the T. There was unlimited substitution, double platoon, when I came along, but then it changed in my sophomore year and it was tough because we had boys who weren't cut out for playing both ways. It got all screwed up. You could play all but two minutes of a quarter and then you had to come out. If you went in the third quarter, you could play one quarter, but you couldn't play two quarters. I was all screwed up. I have no idea how they kept up with it.

Ole Miss had a tough year in 1949, my freshman year, and then that year, in Spring practice—there were no limitations on Spring practice back then; you could practice every day of the week—I broke my foot. I was running the ball and I went down the line of scrimmage and I turned so that my foot shifted. I broke it and that ended my year. They had to take me up to Campbell's Clinic in Memphis and operate on me a couple of times and put a pin in there so the foot would be right. I couldn't play my sophomore year. I remember they tried to get me to play but the game is so fast that if you are away for a period of time, it's frightening because you hear all these bodies hitting one another. People are hitting on you trying to break your neck and I couldn't get out of the way. I couldn't move. They should have redshirted me because I was useless but for some reason, Coach Vaught didn't. I did kick extra points that year and the next year, my junior year, Rocky Bird was the quarterback. We were playing Memphis State and he hurt his shoulder—someone pushed him down on his shoulder and separated it—so I was the second quarterback and I came in and began playing.

Bobby Jabour was from Vicksburg and they tried him at quarterback but when we were freshmen there were about fifteen players who had come back from the war. The University gave them their scholarships and we had to scrimmage against them every Friday afternoon. We ran defense against that group of 23, 24 and 25 year old guys and I'm telling you, it was terrible. We played three freshmen games: Vanderbilt, Memphis State, and Mississippi State. They kept telling us they were going to shave our heads again if we let Mississippi State beat us. And they beat us. You know, a lot of our upperclassmen had been in the war and they were tough. I had just turned nineteen and some of them were 21, 22, 23 and 24. I think we had two who were 26. And they were men. As freshmen, we would scrimmage the varsity. There would be just eleven of us on the field and coming at us were three teams of the varsity. The first team would run a play and when it was over, we had to hustle back to our positions because the second team was getting ready to come at you. So you'd have to tackle them and get rid of them and then the third team was going to come at you and by the time you'd been there about six plays, it got pretty rough. I didn't like that.

Coach Swayze didn't coach football, only baseball. He would come out for practice but he had no part. Coach Swayze was a wonderful recruiter. Wobble was the freshman coach. He was tough and it didn't matter who it was. He'd get on them and he'd eat them up. And he'd get him two or three he didn't like and he'd wear them out. If he liked you and you did what you were supposed to do, he was fine but if you tried to fool with him he was tough.

We had an athletic dorm—Heddleston. The freshmen were on the third floor and the varsity were on the second and first floors so every time you went out to go to class or do something you had to go through their floors. You were assigned to a varsity player as a freshman and you were kind of a servant for the first six or eight weeks, then they backed off. Babe Pearson had come back from the war and he selected me as his freshman and I mean I was scared to death of him. I'd go to the other end of the dorm to go to the third floor and get away from him. He called me one day and said, "Freshman, come up here." He said, "I've gotten the word from the Lord and I'm leaving." I said, "Okay." He said, "Pack me up." So he left me and I packed his suitcases up for him. He got back in about thirty minutes and he said, "Let me look. I've gotten another message." "What's the message?" I asked. "I'm not leaving." I said, "Thank you very much." A lot of funny things happened.

They didn't harass us much when we were freshmen. But the M Club was terrible. Whooo, terrible. They'd put plaster of Paris under your arms and then down in your crotch and the last thing they did they'd put us down on the golf course without clothes and we had to get back to our dormitory. It was terrible. They finally stopped it.

The assistants were Johnny Cain, who coached the running backs. He had played at Alabama. And Coach Vaught really stayed with the quarterbacks. Buster Poole was there. Wobble was there. Bruiser was there. Junie Hovius coached the freshmen with Wobble. Spring practice, if you got hurt, it was get well and start again. Football back in those days was not nearly as complicated as it is now. I think we might have had fifteen plays and that was about all. You'd run them over and over. We did put people in motion. That was a little ahead of the times. Coach Vaught developed it when we went to the T. I think he learned it from someone in Oklahoma. It's not that complicated. You just line up on the line of scrimmage and do what you're supposed to do and it works out well. We didn't throw a lot, maybe twelve or fifteen times a game. You'd ride the fullback into the line and either hand off or keep it, then either pitch it or throw it. Rocky left and I was the quarterback. There was a boy named Tommy Spears from Arkansas who played quarterback and there were a couple of others. Houston Patton played quarterback and that was about it. Jimmy Patton was a class behind me. He wasn't on that 102-point Greenville team.

My first year to start was 1951. In the 1952 season, I was the quarterback and I graduated in 1953. The Maryland game was my senior year. I think it was my most memorable game. There wasn't a lot of hype back then like it is now but Maryland was good and they were tough. They had a big tackle—two of them, actually—named Modzelewski. They were brothers and they were big. Jack Scarbath was their quarterback.

I never played professionally. When I broke my foot that hurt me a lot and I didn't have the speed I had before. I was drafted by the Chicago Cardinals. Their coach met me at the hotel in Oxford and we talked. He said, "We'd like to have you. What do you think about money?" I said, "I believe $12,000 is about right." He said, "Good God, boy. What're you talking about? 12,000?" I said, "Well I don't believe you want me." I knew what they were gonna do. They were gonna put me at cornerback and they would've gotten me killed so I said $12,000. I was talking to Roach Conerly one day and I said, "Roach, how much did you make?" He said, "I made $15,000 the season that we played the best game ever played (1958: the overtime NFL championship game against the Baltimore Colts)." And I thought to myself: I knew I was gonna get killed, so I passed.

I joined Phi Delta Theta when I was here but I was not a good Phi Delt. Football demanded so much of your time that it was just difficult to do both. I'm sorry to say that I didn't participate that much and I wish I had done better. I just couldn't handle it: studying and then you'd go to football practice and play a game and come back and just do it all over again. Plus I was doing other sports.

Baseball at the college level was not very good. We probably played 25 or 30 games, something like that and we had pretty good teams. You may remember Jack Reed. He played with the Yankees, was Mickey Mantle's backup. I played baseball and was on the golf team. I had a friend I played golf with named Jerry Barron from Yazoo City. And another, Willis Connell from Clarksdale. We had about six or eight guys and we'd play for position. I liked golf. I had learned at the Greenwood Country Club. A lot of boys played there and we played every day. I also ran track. I had broken my foot that freshman year and then wobbled through the sophomore season. Then spring of my sophomore year is when I ran track. I played baseball my next year and also played golf.

Doc Knight was a lovely guy. Back when I broke my foot there wasn't much time spent to help you. No rehab, no physical therapy. And they just didn't know a lot about that stuff back then. Doc was an inspiration, I thought. He was always upbeat. Doc had come from Fordham. He would tape my foot and he would help me out. I enjoyed knowing him. I was quarterback when Showboat Boykin scored seven touchdowns against Mississippi State and my claim to fame is that I kicked seven extra points. It was the same play over and over. It was a trap play. We called it an even or an odd: if there was someone on the center, that was an odd defense. If there wasn't anyone on the center, then that was an even defense. So that's how you called your plays. It was a trap play, and it just worked. People say that someone had given Showboat secret instructions maybe to move over a little bit but I don't know about that.

Kayo Dottley was there when I was there. He was a good player and held the rushing record for the longest time: 1300 yards. He married Nina Nosser. One of the Nosser girls married Crawford Mims. Betty, I think. They called her Boop.

We didn't have a good year my freshman year. We had a terrible year, in fact, and we didn't have a good year my sophomore year. So there were people that were of a mind that Coach Vaught needed to be let go. And I can remember him saying, "If I go, I'm going to take a bunch of the players with me." I thought that was unusual but we beat State that year, 26-0. Coach Vaught was a strong disciplinarian and we couldn't have a car on campus during football season, so you walked from the dormitory down to the football field. That's how you got there. Nobody had cars. He made the rule between my freshman and sophomore years that you can't be married, you can't have a car, and you better not smoke and drink. So that's what the rules were. Some of those big old guys who had come back from the war got caught but that didn't hurt anything because they weren't going to play anyway. The marriage rule later cost us Lance Alworth from Brookhaven who went to Arkansas and later went on to San Diego as a wide receiver. He was a wonderful player. But he got married right before the season started and Vaught didn't take him. He was going to come to Ole Miss until he got married.

The practice schedule during each week of the season was scrimmaging by position. Like the tackles would work on blocking and the backs would work on running and passing. And then, if we were going to scrimmage, we went at it. In spring practice, it was horrible. Horrible. We'd been out there since January 15 and here it was almost April and we were about to die. Teddy Millette, Wissy Dillard and I roomed together and we came back from lunch one day. Wissy was in the room and he had a beer in the lavatory. So he said, "I'm absolutely sick of this. Sick of this." So he took a sip and I took a sip and Teddy took a sip and it kind of braced us up a little bit so I said, "What're you gonna do?" Then Wissy and Teddy said, "We're gonna leave." I was the only one with a car, and I said, "We don't want to do this. Coach Vaught will come get us." They said, "No, he won't get us because we're going to Miami." Of all places, Miami. I don't know how they came up with that. Wissy then produced another beer and we said, "Well, maybe we will go. That'll show them."

We put all our clothes in our car and packed them in. Then we drove about twenty or thirty miles and looked to see if they were coming to get us but they weren't so we drove on. Teddy lived in Greenville so he was our first stop and we put him out. His mama said, "Son, what're you doing here?" He said, "Well, Mama, we left." She said, "All right. Well, put your clothes back there in the closet." Then Wissy was the second man I let out of the car and his daddy said, "I don't think you better do this." Well, I put him out with his clothes and I went on home to Greenwood. When I walked in the door the telephone was ringing and Daddy picked it up and said, "Coach Vaught wants to speak to you," and I said, "Yessuh, Coach, I think I'm gonna be able to get them to come back tomorrow and I'm really working hard on it." He said, "You better get yourself up here and be ready to practice at three o'clock." I said, "Yessuh, I'll sure get them back." Well, that was this the coldest day I've ever practiced football. We started scrimmaging and we scrimmaged from 2:30 to almost 5:30. He changed everyone out of the routine. Like he'd run two plays and then he would rotate it around and take people in and out but he left me and Wissy and Teddy in there the whole afternoon. We never did get a rest. He just ran us every play and he almost killed us but never said a word about it to me, or Teddy or Wissy. Just never did. But we got our tails back over there.

Coach Vaught was cool and reserved. He didn't have a lot of fun but he was a good motivator and a smart football man. We always felt prepared when we went into a game. And he didn't call the plays. The quarterback called the plays. If he thought something was good, he'd send a substitute in and tell you what to run. But he'd say, "If you got something better, go ahead." I wasn't going to go ahead. I just ran what he said. We had a printed game plan and we had about fifteen or twenty plays that we were going to run. We had the sheets and we would study them during the week. Of course, once you played the first game of the season, that was the basis of what you were going to do. You carried the same learning process to the second game and you got to the third game and made some changes in there because of the way they were blocking on certain plays but he got you prepared.

Coach Vaught was a lineman but he coached quarterbacks. He probably learned that in the Navy. He was kind of a perfectionist. We'd get to running plays and if we weren't running them right, he'd stop everything and you'd get cussed out. Then you'd do it again. He had his quarterbacks down with the footsteps you'd use on every play. In other words, if you were going to run off the right tackle, it would take you three steps to get to the right tackle—no more, no less—and every play was set up that way. Some worked well and some didn't work well. He could teach the fundamentals of the position. How you took the snap, the footwork. I never will forget this. We were playing Tulane and some way or another we fumbled on about the ten yard line. I think it was my fault, but I wasn't going to let on. So I came out of the game and said, "Mama (Billy Hitt) didn't get me the ball, Coach. I just couldn't handle it." Well, Mama came off the field and the coaches said, "What in the hell are you doing? If we can't get the ball from the center then we can't do anything."

And Vaught knew the mechanics of passing. You worked on repetition so much so that you could do it all with your eyes shut. I can still remember some of them. I can remember how they were numbered. If you were going to call a play, say slot right, 32, on four. The slot right told you where the backs were going to be. One back would be in the slot on the right. Nowadays they are making it hard. Thirty-two would be the three back through the two hole. We had a back named Harold Loftin and he couldn't remember the plays. And of course he's back there with another back, the two of them back there, and I was up there under center. So we would remind Harold which way he was supposed to go because he would forget. If you called it to go to the right, well Harold would forget it and he'd go to the left. The back going to the right would be going full speed and Harold would be coming up, going in the wrong direction, and POW! So we'd have about six people say, "To the right, Harold, to the right."

Houston Patton followed me as quarterback. The boy who had been recruited to play quarterback, Tommy Spears from Arkansas, didn't come back. For some reason when we played Georgia Tech in the Sugar Bowl Coach Vaught started the second team at the beginning of the second half, and everyone to this day never figured out why he did that because we were playing pretty good. We scored the first time we got the ball. And the second time we got the ball the refs took a touchdown away from us. And the third time we got the ball I fumbled on the two yard line of Georgia Tech, so we were doing good, moving the ball. Then we got some bad breaks. We punted and the receiver waved his hand at the last second and no one saw it. Kline Gilbert tackled him. They would have gotten the ball on about the thirty yard line. Instead they got it on about the 45. They said he had given the signal. That was a controversial game. The second touchdown we scored, they didn't give it to us and I grabbed the official.

I almost got kicked out of the game. I don't know why they didn't do it. Wissy Dillard was running it and all I did was come to the line of scrimmage and hand it off to him. He got it over. The ball crossed the goal line and everybody said that the officials were from Georgia Tech. Nobody liked Georgia Tech. Bobby Dodd was their coach and he was a good coach but he was sort of arrogant.

For the Maryland game, we had a pep rally the night before the game and that kind of pepped things up and then for some reason everything just clicked. Thank goodness, because no one had ever heard of me, and I was appreciative. I left a lot of points on the field. I fumbled on the two yard line and I thought I could sneak it in but I got stripped, and then a couple of times that happened and we got down there some more and it happened. Years later, I was talking to Coach Vaught about it and I said, "Coach I don't think I played too well. I fumbled three times." He said, "No, you fumbled four times."

We had good social interaction with the students, went to parties and dances. Most everyone got a wife out of the deal. We had a good time. The football players as a whole mixed with the students pretty good. You had to have your date in by nine so you didn't have time to go anywhere. To get to town to see the movie, which cost fifteen cents, it cost you a quarter to get to the movie in a taxi. We used to get six or seven people in the taxi. Ole Miss had about fifteen hundred students at that time.

My major was general business. We had so many games in baseball, I didn't do that much academically. We'd go on a baseball trip and come back two weeks later. And they would have gone through another book. You needed a lot of spare time in the spring up there. It was a great place to be and lots of good things to do but we didn't have the time.

Teddy Millette ended up on the coast and married a gal whose daddy—Dick Walker—was a construction man who made a world of money. He had a daughter named Jackie—Jackie Walker—who married Teddy and out of that marriage there were a doctor and a lawyer but anyway, she was a beautiful girl. They were both kind of high strung and they divorced. We thought Teddy was going to be a savior. We played Arkansas as freshmen over in Little Rock in that big War Memorial Stadium. Teddy was the ideal runner. He had strong legs, good balance and he was just plain good. I had played against him my senior year in high school when he played for Greenville. I think he got where he just didn't like football. He and Jackie, during spring practice, would play bridge upstairs in the Union building, and if we were supposed to be at practice at 2:30 he'd get there about 2:35. The previous year, we played Boston College in Oxford, and Teddy ran 85 yards for a touchdown. Never had a person touch him, hurt his knee and never played another down. I think he just got tired of it. He had Jackie there, and they'd be kissing one another and the next thing you'd know they'd be fighting.

I guess of all the ones that were there, Teddy was probably the best player that never got to play. He was really good. He'd get tackled and he'd walk up to the player and say "That's nice. You're a pretty good tackler." He was a free spirit and he never met a stranger.

Jackie Parker was the best player I ever saw. Now this boy that's so good for Texas A&M, Johnny Manzeil, Parker was the same kind of guy. In those days, when the game was over, you didn't go meet the other players. You just went on to the showers. It never was any togetherness like that. You know, I never met him or never met any of the boys who played on the Maryland team. It just didn't happen. But Parker was good. There wasn't any question about that. We beat them but at the end of the game they were marching down the field. We were two-platoon at the time, so I didn't play defense against him. I'm glad.

Then the next year it was one-platoon but I was gone. All in all, I wouldn't take anything for the experience. Sometimes, I wake up late at night and I'll wonder, now how did I do that? I remember Junie Hovius coaching us over at Arkansas and the first time I got back to punt and I faked the punt and ran. Coach Hovius let it go. The second time I did it, he let it go, and the third time we had to punt he called me over and said, "I'm not gonna let you punt anymore." I asked, "Why?" And he said, "If you're gonna stand back there twelve yards behind the line of scrimmage and think you can run up there and get a first down every time then you ain't got any sense." I was just doing it on my own, but he put a stop to that.

My feeling about my time at Ole Miss is the good times I had and the people I met. So many of them are dead now. We had a reunion not long ago of the team that played the Maryland game, and we had twelve guys there. From the football experience I guess it would be knowing these guys and becoming good close friends with them and the camaraderie. I stayed active in M Club but the hazing was so bad. They got us out on the golf course. It was just a bad experience.

SNOOKY WILLIAMS

1950-1953

I grew up in Philadelphia and was at Ole Miss from 1950 to 1953. My oldest brother, Brown, had come to Ole Miss as did my oldest sister, Pat, who was President of Women's Student Government. My sister Helen also came. She married Bill Schneller, who played football up here in the late 30s. And then Janie, my youngest sister came; she married a Pickering. Harold, my other brother, also graduated from Ole Miss.

My first time to visit Ole Miss was in 1938. Brown was on scholarship playing football, and we left Williams Brothers Store and loaded the car with a case of apples and a case of oranges, crackers and smoked sausage. We didn't have coolers and it seemed like it took us all day to get there. There were like ten cars on the campus and we were probably one of the first tailgaters. We had Cooper, my cousin, and Brown. And that's my first memory. I really don't remember the football game. When I came up in 1950, there were maybe 2000 students. Ours is a large family. I am related to the Manning boys—Cooper, Peyton and Eli—through Olivia, and Curtis Wilkie's wife, Nancy Roberson Wilkie, is my cousin.

For football games we dressed up, wore coats and ties. The ladies, when they left to go to school, they would put all of their clothes in trunks and ship them by rail, or if they were from Philadelphia, send them on a truck from Williams Brothers. When they went up there they took only winter clothes, no summer clothes, so those first games, you'd go to the games and the girls would have on winter clothes no matter what the weather was. They didn't show everything like they do now. We were born too early.

I went to the games in Memphis and went to the Peabody and would see those cheerleaders around the duck pond and the balconies full and everybody singing and hollering. The first game we came out of Crump Stadium and couldn't find the car. The car we had gone up there in with a student friend was stolen and they didn't find it until he was a senior. So we had to find us a ride home. Telling his daddy was something. You see, you parked way out in the residential area and we walked for an hour looking for it. I don't think his daddy believed him.

We rode the train down to Baton Rouge. Cooper Williams, Archie's father-in-law, took his brother and me when we fourteen on the train to Baton Rouge. We caught it out of Meridian. The train pulled right up by Tiger Stadium and they let us off there for safety. The LSU people were throwing oranges at us. What I remember about that game was that it was wild. I'd never seen so many people so mad at Mississippians and throwing at us and yelling and cussing and drinking. You just didn't feel safe down there. Their fans were so rowdy and noisy. They'd get in there an hour before game time and just roar. It was unbelievable to me. I don't think I've ever heard anything like it, that long and that continuous. There was also a train out of Oxford down through Water Valley. I made several other trips down there to Baton Rouge and New Orleans that were not on the train.

JOE NEELY

1951-1955

I arrived at Ole Miss in August of 1951 in the backend of a pickup with about two pair of pants and three shirts and two pair of shoes. We checked into our dormitory, headed out to the football practice field and checked in with the coaches. There were about a hundred of us for the first day— all freshmen—and by the end of the week about thirty or forty were gone. Practice was hard. We had two-a-days and I was ill-prepared for what was going to happen to me when I arrived at Ole Miss. I was only seventeen years old and weighed about 190 pounds and it was just absolutely tough for the first month. What was tough were the workouts. The first three days I would get up in the morning and put my feet on the floor and then just jump up and down because my legs and my back were so sore. I was hurting all over

During two-a-days we practiced about 8:30 in the morning for one and a half hours. We would finish up, drink orange juice, shower, clean up, go to the cafeteria, have lunch, sleep for about thirty minutes, then go back down there at 1:30 and practice for another hour and a half or two hours, then orange juice, shower, food and sleep. After a week or so, I toughened up a little bit and practice wasn't nearly as difficult as it had been but classes started and studying became very difficult. The school I had gone to was small, and really, it was pretty amazing that three of us out of that small senior class got scholarships to Ole Miss now that I look back on it.

Wobble Davidson was the freshman coach and he and his wife and two small children lived in the dormitory with us, right across from the cafeteria. Wobble was the freshman coach and every once in awhile they'd send us down the hill to scrimmage against the varsity. They'd almost kill us and we'd go back up the hill and Wobble would fuss at us awhile and then we'd be off again.

When school started, we just had one practice a day. The practices were very organized. Johnny Vaught was one of the best organizers you've ever seen. The typical practice session for a lineman, which I was, started with a tackling dummy drill or a blocking dummy drill, and then we would practice running the regular plays. After that, we'd do conditioning drills—wind sprints—then we would do a mile around the outside of the practice field. Next, we'd go to the stadium and run up and down the stadium steps. I gained weight fast and wound up at 235 pounds.

Our Freshman quarterback was Eagle Day, and he ran around campus all the time saying "Ta-rah-rah boom-de-a, my name is Eagle Day, I'm up to run and play." I never was any good. I was just sort of there, never did make first team. But the football scholarship gave me the opportunity to get a college education, which I never would have been able to do without it because my parents simply could not have afforded to send me to school.

The upperclassmen harassed us quite a bit the first two or three weeks we were there and then it died down and wasn't much at all. They did shave our heads. Mine was shaved the first day I was there. We had our own cafeteria in the vicinity of where Paris Yates Chapel is now. The cafeteria was a white building they had probably gotten from the military after World War II. It was near the athletic dorm, which was next to the medical dormitory, and only the athletes ate there.

Ole Miss had good teams while I was there. I still have the silver cup we got for winning the SEC one year. We went to two Sugar Bowls while I was in school, played Georgia Tech and Navy and lost both. When we went to the Sugar Bowl on the plane, the guy sitting next to me was named Charles "Billy Goat" Sullivan. He wore a hat that looked like a billy goat had taken a bite out of it. It was his first plane ride so we left Memphis and got up to a certain altitude they changed the pitch on the props and there was a quiet period. I turned to Billy Goat and asked him why he thought we were stopping up there. He almost jumped out of his seat.

The Georgia Tech game was very controversial because we thought that the refs missed a call on a touchdown we made. But what I remember most is the party after the game in the Roosevelt Hotel. That was the first time I'd ever seen liquor served. Then everyone went down on Bourbon Street and walked up and down the street, which was so crowded you couldn't believe it. We stayed up all night then came home the next day. I slept for two days I was so tired. They served liquor to everyone who was there at the party, and it was the first time I ever had anything to drink. I had two bourbon-and-cokes and that was enough for me. It just didn't set right. We went to strip shows and saw the Cat Girl and Evelyn West and her Treasure Chest. Then we went to Pat O'Brien's for a Hurricane and of course you would always go eat at the Court of Two Sisters. We didn't get travel money for those games. You were on your own. They provided everything but money—food, travel, hotel—but if you wanted anything else, you had to pay for it yourself.

My scholarship covered tuition, room, board, books and $15 a month for laundry. It was a four-year scholarship. I was also on the track team at Ole Miss and of all things, the only injury I ever had at Ole Miss was from pole-vaulting. It was in a meet with Vanderbilt. I ran down the lane and started up and the pole snapped and I came down on the part that broke off in the box and messed up my knee. That ended my track career.

My major was physical education. I didn't finish in 1955, although I had 154 hours. I had failed to take a history course, so I left and went into the military. As I said, I was ill-prepared academically for college. I was on probation after the first semester and the coaches got us a tutor who taught us how to study. I went to the "how to study" class and things started getting much better. I took sixteen hours first semester of my freshman year and from then on either twelve or fifteen. My final semester I took 21 hours plus a six hour correspondence course. I made As and Bs on everything. And then, right before graduation, I found out I couldn't graduate because I had missed a three hour history course my sophomore year. I had 154 hours with a B+ average and I only needed a hundred twenty to graduate, but I needed that history course to graduate so I went back the in summer of 1959 and picked up that course and finished out my degree.

There was one professor who stood out: Dr. Green in the English Department. I failed Freshman English the first time, and the second time, I studied hard and stayed up the night before the exam. Then I said, "I'm gonna lie down for a couple of minutes," so I did and then slept right through the exam. I got over there just as they were closing the exam and the professor said, "Sorry, do better next time," so I wound up having to take Freshman English three times. Dr. Green taught literature and he was absolutely a great instructor and a nice person. He would allow you to memorize things for extra credit and I always had a very good memory so I memorized the thousand lines of Chaucer's Canterbury Tales in Old English.

The players who stood out on my freshman team were Eagle Day. David Dickerson was one of the better ends who played at Ole Miss. The guy who was probably the best football player was Jimmy Patton. Jimmy went on and played with the New York Giants but was killed in an automobile accident out east of Jackson. We had a center named Ed "Straight Ass" Beatty. There was a straight line from the back of his head to his heels. He had no fanny at all. He played with the Rams, I think. Another good player was Jack Reed, who went on to play professional baseball with the Yankees behind Mickey Mantle. You never heard that much of Jack but he was fast as greased lightning. He was a defensive safety and cornerback.

We played two-platoon until 1954 or 1955. Lea Paslay was from Sardis and was one of the most heralded freshmen who played at Ole Miss while I was there. Lea was a very good runner and was probably in the class of 1956.

We called Kline Gilbert "Goldie." He was like a hero to us, especially the linemen. Kline was in the class of 1953 and went on and played for the Giants. In fact he got bigger when he went up to New York. Goldie was a leader, was a good-looking guy with a good head on his shoulders. He was able to think for himself and make good decisions. Of course, Kline was an All-American. I was here for the Maryland game in 1952 but I was so excited during the game that I can't remember much. They were either number one or two in the nation and we beat them. I remember one play: we had a guy in the end zone and he was wide open. There was a hush in the crowd and the only thing you could hear in the stadium was this guy hollering, "throw me the f-ing ball." So they finally did throw him the ball and he scored a touchdown and we won the game.

Rex Reed Boggan was a tackle. He had played several years, then did three years in the Marine Corps and come back for his senior year. Rex Reed was one heck of a football player. If you were scrimmaging against him you better hit him hard because he was going to hit you hard. There were a couple of guys who were in their mid-twenties who were playing then, and a couple of them had been to Korea and had come back and played.

We had concerts in Fulton Chapel. The best was when Lionel Hampton came there. The student body filled the place and the people in the balcony started jumping up and down to the rhythm of the band. They cracked the balcony. A guy named Reed Funderburk, who was one of the football players, was overcome by the music and got up on the stage and started dancing. He was a great dancer and was in a trance. They finally went up and got him off of the stage but he was really having a good time. He later became a protocol officer at the Pentagon. I ran into him once in the military.

Showboat Boykin was here with me. He carried his dog with him to class all of the time. The dog was short-haired, either a boxer or a German shepherd. It lived in the dorm with him and went to class with him and sat right by his seat.

Pete Mangram was one of the better football players. He dated one of the cheerleaders, but she married a basketball player. We all looked up to Pete. There were some bad characters at Ole Miss, too. Guys who would steal stuff. We had two of our freshmen players who would get in your room and steal your clothes, steal your shoes, and the coaches kicked them out and they left Ole Miss. We had another guy who got kicked off the team, Marvin Trauth, but it was not for stealing or anything like that. Marvin was a tackle and he had huge arms and small legs and he dressed right next to me. Marvin would put his leg up on the bench and put his forearm down by his leg and say, "Joe, you think my arms are too big and my legs are too small?" You always said no, because if you said yes he'd knock the hell out of you. Marvin was from Gretna, Louisiana. One time during his senior year he decided he was going to miss practice. He was All-SEC but he didn't show up for practice and Coach Vaught kicked him off the team. Marvin came back and tried to get on the team. He talked to Coach Vaught and everything but Coach Vaught said, "I'm not going to take you back but I'll take you down and we'll talk to the entire team and if they want to take you back that's okay but I'm not taking you back." So he got Marvin up in front of the entire team in the field house and explained what Marvin had done wrong and told the team, "I kicked him off the team and I don't want him back if he can't do what I say. I don't want him around me. Now, if you guys want him back, if you think he's gonna behave himself and you want him to play on your team, then you can vote on it. So, Marvin, get out of the room and they'll vote." Marvin left the room and Coach Vaught said, "Okay, now everyone who wants Marvin on their team hold up your hand." So everyone held up their hand except maybe one or two people and Coach Vaught went out and got Marvin and brought him in and said, "Okay, you're back on the team again." From that day on Marvin practiced harder than anyone else on the team. It was a great way to do it.

Coach Vaught and I never got along very well. He was a very good coach. I thought for the first two years he thought my first name was "damn you" because that's about all he ever said: "Damn you, Neely, why'd you miss that block?" or whatever. But you can't argue with success and he was very successful. He had a very limited relationship with the players and had only one or two favorites he would talk to: Jimmy Lear he would talk to. Eagle Day. Generally it was the quarterbacks, but other than that, he was pretty much standoffish.

Bruiser Kinard was exactly as his name says. He was tough but he was fair and if you did what he said, you were okay. Now if you didn't do what he said, you wouldn't be there. Bruiser coached the offensive line. The defensive line coach was Buster Poole. Buster was always a very, very thorough defensive coach. He had only three defenses he ran but he wanted each of the players to do exactly what they were supposed to do in each one of the defenses. The three defenses Buster ran were a two-gap, where the linemen would line up between the opposing offensive linemen and you were all supposed to meet where the QB was standing in the backfield. We had four down and two back. He also ran a four-three where'd you have four down linemen and three linebackers and you would do stunts off of those. You'd either go right or left. I cannot remember the third defense. His schemes were fairly sophisticated for that time. He brought those from when he played professional.

Buster was a real taskmaster. He led all of the exercises at the beginning of practice. He was a nice guy, very likeable. I also liked Hurricane (Johnny Cain). He was like a little gadfly: he was everywhere at the same time. Coach Cain was a very excitable individual. He would jump up and down when he wanted you to do something. Hurricane was kind of short but he would jump up and get in your face and tell you what you needed to do. Junie Hovius, I remember, was a good guy.

Wobble had a difficult task in that he was supposed to make sure that everyone was behaving themselves in the dorm. He had a wife and maybe two children with about a hundred kids from 17 to 25 years of age living in the same building and it was pretty doggone difficult to make them behave themselves. He would come in and do bed check every night and I remember him being very fair but very, very tough. Wobble was very knowledgeable about the game. He was a teacher. I liked Wobble. I thought he was a really nice person. When I left the freshmen and went to the varsity, they continued to teach all the time I was here. We worked on fundamentals. They drilled on blocking and tackling. Fundamentals were just a big part of the game. I remember Doc Knight so well. We all loved Doc Knight. His favorite saying was, "You jughead, you." When anyone would get hurt he'd say, "You're a jughead for getting hurt like that." He not only was the trainer but he was also a teacher at the school. I took two classes from him. One was on sports injuries and the other was how you learn how to tape different joints. Doc Knight was a very good teacher and an excellent trainer. He worked harder than you can ever imagine.

My feeling about my time at Ole Miss is that the overall experience was great. My father was a sharecropper and in my family only one person had ever graduated from high school before me and I was the first to go to college. College was overwhelming and then it became routine and toward my senior year it got to the point where it was an uplifting experience. I remember individual things like the Grove before it became the big thing that it is now. I remember a guy from Columbus named V. P. Ferguson who had a picture of Jesus on the wall that he had cut the eyes out of and put in blinking blue lights. Down at the bottom it had "To V.P. from J. C." He would also occasionally get the PA system, which used to be at the student union, and in the morning he would play reveille. He was a heck of a good trumpet player and he would say over the PA system, "With the help of God, V.P. Ferguson presents the sun." He was a true character. His mother and father were separated. They decided to try to get back together when V.P. was in college and they went off on a trip somewhere. V.P.

decided to give them a house-painting present when they came home. They had one of the big southern mansions with big columns and things in front and he and a couple of his buddies painted the house black while his parents were gone. V.P. used to wear a hunting jacket around all the time with shotgun shells in it.

There was a football player there named Crawford Mims who married Boops Nosser. Her family owned grocery stores throughout Mississippi and Boops always had the saying, "I was amazed." Anytime they posted anything on the student union bulletin board someone would always come by and write, "I was amazed." Boops was also the head cheerleader.

The one thing that stands out was when I went back in 1959 and I was sitting in class and here was the girl sitting over to my right. I asked her where she was from and she said Tupelo. I said, "I know a lot of people there," and I started naming all of the people I knew who went to high school in Tupelo and she didn't know any of them. I thought boy that's strange, she must be a little bit on the dumb side and then I got to thinking about it and she was in the first grade when I was there. I'm so glad I went back and got that degree.

I think Ole Miss played a part in forming the basics of my life. It was absolutely a very positive experience and I feel good when I think about Ole Miss. It is a great school.

HARDY STENNIS

1952-1954

We had a very good football team my freshman year, 1952. That was the year we beat Maryland. King Lear was the quarterback and they called him that because of the Shakespeare character and because he was king of the football team. Lear was a terrific quarterback. I was at that game. We beat them 21-14. They gave us the next Monday off. Johnny Vaught ran that University then. Whatever he wanted, he would just call up the Chancellor and say, "I think you ought to do this," or "I think you ought to do that. You ought to give the student body a day off if we win. This game is the biggest thing that's ever happened at Ole Miss." And the Chancellor would say, "Oh, that sounds good Johnny. We'll do that." He was the king. The whole Ole Miss crowd—alums, students, foreigners; it didn't make any difference—stood up the whole game. They wouldn't sit down. It was like Texas A&M, those uniform-wearing Army boys, who stand the whole game. But they make the A&M students stand up the whole game. For the Maryland game, we just did it. I went to the first game in Memphis my freshman year. The first thing that happened was when some of my freshman buddies and I walked through the gate and showed our ID cards, going to our seats, a Memphis State boy ran by me and took my freshman cap off of me. It made me so mad and I chased that son of a bitch but I didn't catch him. He left the stadium. And it was cold, man it was cold. I froze that whole game. We beat Memphis (54-6). We always beat Memphis.

We went to the Peabody before the game for a pep rally. All the cheerleaders got up there and stood around the fountain. There was a little rail that was about two or three feet above the floor level. All the cheerleaders just circled that fountain and led us in the yells. And the band came in the lobby and played all the fight songs and the people were just packed on the mezzanine overlooking the lobby. They were just hanging off the rafters of that mezzanine. Man, it was exciting.

CLIFFORD FOX

1952-1956

I remember several games: Maryland was number one in the nation when they came down to play us and we beat them. As a corollary to that the next weekend LSU beat them. Their quarterback was named Jack Scarbath and he was supposed to be the second coming of Johnny Unitas. We played Kentucky at Ole Miss and they had a quarterback named Vito "Babe" Parilli. He played in the pros later on and I thought he was the best quarterback I ever saw. Kentucky beat the heck out of us. Conerly was a great quarterback. When Vaught took over he told Conerly, "You can either drink or you can play football." Conerly decided to straighten up and play that year. And of course he set a record for completions in 1947. The Pooles were memorable. There were so many of them. Ray Poole was a pitcher on the baseball team and Southern Illinois came in here at the first of the spring to play a series. Ray was the starting pitcher and he hit the first four batters who came up. So their coach said, "I'm not going to play." Tad Smith was the baseball coach and he took Ray out of the game. Ray was dangerous. He could throw a ball through a board fence. We were giving blood at a Red Cross blood drive and Bruiser Kinard was next to me. He was a monster—a big guy—so when we got through giving blood they unhooked us and gave us a glass of orange juice. We were on the second floor of the old YMCA building and they told us to sit there for a few minutes. And they said, "Now wait here a few minutes before you go," but Bruiser said, "I got to go." He got up and turned to go down the stairs and fainted and fell all the way to the ground floor. It sounded like the building was going to come down.

WALLY DAVENPORT

1953-1955

We played Maryland up at College Park and Irby and I talked with the administration about that trip. So the school said, "Well anyone who wants to go we'll let you off early in the week and give you plenty of time to get up there but you've got to be back on Monday." Well, we decided, "What the hell?" so we took off on Wednesday and went to Memphis. Then his mother was sick and he decided that he really needed to stay there and take care of her so I had to make a big decision on what to do. I said, "Hell, I'm this far already so I might as well go on." I got my thumb out and left Memphis that next morning and got in to College Park Friday night. It was dark and I didn't have a place to stay but others did so I found someone who had an empty corner and curled up in it. We woke up the next morning and it was raining and cold. The stadium was only about half full and they beat the hell out of us. Now Irby had told me to sell his ticket and to bring him the money but you couldn't sell anything because it was just too cold and too wet and nobody was buying. I decided that the weather was so bad and it was supposed to be that way all the way to Memphis that I caught the bus Sunday morning and got in to school late Sunday night but I was ready for class Monday morning.

I went to the Sugar Bowl with the band for the Navy game, January 1, 1955. We met back at the University after Christmas holidays and then bused down. The band stayed a couple of nights in New Orleans. They didn't give you spending money; if you got out on the town, well, then that was on you. We played Dixie and Forward Rebels and rolled out the big Confederate flag over the band at halftime. Everyone was underneath it with poles holding it up. That was a good trip and everyone had a good time but the ball players. The night before the game the Navy guys were locked in their hotel rooms and our guys were out on Bourbon Street.

GENE VAN CLEVE

1953-1956; 1958-1960

I played on the golf team, which was a great experience. We had the opportunity to go to the Masters with Coach Junie Hovius, a really fine man. Back then they would get colleges to send the players over there to act as gallery guards to control the crowd. The year I went was the first year Arnold Palmer won it and I followed him down the 18th fairway. It was a tremendous experience.

There were six of us on the golf team. We played in the SEC tournament over in Athens, Georgia, and we went to Vanderbilt, Memphis State, and Mississippi State. We went by private auto and they reimbursed us for gas. The other members of the golf team were Raymond Dearman, now an engineer in Hattiesburg; Jack Pittman, an attorney in Hattiesburg; Larry Wagster, who later became the girls' golf coach at Ole Miss and had a previous career with the FBI; Floyd Davis, who went to medical school, and the last one was Greg Lawrence. Larry Wagster was from Missouri and played basketball, too. Junie Hovius was about as fine as they come. He was a football great in the late thirties and early forties. Junie was from Vicksburg and used to run back punts. He was a good golfer and he was very good to us and fair to all of his players. When we traveled, the school paid for meals. We wore slacks and knit shirts on the course. I played three years and my last year I played number one several times. Jack Pittman and I alternated.

I was initiated into the M Club. You had to go through a beltline and sit on a block of ice and they'd shock you with an old telephone. Then, after you finished all of that, you had to run back to your dorm with no clothes on. It was in February and it was pretty rough running from the field house back to your dorm. They painted you red and blue from top to bottom. It was about one or two in the morning. A professor saw me running by and it stopped him cold. It was tough but I'd do it again. I was the first one to letter in a minor sport and be initiated into the M Club.

JOANNA POOLE HEIDEL

BUSTER POOLE

M y father, James "Buster" Poole, grew up in Homochitto, a small community that lies between Gloster and Liberty, in the piney woods area of south Mississippi. The Pooles had a community of people who lived around the little Homochitto school and Mt. Vernon Methodist Church. Daddy's father, Willie Poole, and his two brothers married three Berryhill sisters, so that's how it ended up being many Pooles who played at Ole Miss. They were Daddy's double first cousins. Daddy's two brothers were Barney and Ray. Daddy was the oldest—he was born in 1915—and he played at Ole Miss in the thirties, maybe starting in 1933. He told me how he came to Ole Miss: "I really didn't intend to go to college. The principal at the high school told me I wasn't college material and it wasn't necessary to go."

Daddy was one of nine children: two died and there were seven surviving children. Daddy was nine when his father died and Daddy was the oldest boy. When Daddy was in the eleventh grade, they closed the community school. They had like three grades to a teacher and so the rest of the Pooles ended up going to Crosby to school. Daddy didn't have any place to go and he liked school and wanted to finish. The only place he found that would take him was Natchez. That was about 55 miles from Homochitto, so he said that he hitchhiked down to Natchez. He didn't know anyone, but the boys on the football team saw him—Daddy had never seen a football in his life—and they said, "As big as you are, if you'll come play football with us, we will take you home and you can eat with our mamas at night." He said, "I would never have played football, but I really wanted to eat," so he first went to the sheriff who said he would let him sleep in the jail if Daddy would sweep it when he got up. Daddy lived there and said he was able to get breakfast every now and then. He was there until the Board of Supervisors counted heads and realized there were too many people in the jail. "So they tossed me out of there and I ended up living on the top of the drug store. The man who owned it let me sleep up there and I cleaned the drug store for him." School was very hard for him because that one-room schoolhouse he went to hadn't prepared him for Natchez High School. Daddy said that the Natchez schools were good and it was very hard but he graduated. He played just one year of football in Natchez but he and the Poole boys had always played baseball for a team on which everyone had the last name of Poole. He had also played basketball but they didn't have the equipment to play football at Homochitto.

Tad Smith came to Natchez and offered Daddy a scholarship to play at Ole Miss. So Daddy went home and asked Mama Poole whether he ought to stay and help her or go to Ole Miss. She said, "As much as you eat, I'd be a lot better off if you'd go on up there to school." He said that he really didn't want to go to Ole Miss. "I didn't know a soul at Ole Miss and I really wanted to go to State because they taught you how to farm." So he came to Ole Miss and played football, basketball and baseball. Daddy lettered every year in all three and then was the first Ole Miss player drafted into the NFL. When he was in New York, the pay was terrible, but they didn't know better and thought it was good pay. When Daddy died, we found a telegram from Wellington Mara, the owner of the Giants, and he and Daddy were very good friends, and the telegram said, "Buster, if you will come back and play one more year, we will pay you $125.00 a game." But Ole Miss had already called and asked him if he would be willing to come coach the basketball team. He said he made so little money in New York that he decided to come coach the Ole Miss basketball team and go to graduate school. He said it was a wonder he didn't die of a heart attack, because "Nothing is as up-setting as watching those basketball players." They didn't just play college teams: they had a little local team at Tupelo they played on their way up to Nashville. They drove all around Tennessee and Alabama with all of them in one car, playing local teams. That was around 1946 or 1947.

We had a player back in the thirties named Merle Hapes, whom Daddy called "Big"

COMPANY __"M" SECOND__ REGIMENT

UNITED STATES CORPS OF CADETS

WEST POINT, NEW YORK

9 August 1946

SUBJECT: Resignation from United States Military Academy

TO: The Superintendent of the United States Military Academy

1. I desire this to be considered as my resignation from the United States Military Academy. It has been my belief that I could resign upon graduation, but this was disproved by the Commandant of Cadets. Therefor, I am submitting this resignation immediately.

2. It is my desire to continue study in the field of physical education which subject has commanded all of my attention both before and after entering the academy. The past two years have failed to develop any interest in the army; further continuation in this career would be undesirable both to the army and to myself.

3. Financial responsibilities toward my mother have become increasingly urgent during my period in the service. Her income from a small farm is insufficient for her support.

4. I am quite sure that my indifference both to the military and academic services would necessitate my dismall from the academy at the termination of this semester.

5. I should like to state that I desire my football proficiency to be disregarded as a cause for rejecting my resignation.

6. I request immediate action be taken on this subject in order to permit me to enter my last semester of college.

George B Poole

George B. Poole
Cdt Sgt, 1° Cl, USCC

Hapes, and after the war, there was a shortage of housing so Merle, his wife and child, and my parents and I lived in a hotel in New York. The Giants were going to play in the championship game. Mother had gone out to eat with Big Hapes and his wife, and the Mafia was in the restaurant. She heard them talk to Big Hapes about bribing him, which they did. They subpoenaed Mother and I think Big Hapes got kicked out of professional football. Mother was scared to death. It was in the *New York Times*. So Daddy came back to Mississippi and coached because he didn't want to go back to New York.

All of the Poole brothers were very competitive people. Uncle Barney was no exception. He was at West Point when the war ended and they had three times as many soldiers and officers as they needed or wanted to pay. So Uncle Barney wrote a letter resigning so he could go on and play elsewhere, but they wouldn't release him. The only way he could get out, I always heard, was to fail a senior class, so he did and went to North Carolina and then came to Ole Miss.

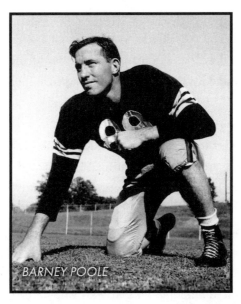

BARNEY POOLE

We moved to Oxford when John Vaught hired Daddy to be on his first staff. Then John got Bruiser, John "Hurri" Cain, and Junie Hovius. There was a big apartment house that faced the Grove and we lived there with the Hoviuses, and the Cains lived in one of the faculty houses. The coaches loved the alumni and considered them very good friends. Now, the coaches are kind of like celebrities and don't mix with the alumni like they did then. Daddy and Mother had a house full of alumni for every home game. Mother would cook all week and there would plenty of liquor. They loved those people and hunted with them in the spring. I think there was a wonderful camaraderie between my parents and the alumni. My mother was a people person. Johnsie Vaught, on the other hand, was not a people person.

She was feisty but she didn't hang out with the other women. The coaching staff was like a very big family. We vacationed together; we spent holidays together; we lived near each other. But Johnsie stayed very much to herself. That was just her nature. John and Britt Cain had both gone to Alabama so they didn't know the alumni like the rest of the coaches did. They had one daughter, Johnnie Britt, but we didn't see them like the others. Mother and Daddy had a lake house, which is where the Chadwicks live now, so the coaches went out there a lot. They'd fry fish and have fun, but Britt and John were kind of standoffish. They just didn't know everybody. John didn't hunt and fish, and the rest of them did.

Junie and his wife Kitty both were from Vicksburg and both went to Ole Miss. Junie and Kitty were wonderful people. Junie accidentally shot Kitty and killed her. They had finally built a house on a very large piece of property near the University, part of which is where Dick Scruggs built his house and the rest—Faulkner Woods—has a number of houses on it. They were having a problem with wild dogs and Junie got the shotgun out to scare the dogs. He walked through the room and the gun discharged and it killed her. So he had those four little boys. Everyone really loved her and he grieved a long time. They had a grandmother who came and lived with them for about ten years and then he married again, a lady named Anne Hale. He and Kitty—she was Kitty Tellant—were both from Vicksburg. She was a wonderful person.

In the fall we'd walk over to the Student Union to watch the boys get their head shaved. They would bring a flatbed truck and the Cardinal Club would shave them into mohawks and other assorted goodies and we would just watch and cheer. We just thought it was wonderful. We had the University as a playground. Paige Cothren was my cousin and in order to get to use our car, he would babysit us one night.

The coaches back then worked so hard to get those boys to Ole Miss. One of Daddy's responsibilities was to get a summer job for every boy who needed one. He had alumni who would hire them, like John Boyd, who was in the construction business in Grenada. He always would put five or six boys to work all summer. Daddy liked to put boys on construction jobs because it would get them in shape. And then after the boys got here, Daddy would talk to the professors to be sure the boys were going to class. We had a professor here who taught Jim Poole and Archie and Jimmy (Heidel). His name was Ron Pruitt, and he was in a wheelchair. One night he came up to Daddy at a dinner party and said, "Buster, you need to talk to Archie Manning. He's not studying very much and he's not going to pass if he doesn't get on the ball." Daddy looked at Ron and said, "Ron, do you know how hard it is to find a quarterback of Archie Manning's caliber and how easy it is to find an economics professor?"

Ron told that story for years to come.

I really saw a great deal of the boys and I didn't know any who didn't graduate. They were doctors and lawyers and presidents of banks and preachers. They all did something with their education and their lives. It is so different today. They are here to play pro and so few of them will make it. When Jimmy was drafted, out of sixty rookies on the pro team—some were drafted and some were walk-ons—two made the team and two made the taxi squad. When Daddy was coaching, we had more players in the NFL than any other school. Daddy used to get calls all the time because he played pro football a long time. His best friend, Jim Lee Howell, was the coach of the New York Giants a long time. Daddy would tell these coaches about the players and he would compare them to other Ole Miss players who were already playing pro football. He'd say, "I think he's faster than Jimmy Patton," and stuff like that. You know it's amazing that of all the men who came here to coach under John Vaught, none of them ever left until after John's heart attack. Then things starting falling apart. The assistants never made over $12,000 a year. John, when he quit, was probably making $20,000. Those assistants could have gone anywhere they wanted. Daddy went to pro training camps in the summer and helped coach the pro players. He worked for the Lions a bunch of times and then Pittsburgh for several years.

Tom Swayze always coached baseball but he also oversaw recruiting for Coach Vaught. He would have you think that he singlehandedly signed every player but each coach had an area that he recruited. Daddy's was West Point, Amory, Aberdeen—up in that part of the state. Bruiser worked a lot in the Delta. Uncle Ray worked south Mississippi. He was a great recruiter. He had a great touch. Uncle Ray never had a specific coaching function, so much.

TOM SWAYZE

He coached redshirts, but he was a great recruiter.

Wobble kept the dormitory, and Sara was always a delight. Wobble was the disciplinarian for the team. People have built him into a huge, bigger-than-life figure. When I was growing up he was the dorm guy, and if any of the coaches had a problem with one of the boys, Wobble would go run the boy in the stadium. Wobble was never elevated past the freshman team and I think he and John did not get along. Wobble was a very hard, hard coach, and he resented the fact that he never got elevated. He never got to work with the varsity.

WOBBLE DAVIDSON

Billy Mustin came later and took Wobble's place in the dorm with the boys. Wobble would walk outside and look in the windows to see what the boys were doing. Jimmy (Heidel) said one night he was studying and Wobble rapped on that window because he thought Jimmy was playing cards. Of course they had a lot of people who would slip a woman in there. They were certainly not jewels but Wobble stayed right on top of it. I think because he did and was so hard on them, people have built him up into this bigger figure than life, but once they left the freshman team, that was it.

The coaches loved each other, and I think they didn't leave because they had a marvelous time with each other and they cared about one another. It was a very, very sad thing when it began to fall apart. John had his heart attack and Bruiser took over the team, then Archie broke his arm. When Bruiser came in as head coach, he sat Jim on the bench. Jim was a junior and then his senior year under Billy Kinard, Jim sat on the bench. We realized later that Bruiser was very sick. He had a personality change. Mother and Daddy remained close to John Vaught and Daddy and John hunted together. I think John Cain was the first to die.

The boys loved Doc Knight. They had five or six children and lived out in the country. They raised chickens and Doc adored the boys. Before the game, he would write each boy a letter. He'd tell them who they were supposed to cover or what play they were supposed to run and he made each one feel very special. Doc spent an inordinate amount of time with those boys. He was from up north. I don't know how he got down here, but he never left.

The boys loved Nub Sanders, loved to imitate him, and Blind Jim was a symbol for them for many years.

Daddy, John Cain and Bruiser had a little office in the old gymnasium, right to the left of where you walked in. There was a little room and a secretary and the coaches kind of rotated around, using that office. Most of the time they coached they were there. Then they built that little building behind the gym. Most of the football coaching staff had other jobs. Junie coached golf. John Cain coached tennis. Doc was the track coach and they never signed a boy just to run track. The football boys ran track, and really, most of them played two sports. Uncle Ray coached the freshman baseball team. He had played pro baseball with the Cubs while he was playing pro football. He was a great pitcher.

All of the coaches played gin rummy, and if there was any way to compete, Daddy competed. He loved competition. They played in the office; they'd close the door and play. It was so different then: they'd watch one or two films of the other team and that was about it. They'd tell the boys who they were supposed to cover or who they were supposed to block or what play they were to run and then they played gin the rest of the time. They played in pairs. Daddy really liked to play but I don't remember John Vaught playing.

John Vaught was to me a very warm, loving person. He was always so dear and sweet to me. When I was a little girl I always liked him because he gave me some attention. He cared about his boys later in their lives and he loved it when they came back to campus.

Having grown up in a coach's family and having gone to Ole Miss, I feel really blessed that I was there at the time I was there because I could go and watch practice with Daddy and then ride home with him. I would go and drink an orange drink while they showered. The boys were really nice to me. It was a really golden time at Ole Miss. People weren't concerned about money.

SHIRLEY WAGNER CRAWFORD

1953-1957

EDDIE CRAWFORD

I was going with Eddie Crawford and we decided to get married. Eddie was to sign a contract with the St. Louis Cardinals to play baseball so we could get a little money. It was in December of his junior year and he went to see Coach Vaught to tell him he was getting married and was going to sign to play professional baseball. We drove over to the athletic offices and I waited in the car while Eddie went in. Coach Vaught listened to him and then said, "What did you sign here for, to play baseball or to play football?" Eddie said, "Football, coach." Coach Vaught said, "Then I expect you back for spring practice. Go tell Shirley you're not going to play baseball and you're not getting married." Eddie came back to the car and I asked, "What did he say?" Eddie said, "He said we're not getting married and I can't play baseball." So Eddie didn't sign with the Cardinals and we didn't get married and that was all there was to it.

BERNARD DANZIG

1954-1959

BERNARD AND MIRIAM DANZIG

I grew up in Rolling Fork and had a cousin who played football at Ole Miss named Sollie Cohen. He was an All-American back in the twenties and early thirties so I had that identification with Ole Miss. I felt that I wanted to go to an in-state school and I had this feeling for Ole Miss, so I went there. Solly was Jewish and The Commercial Appeal used to do stories about him after football games and the headlines would be "Jew Cohen runs for xxx yards or xxx touchdowns." He played fullback.

BOB BLACK

Boyhood

The Rebel Drive-In movie theater opened in about 1954 or 1955. The Ole Miss Drive Inn restaurant was across the highway (West Jackson) and they had a big parking lot. There was a creek running by the drive in movie, just beyond where you turn off Jackson to go to Home Depot. I was in the sixth or seventh grade and I'd help them take up tickets and I'd work in the concession stand selling hamburgers, hot dogs and soft drinks. The students were infamous for sneaking people into the movie in the trunks of cars. The older Mr. Adams could spot cars with people in the trunks. They'd come in with one guy driving, which was a dead giveaway. There was small theater seating inside the concession building. One night Mr. Adams noticed that there was a big group sitting in the theater style seating in the concession building and wondered why they were sitting in there rather than the automobiles. So one Saturday night he sent me over to the ditch, which ran along the west side of the drive in movie. I was over there and it was dark as pitch. Then I became aware of these people coming up out of the ditch. Well, I was supposed to catch these people and make them pay. The first batch of people I saw was about five people, all sizable. When they got closer, I recognized Crawford Mims and another guy named Blackledge. I was faced with a dilemma: I didn't want to hassle these guys for admission money but that's what I was supposed to do. Crawford had student-taught PE at Oxford Elementary the year before and I had been in his class. I just knew I knew him and that he would remember me, so I felt that I could approach him. I did and we struck a bargain that one of them would pay and the rest of them would come in. It was a practical thing because it looked like an invading army coming up out of that ditch. They were some big guys. I was a little peanut. The bad thing is they continued to send me out there and I guess I developed a reputation that if you pay one or two I'd let the rest of you in.

When I was at University High School we had coaches who were football players who were majoring in PE and they would come there and work with us in Spring football practice. We had Jimmy Patton and a guy named Dickerson (probably Dave), a big guy, and Dewey Partridge. Gerald Morgan coached us. Gene Hickerson used to work out with us. He worked at the Ole Miss service station in the summer. He was a big guy and he would come down and work out with us. We weren't doing much. It was a couple of weeks before practice officially began. Gene appeared several times. He was like the Jolly Green Giant: very approachable. He would do pushups with someone on this back and deep knee bends with someone sitting on his shoulders. Vaught didn't allow them to lift weights. He didn't want any of his players lifting weights because he was afraid it would make them muscle-bound and slow them down.

Ron Franklin was a year behind me. He played football but got hurt at some point. He was very competitive and loved sports: basketball and football and may have played baseball. He played center on the football team and my senior year he was playing center and he got injured with a concussion. Ron was in the hospital a few days and then had bed rest at home. He was in the chorus and had a great voice. Ron started out at WSUH, which was out on the hill at the end of University Avenue where the FBI building is now. He started doing high school football games there and then got involved out at Ole Miss. I think he was majoring in music and voice. I lost track of him when I went to Dental School and the Navy and then, when I came back, I found out he was working TV in Oklahoma. He went on to do play-by-play at Texas and then the Houston Oilers and then ESPN. He may have been in New Mexico at one point. Ron loved to fish and had a TV program on ESPN on bass fishing. It was on Saturday mornings. He once said that he enjoyed his work so much he felt like he was stealing from ESPN. I think he got a bum deal from ESPN. He called some lady a "babe" and they fired him. Give me a break.

RAYMOND BROWN

1954-1958

I was from Greenville and was recruited to Ole Miss by Coach Vaught. He came to our family restaurant in Greenville a couple of times. The coach at State was Murray Warmath. Coach Warmath told me that I didn't really want to go to Ole Miss. He said, "They've got quarterbacks just stacked up over there. It'd be four years before they'd let you play." So I mentioned that to Coach Vaught and he said something along these lines: "Do you believe in yourself? Do you think you can compete? I think you can but if you don't think you can compete over here then you go on to Mississippi State." That made a lot of sense to me, so I decided on Ole Miss. Ole Miss ran the T formation and we had run the T formation the whole time I was in high school. At times it was a wing T but mostly a straight T.

Wobble was the freshman coach but he didn't do a lot of coaching with the quarterbacks. Sometimes the varsity guys would come down and help. In my case, after I did my four years at Ole Miss and went to Baltimore, I came back in the middle of the year to enroll in law school. Coach Vaught, Coach Cain and Coach Poole were in the Alumni House grill and Coach Vaught called me over and offered to put me on scholarship, even if it was law school, if I would help them coach the quarterbacks in the spring and primarily work with the freshman quarterbacks. So I did that and when I would come back in the spring the next two years, I coached the quarterbacks. I played defensive back in Baltimore three years, and we won two world championships. There were 36 players on the pro team dress-out roster, so if you could do two things, you were more valuable. I started at safety on defense, did the punting and was the backup quarterback. The first year I was third quarterback and the next two years, I was the second quarterback behind Johnny Unitas.

When I arrived at Ole Miss it was pretty rough for freshmen. By the time we got to be seniors, we had toned that down a great deal. It went on pretty much all year, too. There was no restriction on the numbers you could sign back then and we had a huge freshman class. Coach Vaught would go out and recruit and sign just about anyone who could go out and play for Mississippi State or Alabama or whomever. We had four quarterbacks in my class and he also liked fullbacks whom he could change into linemen. Notable among those were Jackie Simpson and Gene Hickerson.

When I got to Ole Miss, Eagle Day and Houston Patton were there, and John Wallace Blalack was the third quarterback. By my sophomore year, Houston had gone, Eagle was there, and I began moving past Blalack. We played three games as freshmen and won all three. The varsity went 9-1 in 1954, losing to Arkansas, and we were 9-1 in 1955, losing to Kentucky in Lexington. Both of those would have been big bowl teams today, but there were only five bowls then, and the Rose was locked up with the Big Ten and the Pacific Coast Conference. In four years, we went to three bowls: two Sugars and a Cotton.

Jackie Simpson was an All-American my senior year and Gene Hickerson was an outstanding lineman. Coach Vaught's offense was a sprint-out, roll-out offense where responsibility was on the quarterback's shoulders to either run or pass. Eagle Day was a really, really good running quarterback. He would sprint out with the ball and choose his option based on where the cornerback and defensive end were, and he would either run or throw. The fullback was really important in the sprint out because the fullback had to take on the defensive end. It was a running offense because we had great fullbacks: William Otis Hurst, Charlie Flowers, Slick McCool, and they could take on that defensive end and open it up for the quarterback. Darrell Royal's old adage was that if you throw the ball, three things can happen and only one of them is good. William Otis Hurst's nickname, given to him by Wobble, was "Mama" Hurst. Wobble had a nickname for everybody, and he called him Mama because he said, "Hurst, you look pregnant."

One of the scrimmages I remember was when Richard Price was a freshman. We ran a quarterback sneak and they were in a gap six defense. I started up and Price almost took my head off. He was tough and played low to the ground on the running game. He was good.

Wobble's practices were pretty tough. Wobble's job, we understood, was to weed guys out of those big classes. Those who stuck were tough and those who weren't tough went home. And he did a lot of that. There was a guy from over in the Delta and Wobble tried and tried to run that guy off. Having largely failed, he took to finding some cause at practice to make the guy run around the field, over and over, and Wobble would holler over there at him, "Speed up! Speed up!" One day, the guy didn't show up. We learned that he didn't quit and go home, Wobble and Vaught just met with him and told him they would honor his scholarship, but don't come back out to practice anymore.

For the 1955 Sugar Bowl during my freshman year, I was not going to travel with the 1954 team as a freshman. I had been a member of the Greenville High Band, had played trumpet and in fact, was in the Greenville band in the seventh grade that won the state band contest and went to New York. The call went out from the Ole Miss band my freshman year when the team was going down to New Orleans to play Navy, so I went over there. I thought they needed a trumpet player, but it turned out that they weren't looking for band members, they wanted to recruit several people to carry that big Confederate flag over the field. They had plenty of people to do it in Oxford but not on the road. So they recruited three of us football players and told us they would take us to New Orleans. We went down there and stayed a couple of nights and carried the flag out onto the field and held it up over the band. We stayed in a Navy barracks that was close to New Orleans those two nights.

I lettered my sophomore year, which, of course, made me eligible for M Club initiation and it was tough. I got painted largely red and blue, nude, and was told that I would have to get back from the field house area to the dormitory on my own without my clothes. So some other guys and I darted across campus behind trees and bushes and whatever to get to Garland Hall, which was not very far from the old infirmary up on top of the hill. We're talking about three or four blocks. But it was late at night, so there weren't many people out on campus. And before they let us go, they paddled us—a lot. They also put plaster of Paris under our arms and between our legs.

In practice, Coach Vaught worked with the quarterbacks. I don't know where he picked that knowledge up. The rollout was part of a running offense. You turned upfield with the ball and ran or you threw it on the run. We didn't have but about a half-dozen drop back passes and we didn't use them very much. It was rollout and sprintout. On a sprintout right, you'd take your first step with your right foot in the direction you were going. On the rollout, you'd turn out about 75 percent of the way around and go out, which would allow both backs in the backfield to lead you. So on a rollout right you'd take your first step with your left foot and circle around and go right. We threw off of both types, and if we threw 20 or 25 times, all of them would be either rollouts or sprintouts. Sometimes, every once in awhile, if you needed a first down you'd drop back and the end could go down there seven or eight yards and hook and you'd hit him. We didn't throw long very much. Typically, the pass would be eight to 12 yards, but on each sprintout or rollout, you'd have an end going down farther and a back shorter and you would have a safety outlet in the form of the halfback who was rolling out ahead of you. You'd then have three receivers out there. The fullback would be taking out the defensive end. Coach Vaught pulled his guards on a lot of plays but not on the rollouts and sprintouts.

I had a lot of interaction with Coach Vaught. On the days we practiced, the quarterbacks would meet with Coach Vaught in his office. It might be prior to noon if our schedules allowed it and it might be after lunch but there was a time when we sat with Coach Vaught, not down at the stadium and not around the other guys. We'd sit and go over the game plan, go over the scouting report, in addition to the film session we had with everyone. The quarterbacks called our own plays based on the game plan we had put together all week long. So we would know in certain situations which plays we wanted to run. For example, we would know what the best short yardage plays were against a particular defense. Say it was third and two, you would have a few plays that you wanted to call in those situations depending on the defense they were running, but you would also have an alternate play. If you approached the line of scrimmage and instead of being in the kind of defense you had expected, they were in something else, like a gap eight with the linebackers up close, you had a couple of checkoffs that you could make to get out of the play that was called into one that would be a better gap eight play. You would do those checkoffs at the line of scrimmage. The way it worked was you had colors, like the "B" colors—brown, black, blue—and you would call one of those. That alerted everyone that a new play was coming, and so you would call a number right after the color. But if you called any other color, it was a dummy.

We played both ways all four of my years. Later, of course, Archie for example, played every offensive down, no defense. When I was there, when Bobby Franklin was there, we would play both ways for a period of time and then in would come another unit that would play both ways, and sometimes, a third unit that would play both ways. We called them the red team, the blue team and the green team. So instead of sixty-plus plays that you would have back then, your starting quarterback might get 35 of those, and if you were putting the other team away, you might get half or less. So in comparing total offense, whether it be running backs, or quarterbacks, or receptions or whatever, the numbers weren't nearly what they'd be if you played only offense the whole game. Back then, a thousand yards of total offense was a lot. Today, of course, quarterbacks get 3000.

We would start practice and we'd have passing work without the offensive line. We'd have skeleton backfield, practice handoffs, run the plays for the next game, then we'd all come together and begin working with the offensive line to get our spacing right and where to make the steps. Coach Vaught would work with us on footwork, on when you ought to release the ball and things like that. He didn't really teach passing techniques. He might say, "Son, you've got to get rid of the ball quicker. You can't loop the ball down around your hip and come back up with it. By that time, the defensive backs have closed in on you. So carry that ball up higher."

Leroy Reed was one of my running backs. He was really a bright guy, a Physics major. Kent Lovelace was a good running back. Hoss Anderson at fullback came along, with Charlie Flowers and Mama Hurst. Cowboy Woodruff was in there. Jimmy Hall was there. They were the backs we played with.

Teddy Millette was from Greenville. He was a star when I was in junior high and was a high school All-American running back. Unfortunately, Teddy bummed up his knee against Boston College his sophomore year. Jimmy Patton was also from Greenville. He was a good two-way player and went to the New York Giants and played in the defensive backfield. In fact, when I played in the 1958 NFL Championship game in Yankee Stadium, I played defense and punted. In that game, the defensive safety on both teams—Jimmy and I—played college football at the same place and high school football at the same place. You can look it up. My punting in that game was 51 yards on four punts, all fielded in the air by Jimmy Patton and Don Maynard, and nobody before or since has punted for 51 yards in a championship game. All in the air, too. No bounces, no rolls.

I was the third quarterback on the 1955 Ole Miss team, which was nine and one and went to the Cotton Bowl. I didn't play in the Cotton Bowl; it was too close a game. We played Georgia in Atlanta that season. It was a doubleheader. I think Georgia Tech played in the other game. We beat LSU 29-26 in Baton Rouge. It was a barnburner. They had a monster guy named Earl Leggett, who played a number of years with the Chicago Bears.

In 1956, my junior year, I had a good game against Kentucky in Memphis (37-7). That was the game that probably solidified my role as taking over the quarterback position against the competition, which included John Wallace Blalack. As a result, he went home. He quit and they had to go get him. They did and brought him back. Coach Vaught promised him that he could start the next game to give him an opportunity to win the position back. We went down to Jackson and played Tulane in a rain storm and got beat (3-10). Blalack was the quarterback most of that game and that was it for him. Fig Newton ran a long touchdown off of an option play. I've seen him a number of times over the years, and it wasn't too many years after that game that I told him, tongue in cheek of course, "If I had been in that game instead of Blalack when you ran that play, you wouldn't have gotten ten yards." My bunch and I drove the length of the field and time ran out on us at the ten yard line. We blew out LSU 46-17 a couple of weeks later. I started a sprint out in that game and somebody had busted through so I pulled up and I saw Eddie Crawford who had started to the outside. I could see that he was cut off so he turned around and I led him back to the inside. Eddie caught the ball and went for a long touchdown. Tiger Stadium got real quiet.

We had a bad loss to Tennessee in Knoxville. They had Johnny Majors, Tommy Bronson and those guys. I went back to pass, somewhere around the middle of our half of the field. Eddie Crawford again was the guy and he thought he was cut off from the outside and pulled up. I was going to the left on a sprint out so I threw it to the outside, and Tommy Bronson intercepted that ball, which was out in front of Eddie, but Eddie wasn't there. Bronson returned it for a touchdown. That was the year that Johnny Majors was runner up for the Heisman Trophy. He weighed about 165 pounds. Tennessee was still running the single wing and ran a lot of power stuff to the outside. We practiced for it by getting two or three additional—and expendable—defensive ends. We'd send them to crash in and bust up that tandem coming out of the backfield. They would tell them, "Don't worry about getting hurt. If you get run over, that's fine."

I had a lot of interaction with Doc Knight, who was absolutely a friend to all of the guys. He looked after us, took care of us, and would intercede for the players from time to time with the coaches. He was just a great guy. Johnny Cain was probably the toughest of the coaches. Bruiser, in spite of his gruff appearance was a gentle, nice guy. If somebody got on a player, Coach Vaught would a lot of times put his arm around you and say, "Son, you got to do better." It was sort of a "good cop, bad cop" kind of thing.

My senior year we opened in San Antonio against Trinity. Someone said something to Vaught about playing Trinity and Hardin Simmons, Chattanooga and some of those. He said, "You got to have a couple of games where you can play bad and still win." Kentucky had a damn fine halfback and he broke through the line and headed upfield. I caught him straight from behind. For the next week, our coaches couldn't believe that I had caught that guy straight away flat-footed. We beat Vanderbilt 28-0 and we got our revenge on Tulane 50-0. I had a good game that night. Our passes were working. One time, I ran a bootleg from our end of the field and I never saw a receiver as wide open as ours was. The whole Tulane team had gone in the other direction. I could have floated it to him.

We lost to Arkansas in Memphis 12-6. At some point in that game I got hit in the head and from whenever I got hit in the head to the end of the game, I must have done it by rote because when the game was over, I didn't remember anything after the early part of the game. It was a complete blank. I had retrograde amnesia. Apparently, it wasn't obvious to the coaches and I didn't have enough sense or know what to do. I probably didn't execute the game plan very well. We then played LSU in Oxford and beat them 14-12. That was Billy Cannon's sophomore year. We were somewhere around midfield and Jim Taylor came running up the middle. He and I were going to have a hell of a collision but he juked one way and I went for it and all I got was a hand on him as he ran by. Someone else had to catch him. I caught Billy Cannon in that game, too. He was running up the sideline. The winning touchdown came off a sprint out where I pulled up and hit the end coming across from the opposite side. About that time I was going to lead Don Williams with the ball into the end zone, Jim Taylor, playing defense, appeared in my sight, so I had to change the course with the ball and throw it downward. Don Williams did the finest home plate slide you would ever want to see. He slid and caught that ball about eighteen inches off the ground for the winning score.

State tied us 7-7. After our game in Memphis when we beat Tennessee 14-7, we came into the dressing room and were celebrating. Coach Vaught yelled for our attention and he said something like, "Fellows, this man here is a representative of the Sugar Bowl and what he wants me to tell you is that if you guys want to go, we can play in the Sugar Bowl on January 1." We said yeah, yeah. Then we went to Starkville with the Sugar Bowl in our pocket. It was anticlimactic (7-7 tie). I'm certain to this day that had we not had that Sugar Bowl bid in our pocket and had to play for a bowl bid we would have beaten them.

We played Texas in the Sugar Bowl and part of our offensive setup was that we were go-ing to run some plays from an unbalanced line with both guards on the same side of the center. The coaches figured if we ran that just a few times and didn't stand up there on the line of scrimmage too long, they might line up on the ball as opposed to counting the men, and we might out-man them to one side or the other. We made the quarterback run option go for a good bit of yardage. I did, Bobby Franklin and Billy Brewer did, running a few of those off balance things. They didn't pick up on it and we made a good bit of yardage off of it.

Then, in the huddle for a punt I told the guys, "Look, I may not be able to kick it very far. I'm damn tired. You guys get down there and cover that ball." So we lined up on the eight yard line and they snapped the ball to me. I'm really not sure whether the snap was a little off or I bobbled it a little. But about the time I'm going to take that last left-foot step, I felt the Texas defensive end coming in from my left. So I planted my right foot, juked, went around him and headed upfield. I had one more guy to avoid and I did. Pretty soon there were a bunch of Rebels around me. It actually went 103 yards but since the ball was on the eight yard line it was officially 92 yards. Somewhere around the twenty on the other end of the field, Jackie Simpson was yelling "Lateral, lateral, lateral!" I could hear him but I wasn't about to let that ball fall on the ground. When I got into the end zone I saw stars. I was so exhausted I was afraid I was going to pass out.

My wife Lyn had come down with some friends and she was in the stadium. Somehow she found her way down to the sideline and was there when I came to the sideline. I didn't want to sit down so I went over to the sideline table with the phone on it and turned around to face the field. Then, all of a sudden, there's Lyn, on the sideline, with the game going on.

I was on Ole Miss' first ever baseball College World Series team, the 1956 team, which was the spring of my sophomore year. The team was set pretty good. We had pitchers like Joe Gibbons, Buddy Wittichen and Don Goad who were really good. We had a guy named Moose Scott who played shortstop and made it to maybe Triple A and Bernie Schreiber made All-American. I played infield and had a pretty good year. We won the SEC and went to Gastonia, North Carolina and won that then went to Omaha. Joe Gibbons was a left-hander and pitched for Pittsburgh in the National League. He also played basketball and was a high scoring basketball player. I played two years of college baseball but then had to give up my senior year of baseball, because by playing in the Senior Bowl, for which we were paid, I was ineligible to play my senior baseball season. The rule has since changed, and one can play pro in one sport and be an amateur in another.

I feel wonderful about my time at Ole Miss. How could I have chosen so wisely where to go to school, what to study, whom to play for and be so lucky to meet my wife? There was a guy named Chubby Ellis who was the Assistant Registrar. He tried to recruit people to come to Ole Miss and he recruited Lyn to come up for a weekend. He told her and a friend that he would get them dates with football players. The first night, my roommate Billy Prewitt dated Lyn and I dated the other girl and the next night we switched. Chubby had gotten them invitations to a couple of sorority dances so when she came on campus for her freshman year I was waiting for her. We were married at the end of her freshman year and my senior year.

Authors Note: Ray Brown completed law school at Ole Miss, clerked one year for Justice Tom Clark on the United States Supreme Court (1962-63) and practiced law from 1963 to 2014 in Pascagoula.

LYMAN HELLUMS
(APRIL 19, 1926-JULY 4, 2015)

Broadcaster

I grew up in Tishomingo County and played a steel guitar in a dance band. That put me around some radio stations, and I found that I enjoyed that kind of thing. I served in the Navy where I fought the battle of Norfolk, which I barely won. I got out before the war was over, but it was winding down. I was the only male in our family, and Dr. Bickerstaff was my mother's brother. He was head of the Math Department at Ole Miss and he talked me into coming over to Ole Miss. But you know, after you've been out it's hard to go back to school. The veterans were just coming back that fall. I lived with Dr. Bickerstaff who lived near Tad Smith, Dr. Howerton and several others. It was kind of a professors' row. Lillian, his wife, was an English professor.

I went to Ole Miss for about a year and a half the latter part of 1945 and first semester of 1946. My GI Bill ran out so I had a little money and went to radio school in Memphis. When I finished radio school, I had two opportunities: one in Jackson and one in Wheeling, West Virginia so I chose Jackson.

I joined WJQS, 1400 on the dial, and our studios were on the mezzanine of the King Edward Hotel. We were the CBS affiliate in Jackson and carried a lot of the CBS programs like Jack Benny and all of the real popular shows back then. I did news, sports and whatever had to be done. It was done live back then—no recordings. I was then hired by WSLI in Jackson. Back in those days they didn't want you to go directly from one station to another in the same town. They wanted you to get out of the area for awhile and then come back. So that's what I did. I went to Lake Charles, Louisiana and stayed about a year and a half and then came back. When I came back, we went on the air in television in 1953. Everything was done live. I did news and sports and a couple of variety programs. We had a staff of 17 people. I was out there at the station after I retired and they had about 130 people.

I started doing the Ole Miss games in 1955. The play-by-play man was Maury Ferrill and we worked together for two years. Then a boy came down from Knoxville named Art

Metzler and we worked together for two years. After Art, Bill Goodrich came aboard and we worked together five years. Evan Lewis came on for a couple of years and then Stan Torgeson and I worked together for 17 years altogether. Charlie McAlexander was there when Ken Cooper was coach. And then Stan came back for awhile. A boy out of Memphis came next, and then David Kellum through the 1995 season when I hung it up.

I saw some great years during the Vaught era. That was a great time. He kept the same staff for a long time. Bruiser and Buster, Ray Poole, Roland Dale, Eddie Crawford, Junie Hovius and Johnny Cain. They had a lot of continuity. I got to know them all and they became good friends. I played a lot of golf with them, especially Johnny Cain. Nub Sanders was slick when it came to gin rummy. He would keep moving those cards around and you never knew what he had. He had trouble holding his cards and he'd drop them and pick them up. He was something. He was so loyal. One time down at the Sugar Bowl we played Rice (1961). Coach Vaught liked to talk to his team for four or five minutes after the game so he told Nub to stand over there at the door and told him, "Now don't you let anyone in until I get through." So the Governor (Barnett) came up and opened the door and Nub said, "You can't come in." And the Governor said, "Well you understand I'm the Governor and I want to talk to Coach Vaught." Nub said, "I don't give a damn who you are, you aren't coming in. Coach Vaught don't want anybody in there." And he didn't let him in. Nub would go up to Memphis and get the film for the game the following week. He was the equipment manager.

Doc Knight was like this: Wobble would knock a player down and Doc would pick him up. Wobble was a great guy and everyone respected him, but he was the enforcer. Doc was the guy who picked them up and he was a great guy to have around. And of course, he mended up their broken bones. Doc was a father figure. I remember we were down on Bourbon Street the night after the game and several of the players were down there with us. Doc was right in the middle of them and some guy started hassling Doc. The players were ready to go after that guy but Doc held them back.

That first year—1955—we went nine and one. We lost to Kentucky the second game and then beat TCU in the Cotton Bowl. I didn't go to the Cotton Bowl. The broadcast team didn't go to the bowl games back then. ABC had the broadcast rights so they did it themselves.

Coach Vaught was first class. First of all he was a gentleman. In 1960 I got out of television and went with Wilson Sporting Goods Company as a field representative. They wanted three references so I gave Reed Green of Southern, Wade Walker of State and John Vaught, and they checked them all out. He gave me a great reference. I saw him and thanked him and he said, "I told them you weren't worth a damn but I thought you could sell." He was just a great guy. We wound up better friends after he quit coaching because we played a lot of golf together. One time we had a golf tournament at Olive Branch, just out of Memphis, and he'd invited some of the old alumni and a few players so I played. After we finished our round he came up to me and asked if I wanted to play a few more holes. I said "Yeah, who you got? He said, "Spook Murphy and Pick Randall from down in Gulfport." I said, "You think we can beat them?" and he said, "I think so." And I knew if he thought we could beat them then we could because he always got the schedule right. So the first hole was a dogleg par five, with the dogleg to the right. John cut across the dogleg and knocked the ball on the green in two and made the putt for an eagle. So we go to the second hole and it runs right along the street and he hooked his ball out into the street. I hit second and hit one up the middle and Spook says, "Vaught, where do you get all these damn ringers from?" and Coach Vaught said, "Spook, I always could out-recruit you."

You know, Ole Miss didn't draw back then like it does now. I don't know how many Hemingway Stadium held, but I remember we opened the one down here (Memorial Stadium, Jackson) in 1961. We played Arkansas and it didn't seat but 20,000 people. Frank Broyles was coaching then and they had Jerry Jones, who owns the Cowboys now, and Barry Switzer who coached at Oklahoma and coached the Cowboys, and Jimmy Johnson. We beat them 16-0. Doug Elmore was the quarterback but Vaught usually had three quarterbacks. Archie was the only quarterback to start as a sophomore. Usually you'd be a junior or a senior to start because there was always someone ahead of you.

I was the golf pro over in Tupelo for fifteen years and I played golf with Glynn Griffing. He could hit a ball as far as any man I ever saw. Junie was the best golfer on the staff. Coach Cain was a good golfer. Now on Wobble, I had breast cancer, which men can get and I was over there and I was walking across the parking lot to go in the stadium. There weren't many people out there and Wobble says, "Hey, come here." I said, "Whatcha want?" He said, "Come here and show me your titty." I said, "I ain't got one," and he just laughed. He was a real character. He called his wife Sara the goddess of dawn. He couldn't get her up in the morning. She liked to sleep. The more you were around him the better you liked him. I asked him how he got his name. He said when he was in the first grade in Memphis the teacher said all you children back there sit down. All you young 'uns want to do is wiggle. Wobble said, "I don't wiggle, I wobble," and so from that day on they called him Wobble.

Wobble ran a tight ship with the freshmen. Doug Elmore told me years later, "I still wouldn't smoke a cigarette in front of him." He ran the athletic dormitory until Mustin took over for him.

The football network back then was run by Texaco. An agency in New York—the G. H. Johnson Corporation—and placed all Texaco radio advertising. They had twelve major colleges that they had the broadcast rights to. Jeff Hamm used to handle it and it got to be a headache because people would call up the morning of the game and want to pick up the game. So it became a rat race to try to put the thing together. Then, Texaco bid on the rights and they got it so that's who we worked for. There was Ole Miss, Georgia, Alabama, Florida, North Carolina, Notre Dame, Northwestern, Kentucky and some others. Anyway, Texaco had the rights and if you wanted to carry the game you had to order the game out of New York by a deadline that was certainly prior to Saturday. A lot of them would want to wait till the last minute but when Texaco got it, it was a lot more organized. Back then it was all telephone lines. AT&T would be working right up to game time to be sure you got on the air.

We traveled with the team a lot of the time, but I lived in Jackson and it was sometimes easier to drive from my home in Jackson to Birmingham, LSU or Memphis. I've ridden on the buses with them. They'd ride a bus to LSU and Tulane. We didn't travel that far, except to San Antonio to play Trinity.

JIM TOM ATHERTON

1955-1959

I grew up in southern Illinois, about seven miles north of Cairo, Illinois, and attended Ole Miss on a basketball scholarship from 1955 to 1959. Country Graham was basketball coach while I was there. I actually found Ole Miss; they didn't find me. My parents and I were visiting some friends down in Alabama named Gilchrest and his wife was from Rolling Fork, Mississippi. She knew I was a basketball player. I was a senior in high school at the time and she said, "Well, have you ever considered Ole Miss?" I said, "No, I haven't," and she said, "Let me contact the people up there and let them get in touch with you." So that's how it happened. Coach Graham invited me down to Ole Miss for a tryout and I worked out with the players who were on campus at that time. Then he offered me a scholarship. They couldn't do that now and I don't know whether it was legal even back then.

I entered in the fall of 1955. Coming from southern Illinois to Oxford, Mississippi was not that big of a change. We had a black high school and a white high school in my little town. It was the same for grade schools and was that way in all of the towns in that end of the state. So I had never attended school with a black person before and I didn't think much about it. In fact, when I got to Ole Miss people would say, "Where're you from?" and I'd say, "southern Illinois." I guess people in Mississippi thought that was Chicago and they'd say "How'd you get way down here?" I ask, "Where are you from?" They'd say, "Biloxi," and I'd say, "I'm forty miles closer to Oxford than you are, and I'm four states away."

So it really wasn't that big of a cultural change. I was familiar with Memphis where I'd been several times. I didn't even know where Ole Miss was so I wasn't familiar with Oxford. My parents brought me down and I lived in Vardaman B, which was the athletic dorm for basketball and baseball players. The football players lived up in Garland. We had freshmen parties where the M Club members would whip your ass with a paddle. I came home one weekend and my butt was still red. My mother said, "You're not going back," and I said, "Yes I am." They would gather us all together in the dorm and line us up and paddle us. The scholarship basketball players in my freshman class were Larry Eubanks from Tupelo, who left after one semester; Jimmy Graves, a tall kid from Meridian, and myself. Just the three of us.

When I arrived on campus they shaved my head and I got a beanie. We started basket-ball practice in October but back then we didn't play with the varsity. Cob Jarvis was my freshman coach. He just passed away over in Alabama. We practiced with the varsity but had a freshman schedule. One of the players on the varsity was Joe Gibbons, one of the best athletes Ole Miss has ever had. He was from Hickory and pitched for the Pirates for twelve years. He was the second leading scorer in the nation in basketball his senior year behind Lenny Rosenbloom of North Carolina, one of Frank McGuire's New York boys. Some of the others on the Ole Miss team were Jerry Bynum from Corinth, Bobby Robinson from Booneville, and Bobby Williams from Memphis. Jack Waters, another great player was a freshman when I was a senior. We had very average teams while I was here. Kentucky was the dominant power.

Once we were playing Kentucky in old Ellis Auditorium in Memphis because it was our home game and Ellis Auditorium held a lot more people than the old gym on campus. That was Joe Gibbons' senior year and the benches were on the same end of the floor, like Vanderbilt now. We were leading Kentucky and Rupp called timeout and in that old Kansas twang voice of his—he had a forward who was guarding Joe Gibbons named Roger Crigler —I heard him say, "Crigler, you sorry sonofabitch. We're trying to win this game whether you know it or not." Joe was working him over pretty good. They came back on us. Not many people know this, but Rupp had a farm system. He would send players down to junior colleges like Northeast Mississippi Junior College and then bring them up when he needed them. There was a kid—a guard—named Adrian Smith and of course there wasn't a three point shot then. Adrian had been back from an appendectomy for a week. He hit two set shots outside that beat us by three points.

Coach Graham was an underrated coach. He didn't have a lot of talent during those years. You've got to remember that his main job as far as the Athletic Department was concerned was scouting for the football team and recruiting in both football and basketball. He idolized Coach Rupp. All of his plays revolved around what Coach Rupp had in his book. His practices were pretty intense, a lot of running and getting in shape and battling through screens. I have fond memories of him.

I was about 6'1" and played guard. We had about ten or 12 varsity players, the three scholarship freshmen and some football players who walked on and helped fill out the squad. There was a big old boy from Memphis named Milton Crane who played center on the football team. Dewey Partridge played football and basketball. He was part Choctaw Indian from Philadelphia. He was a running back and a good receiver. I think he lives down on the coast somewhere. Dan Jordan was from Philadelphia and he played. A super guy. He was a Sigma Chi. I thought he should have run for Governor of Mississippi.

I went though fraternity rush and pledged Sigma Chi. I made a lot of lifelong friends: Jerry Hornsby, Joe Pegram, who's a lawyer in Oxford, and Frank Crosthwait stand out to me now.

I went to the football games, including the ones we played in Memphis. We played at Crump Stadium behind Central High School. I remember taking a date to the Tennessee game, which we won (14-7). Herman "Eagle" Day was a senior my freshman year and he was one helluva athlete, too. Played baseball and football. They were playing TCU in the Cotton Bowl his senior year and Coach Vaught sent Paige Cothren in to punt on fourth down and two or three at midfield. Eagle said, "We ain't punting, we're going." Vaught asked Bruiser when they lined up, "Bruiser, what the hell are they doing?" And Bruiser said, "Johnny, I think they're going for it." And they made it. Eagle was a cocky guy, but a great guy. I knew him through M Club. He didn't belong to a fraternity. Raymond Brown, the next quarterback, was a Sigma Chi. Winslow Winston was a Sigma Chi. Raymond was the most notable. I remember the Sugar Bowl game against Texas. He was supposed to punt from about the ten and maybe the snap was a little off and he bobbled it so he took off and ran ninety yards for a touchdown. The story was that Jackie Simpson was running beside him and they got near the goal line and Jackie said, "Give me the ball so I can score." Raymond didn't give him the ball.

I never thought that the basketball team was a step-child to the football team. We got the same scholarships, same food, same books, same everything. I never felt that we were secondary but I knew that football paid the bills.

M Club initiation was my sophomore year. It was the last year they held the famous initiation where they took you down to the field house, stripped you down naked, blind-folded you, and paddled your ass constantly for two hours. They made you do silly ass things, painted you red and blue and ran you back to the dormitory naked. It was about midnight but there was so much uproar about it that Chancellor Williams decided that was out and wasn't happening anymore. Charlie Flowers was a class behind me and only had to carry a football around campus the next year for his initiation.

There was a Quonset hut right across the street from Vardaman and down the hill from Garland and we took our meals there. The food was great. A lady there named Mrs. Calhoun was the manager of the athletic cafeteria and she was a wonderful, wonderful lady. We were really fortunate.

We had a helluva lot of card games in the dorm and some of them introduced me to Boure. There was a fair amount of smoking and drinking going on, too. Leroy Reed was a Sigma Chi who was on the football team. Carlton Garner was a basketball player who stands out now to me. Archie White stood out. He was a baseball player, and he adored Cob Jarvis. Archie was a helluva baseball player but I don't think he went to class much. Buddy Wittichen was another.

When I was a freshman there was a Hansom "Bull" Churchwell from Lucedale. I think he was the strongest white man I ever saw. The freshman football players lived in Vardaman A and we lived in Vardaman B. We were over there in Bull's room and he lay down on the bed and stretched his arms out on both sides. Two people got on each arm and he just picked them right up.

Playing Kentucky in Memorial Coliseum up there stands out to me. You would look around and see the banners indicating NCAA Champs and you thought, "Ummh, those boys can play basketball." After they finished playing "My Old Kentucky Home," it just got worse. We were playing them in Jackson my senior year because again, the gym down there held more people. They had an All-American named Johnny Cox from Hazard, Kentucky, and Coach Graham said, "We're going to play a zone." So Cox sits over in that corner and hits about five one-hand jump shots out of the corner. I said "Coach Graham, I think we need to come out of that zone."

The State football games at home always stood out. We always won back in those days. Coach Vaught recruited fullbacks and turned them into pulling guards. He liked the speed. The records when I was at Ole Miss were 9-1, 7-3, 8-1-1 then 8-2. So we really had good teams when I was there.

We were playing Georgia in basketball at home and they were about like we were, average or below average. They had a coach by the name of Red Dawson or something like that. He and Coach Graham were talking before the game and Georgia's coach said, "Well Country, it looks like we're going to fight it out again for the cellar."

I played against Bailey Howell at State all four years. Of course, State coach Babe McCarthy was a great recruiter and a great coach. He and Country Graham were from the same area up in North Mississippi. They were about four miles apart growing up. Coach Graham hated Coach McCarthy and State with a passion. The last game of Bailey's college career was in our gym and it was packed. The freshman football players had gone over to State and stole the bulldog. They brought it out on the floor before the game painted red and blue. Bailey needed like twenty-something odd points to break Bob Pettit's scoring record in the SEC. We were determined he wasn't going to get it. The score at halftime was like 7-5. We held the ball the whole damn time. And it ended up like 23-19 and Bailey didn't break the record. But he was a heck of a player. I never thought he would make it in the pros because I didn't think he was tough enough. But he did. He has many championship rings to show for it. And there was another player at State named Jumpin' Jim Ashmore. He became a dentist later in life. He was ahead of me by about two years. Ashmore was a great jump shooter. Coach Graham decided that we were going to overplay him and make him go to his left because Coach didn't think he could score going to his left. Jumpin' Jim got 38 points that night. So much for that theory.

Big Gene Hickerson's mail box was next to mine in the post office. So he'd go in there and pull out an envelope. They got paid for how many tackles they made or whatever. And he opened that envelope and said, "Hell, is that all he could send?" We got only $15 a month laundry money. Combine that with the $27 a month I got for Advanced ROTC and I was in hog heaven. Hickerson and Eagle would get their clothes free at Carl Coers. I hung out in the Grill some. It seemed like there was a bridge game going all of the time in the Grill.

And you could smoke back then. It took a knife to cut through the haze back then. We had two Miss Americas when I was there: Mary Ann and Lynda Lee. Bessie Sarphie and Pat McRaney were both beautiful. Ole Miss has always had beautiful women and they still do. It's amazing.

Back when I was playing at Ole Miss we were at a basketball tournament at Louisville, Kentucky. Joe Gibbons was still playing and we were told there would be no black players on any of the teams in the tournament. Well, Iona College had one black player out of New Rochelle, New York, and we were to play them the second game. The Board of Trustees ordered us home and we came home and didn't play. Mississippi State was over in Evansville, Indiana, and they had to do the same thing. So Khayat got in touch with me. He thought it was an NCAA game but I told him it was a holiday tournament. Later, when Ole Miss played Iona College in the NCAAs, Robert invited that lone black player off of the 1957 Iona team to come and sit with him at the NCAA game. Robert's nickname in college was Teddy Bear, and he was the best thing to happen to Ole Miss in the last one hundred years. He is a real hero in the history of the University.

The four years I spent at Ole Miss were one of the most enjoyable times of my life. It was a small school compared to the other SEC schools. It still is. Probably less than 4000 when I was there and everyone spoke. I still have so many friends from my time there, not just fraternity brothers. I know people in Greenville and Biloxi and all over and it was just a great experience in my life. George Falls was a Phi Delt, along with Warner Alford and Bobby Khayat, and I've stayed in touch with them.

WILL LEWIS, JR.

The College Years: 1954-1958

I saw the Showboat Boykin game in Starkville (1951). He scored seven touchdowns off the same play. I also saw the Maryland game in 1952. I was in high school. There was no game to equal that: the tension before the game. It was hard to get tickets for the game. They were number one in the country that day and had been the undefeated national champions the year before. I believe it was the only game they lost. The next year we went up there and they beat us 38-0.

In January of 1953 we went to the Sugar Bowl after the Maryland win. We took the train down there. It was a big Christmas present for me. Mr. Blaylock who was the father of my friend Darrell, was our chaperone. He owned Blaylock Drugs. We played Georgia Tech and thought we had gotten robbed. We got the ball, went down and scored and were up 7-0. Then we got the ball again and went down again and Wilson Dillard ran it on 4th down.

The refs said he didn't score but Wissy and everyone else said he did. It was all downhill from there. They had this great back, Leon Hardeman who was an All-American. Tech filled up one side of the Sugar Bowl and there weren't that many of us. We weren't accustomed to going to bowl games then.

LEE DAVIS THAMES

1954-1960

I was in the band one semester and Banks Shepherd was editor of the annual that year and I started taking pictures for the annual. Then Banks was taking pictures at the spring dances and got me to help him with that so we formed a partnership where we took the pictures at the dances. I didn't get paid for the work on the annual but we made pretty good money taking pictures for the formals. I also started taking pictures at football games and then I started selling pictures from the football games to AP, UPI and all. During football season we always played Tulane and then LSU played someone else at night so I would catch a train down to New Orleans and cover the Ole Miss-Tulane game and then hitchhike up to Baton Rouge and cover the LSU night game. I could cover two games and sell some pictures. I took the picture of Paige Cothren kicking the winning extra point in the Cotton Bowl and sold it for enough money to cover tuition and books for a semester. I just happened to be in the right place at the right time. I made connections with AP and UPI through Memphis and met people on the sidelines who would help me. I would hitchhike to Starkville and other places to photograph games and had a sideline press card that would get me in.

When I was in the band we went to a doubleheader in Memphis where State played in the afternoon and Ole Miss played Kentucky that night. We had to go to the afternoon game and play for State and play "Hail State" and all of that stuff. And then we came back for the night game and I'll be darned if the State band wasn't on the other side of the field playing for Kentucky. When I was in the band we played at the pep rally in the Peabody. It was the first time I had ever been in the Peabody. It seemed as big as the Superdome. The Creel Room was off the lobby. It was a big gathering spot for Ole Miss students.

I came up here for the Maryland game in 1952. They were number one in the country and had the Modzelewski brothers. It was a fantastic game and we won 21-14. After the game two cars were turned over and set on fire. It was sheer bedlam. Jimmy "King" Lear was the quarterback. A great guy.

In those days most of our home games were in Memphis. We also played one game in Jackson. We were undefeated my sophomore year when we played Tulane in Jackson Memorial Stadium. In those days I used an old flash but they had come out with an electronic flash and I borrowed some money and bought one. It had a big battery pack that you wore on your shoulder. At the Tulane Ole Miss game it rained the whole ballgame and every time I took a picture it just shocked the hell out of me. And on top of that, Tulane beat us.

Everyone dressed up for football games: coat and tie for the boys and the girls wore suits and gloves. Even the coaches dressed up. I remember Coach Vaught in a suit and a hat.

We took a train to the Cotton Bowl. It made up in Meridian, stopped in Jackson and stopped again in Vicksburg. It had Pullman and non-Pullman cars and about every third car they had taken mail cars and turned them into bars. And when that train rolled into Vicksburg it was something. We got on the train and went to Dallas. I was with Banks and Mary Ann Shepherd and had a date with a girl from Vicksburg. The only other one I remember is the train trip down to the LSU game in 1959. If you see the film of Billy Cannon's run, when he breaks out on the film there is a flashbulb. That's me. The picture in the 1960 annual of him starting his run is in the annual. I was down on the goal line at the end of the game. We were on the two yard line. Doug Elmore was the quarterback and we didn't score. I think Vaught learned his lesson about punting on third down. He never did that again.

I went to the Sugar Bowl when we beat Texas, the Sugar Bowl against Navy, the Cotton Bowl, The Gator Bowl and the Sugar Bowl when we played and beat LSU in the rematch game. We went to bowls fifteen or more years in those days and that's when there were only five bowl games.

Robert Khayat and Warner Alford were both Phi Delts and great guys. The demands that Coach Vaught put on them didn't give them a lot of time outside of football. Robert was also catcher on the baseball team. They were very good and won the SEC championship two years in a row.

ED WILBURN HOOKER

1955-1959

We did a lot of beer drinking. We'd go to Memphis and go to Milo's, then go to the big metal basket where they put all of the cut rate liquor and buy that stuff. We'd go to Marks to drink beer at Lambert's Grocery. I went over there with some football players and the place was full of truck drivers. Charlie Duck, a football player, was over there near the phone. A fight started and he pulled the phone out of the wall because there wasn't going to be any calling the police. We fought our way out of there and as we did, we loaded up with cases of beer and filled up the trunk of my car. I knew we were going to get caught because they knew we were headed back to Oxford so as a precaution, I cut off the headlights and drove back to Oxford in the dark. We went up in my dorm room and had all of this ice and barrels. Roy Moore was over there asleep and we cut my stereo up so high that Roy sat up on the edge of his bed. Dick Gates sat there on his bed and dealt him a hand of gin rummy. We were playing poker and as the ice melted in the night it dripped down through second floor and first floor. Bobby Fisher and Charlie Duck came up to my room to check on me and there was water running out of the dorm. I lived in the dorm two years.

Mostly seniors lived in the Phi Delt house; I got in there my senior year. We had a poker game going in my room almost every day. People would come there knowing there was a game. Gene Hickerson was a good friend of mine and he would come and watch us play. The regulars were Bucky Hutchison, Ottis Crocker and Cob Jarvis. We had some Korean War veterans who would come play with us. Ross Barnett, Jr. would also play with us. We played table stakes and I got so far ahead that I was playing with someone else's money and could bet like you're supposed to bet rather than worrying about saving money for the picture show. We'd have six or seven players and then you'd have five to seven onlookers. Bo Ball would come up there after he went to the post office to get his mail. He kept cigarettes—Pall Malls—in my sock drawer and he'd come in there and light up a Pall Mall and open his latest letter from Lynda Lee Mead. He'd start reading the letters from her and she'd be telling him how much she loved him and everything and we'd have to stop dealing the cards and listen. Most of the players smoked. Possum Price was a bad smoker. Shed Hill Roberson was a smoker. Coach Vaught sent word to him to come to the coach's office. Coach Vaught said,

"Son, you're pretty good friends with Possum, aren't you?" Shed said, "Yessuh." Coach said, "Son, Possum needs to quit smoking." Coach Vaught didn't want to talk to Possum because where did it go from there if he didn't quit? Coach Vaught said, "Now son, you come back after you talk to him and tell me what he said." Coach Vaught called them "son" because he couldn't remember their names. So Shed went to Possum and talked to him. So Shed comes back and Coach Vaught says, "What he'd say, son?" "Well, Coach, he said he can't quit but he will promise to try to cut back." Coach Vaught made allowances. For example, Gene Hickerson didn't practice. He'd go out there and twirl a football and go down to the goal post and throw it over and catch it. And Vaught let him get away with it. Hickerson thought practice was boring. Gene did the same thing with the Cleveland Browns and Paul Brown let him do it, too.

Gene didn't talk much. He giggled a lot and I could keep him entertained. We'd go to the Haba Grill in Holly Springs. The guy who owned the place loved him. Gene had a trunk of a torso. We got in trouble coming back from some place. We'd had too much to drink and I was on the back seat of my car. Harper Rivers Myers, a notorious idiot, was driving my car. And he went down this bumpy road there and pulled into that half circle in front of Barnard, Somerville and Isom. I told him to slow down, slow down but he didn't and he ran my car up into the flower bed. I got out of the car and was enraged. My date was a girl from Arkansas named Lou Owens. She had a twin sister named Sue Owens. We scattered. Lou ran up in the dorm and the police, such as they were, came and checked it out. Dean Hefley was all over it. Sue Owens came down. She'd been in the dorm all afternoon and she said she had been my date. But I wasn't there at that point. Gene Hickerson had heard the racket over in the student union building and he came over and grabbed me and took me back to Howry B. He stripped me down and put me under the shower and I thought he was going to drown me. It was like a water board. He pulled me up against his big chest and that water was running in my face and he'd hold me there. I had just enough air and I'd think he was letting me go and would try to pull away but he'd drag me back under there just like a water board. Well, it sobered me up. And if I had been at the accident scene, I would have been in trouble. As it was, I had to get a wrecker to get it out.

BILLY KEYES

1955-1962

I grew up in Laurel. I was a senior and my brother Earl was a sportswriter in Laurel for years as a part-time job. He had become good friends with Coach Swayze, so my brother would take Laurel players up to Oxford for the ballgames. He was kind of a contact for Coach Swayze in Laurel and he asked Coach Swayze about me coming to school up there. I figured I was going to Mississippi Southern but one day my brother called and said, "You ready to come to Ole Miss?" I said, "Yeah, but how am I going to get up there?" And he said, "Well, I got a letter from Coach Swayze; you got a scholarship to manage the football team up there." I said, "Hallelujah." So he carried me up there in August of 1955 and that was the beginning of a great time for the seven years I spent at Ole Miss. Those were some great teams through there.

Doc Knight was my boss. Nub was the equipment manager but he usually didn't travel with the team itself unless the game was in Memphis or Jackson. The student managers worked for Nub and the trainers worked for Doc. There were normally two equipment managers with Nub and two trainers with Doc. My freshman year I lived over at the old gym. In the back of it there was a big room under the fire escape. They had part-scholarship-people who lived back there who were on the baseball and track teams along with the managers. We slept on Army bunks back there and we had a shower and a big old room for our closets. We lived there the first year; the second year I moved up to Mayes dormitory and lived there for three years, and then from there I moved over to Miller Hall in 1959. I was the dorm manager when they first opened it and stayed there until 1962.

I lived on the bottom floor in the end room down there away from Coach Wobble. One of my duties was to lock the door at night. Then I'd have people knocking on my window: "Keyes, come open the door. It's after ten and I got locked out." So I'd have to open the door and let a few folks in before Coach Wobble came walking down there. Wobble did a bed check every night and if he found someone missing, well, there were 65 steps in that stadium and they'd be running those stadium steps. Mayes was not the athletic dorm; Garland was the athletic dorm. Mayes was on one side, Garland was on the other side and Heddleston was in the middle. We had the athletic cafeteria in a World War II building down behind there. So I was in walking distance of that. My scholarship included room, board and books. You know, back then, the Athletic Department owned the book store, so we got our books free.

As time passed, on the scholarship side of it, when I became the dorm manager over at Miller Hall, I got money for being the dorm manager. We sent the laundry to Morgan Cleaners so I collected that money from the players and got ten percent of that from the laundry. I was also getting fifteen dollars a month from the Athletic Department for my own laundry money so I was in good shape. And by the time I bought tickets off the players and sold them myself, I was making more money when I left Ole Miss than what I made in the service.

That first year I helped manage the freshman team. Jimmy Stigler was the head manager and we kind of just did both the varsity and the freshmen. On a typical day, I would have classes from eight to 12. You'd get up about six o'clock in the morning and go eat breakfast around seven and then classes at eight and out at 12 and go eat lunch and then go to the field house. Nub Sanders would have the laundry back from Morgan Cleaners in baskets and we'd have to take it out and sort it by size and type: socks, jocks, and tee shirts and practice pants. We didn't have numbered jerseys: We just had red, blue, green or white. There were big bins that we put things into. There was a sock bin and we had the colored things on the socks to tell you what size they were. Maybe red, green, orange and something else. Small, medium, large and extra large. We had the jocks in separate bins by size and so forth.

When practice was over we'd clean up everything and lock up the field house. That would be around five or so. We'd go to the cafeteria between five and six and then go to the library and study from seven to ten. Lights were out at ten o'clock so I had to be organized to get it all done. On game days we'd be getting ready for the game and the day before, if it were a road game, we'd be getting ready to fly out. On Thursday we'd start getting everything ready. We'd make sure each player had little rectangular boxes, about two feet high. We had three large trunks that those boxes would go in, 12 boxes to a trunk. Back then, we only traveled about 40 players at most. On Thursday night before we left on a Friday, we'd put all of the boxes out in front of the guys' lockers and tell them to put the pads they wanted in there and we'd make sure they had laces and everything, all the pads, and a game jersey. We even made sure they had brand new shoe laces and we polished their shoes. They had game shoes and practice shoes and we would keep those separate. We'd go around and pack socks, jocks, tee shirts, and chin straps for the helmets, then put the boxes in the big trunks. They had their names and numbers on the boxes. The drivers would load that truck up Thursday and then they'd leave on Friday morning headed for wherever we were going to play. When we played LSU they always wanted to wear white so we'd wear either red or blue jerseys. Coach Vaught didn't care whether we wore red, blue or green. We wore red or blue most of the time; we very seldom wore white. The colored practice jerseys they wore in practice represented the team they were on: red jerseys were the first team, blue jerseys were the second team, green were third, white jerseys were the fourth team and redshirts. Freshmen didn't play into that because they didn't practice with the varsity at that time. They'd get whatever jerseys Coach Wobble wanted to put them in.

Coaches Poole and Kinard would take the offensive/defensive lines up on the hill and run them through routines: blocking, tackling and so forth. Coach Cain and Coach Hovius would take the backs and receivers and coach them. Coach Vaught would take the quarterbacks and practice them. Coach Wobble would have the freshmen. They'd run their drills, then run plays and then they'd have a scrimmage. When they scrimmaged the managers would be the referees. And let me tell you, we'd blow whistles and the coaches, I'm telling you what, they'd be hollering at you: "Aww, he wasn't down," and so forth. They'd get all over you. "He wasn't offsides." It was like a ball game out there. We had a lot of fun doing all of that, I tell you. Maybe I should have been a referee.

Ray Poole joined the staff after my freshman year. He came down there from Canadian ball. Coach Cain had the offensive backs. He also coached tennis. Doc Knight was the trainer, and he coached track. Bonnie Graham, the basketball coach, helped Coach Wobble with the freshman team. He also scouted every game that Mississippi State played. And he could tell you just about every play they were going to run and what the players were going to do. Roland Dale came later. Coach Swayze didn't do any on-the-field coaching; he was Coach Vaught's recruiting guru.

After a game, the players went to church the next day and then we'd open the field house up and they'd come down on Sunday afternoon. We'd sort through the dirty clothes and put them in the laundry to send to Morgan Cleaners. That's when the guys who had been injured would see Doc Knight and go through the whirlpool and so forth. Doc Knight would come down and see them. Roland Maddox who was a manager lived in the field house. His roommate was a guy named Bill Sistrunk. Bill played baseball and made a career of the Air Force. He got one or two stars and died a couple of years ago.

I didn't go out on the field when the players first went out. I was busy trying to get everyone out on the field so they could practice. Then we went out. Summer practices were pretty routine but the Spring practices were knock-down, drag out. The players would get out there battling one-on-one and get mad and they had some pretty good fights over there. I think Marvin Terrell and someone tangled; and Milton Crane and Larry Grantham. Buck Randall was a scrappy guy. He was a pretty mean little old ballplayer. He was well-built and tough. Buck had a role in the Meredith riot and got a lot of publicity when he passed away. It's funny but Buck never wanted that publicity. Buck wanted his ashes scattered in the Grove when he died. I said just do like those World War II movies where the guys would be digging the tunnels and they'd hide the dirt in their pants and then drop it once they got out. They could just do that with Buck's ashes. Just walk through the Grove shaking it out. That would be apropos of Buck.

Doc Knight was one of the most loving guys, a very religious guy. He cared about his players and was a very inspirational guy at Ole Miss. Before every Mississippi State game he'd put on the wall opposite all of the players his opponent: his name, his number, his statistics, all the week before we played State. He did motivational stuff and did the prayers. He was right up there with Coach Vaught in the eyes of the players. Doc was very focused on what he was doing. He didn't like a whole lot of foolishness. Doc handled most of the routine stuff himself. If a guy had a cold or sore throat Doc would get out his swab and a little medicine and swab the throat. The doctors would give him stuff to use. If you had a contusion on your thigh, he'd treat that. He taught a course on treating injuries in athletes and a lot of people took that course, especially the players and managers. How to tape and how to treat injuries. You got one or two hours credit for it. He would probably be considered a nurse practitioner today. My roommate was Rush McKay and he was complaining about a cold and all of that stuff. Doc gave me a needle and some medicine and told me when I got up to the dormitory to give Rush a shot. I got up to the dorm and I said, "Doc said you need this shot so bend over, I'm getting ready to shoot you."

The food in the athletic cafeteria was great. We had T-bone steaks every night if you wanted it. They could cook some good meals. On your first floor you had your varsity players. On the second floor you had the cafeteria in there and the M Club room and a meeting room in the basement area. We had the lobby out there and Coach Wobble had an apartment up there. There was a phone in the lobby but Coach Wobble took it off the hook every night at ten. I had a phone in my room but I had to keep it locked up in a closet.

The players had more time than we did because our work really started when practice was over. We were the last ones to eat and Doc Knight would eat with us. I had one of the few cars. Bill Gates would drive to Memphis and since only forty could fly, some of us would either have to go on the equipment truck or drive. When they took pictures of the 1960 team there was one picture made with the managers in it and that was it. Don Sheffield and I were in it. Bill Gates told us to get in there and that happened to be the national championship team. That is still the only one that has the managers in it.

The 1960 Arkansas game was when Allen Green kicked two field goals. The managers had to retrieve all of the footballs when they were kicked up into the stands. I was under the goal and we had one manager in the stands. The Arkansas people say one of them was wide left or wide right but I tell you, both of them were good. What happened was, someone called time out or something before that first kick and they had to re-kick it and when they did the fans said it was wide left but both of them were good. We had to go up and get the ball out of the stands. The fans over there were pretty rowdy. One time we were trying to get rid of some tickets over there and Nub went to sell them. He was standing behind a fence and an undercover policemen was on the other side of the fence and he said, "You know, I can arrest you for scalping tickets," and Nub said, "No you can't." And the guy said "Why?" and Nub said, "Because you're on that side of the fence and I'm on this side." And Nub turned around and left.

The redshirts got two tickets to sell, and the traveling squad got four. I'd buy tickets from them for twenty-five dollars and sell them for thirty-five. Between laundry and all of that other stuff and scalping tickets, I was making more money than I did the first two years I was out of school. I never saw any golden handshakes or any of the alumni putting cash in the helmets. I understand it went on but I don't have any personal knowledge of it.

The players got fifty-yard-line seats, so they were premium seats. The alumni knew that and they would pay premium prices for them, especially if we were going out of town to play. My brother was a lawyer in Jackson and of course, those lawyers were playing premium prices for tickets. I don't know what lawyers he was getting tickets for, but I know I was getting a hundred to two hundred dollars for tickets and some of the players were benefitting from that. That was how the players got money. The game we played in the Cotton Bowl we had a whole bunch of extra tickets and Coach Kinard got me out there early to sell all those tickets.

I never had much contact with Coach Vaught. I worked for Doc Knight and among the coaches, I had more contact with Coach Kinard because he handled all of the tickets and I would do things for him. Coach Cain was probably one of the friendlier coaches, too. Coach Wobble was the disciplinarian and of course, I was scared to death of him. But he was just as nice as he could be. Sara was the housemother at Miller Hall so I got to know her there. I'd babysit her kids and I'd babysit Doc Knight's kids some. Sara had a good bit of contact with the players and would make them feel at home. She was really kind of a mother figure to them.

When we got back to the dorm after that 7-3 loss to LSU on the Billy Cannon run, that was one of the most memorable nights we ever had. We got back and locked down the dormitory and everything and all of sudden we heard all of this commotion outside and the students had an impromptu pep rally outside of Miller Hall. I mean there was a crowd out there. They were hollering and wanted the players to come out and speak to them and everything. I went down and knocked on Coach Wobble's door so he said, "Well, open the door and let the players go out there and speak to them." So the players got up and went out and spoke to the crowd. That was probably one of the most tear-jerking moments in Ole Miss history. Of course, the players felt bad about losing the ballgame. And the students showed up there for that impromptu pep rally and it really gave the players a lift. In the week leading up the game there had been pep rallies about every night but that one after the game was something.

After practice we gave the players orange juice and some of them always wanted two glasses. It was the hardest thing to fight those guys off from getting two orange juices because we only had enough for them to have one. There was very little water during practice.

I was also the baseball manager and there were a lot of good baseball moments. My freshman year the 1956 team went to the College World Series. That was a great team and ended up either the number two or number four team in the country that year. We did pretty good in the college world series. I think we won four and lost two. We probably finished as the number three team in the country. We flew up to Omaha and rode the train back. I think we took about twenty people up there. No more than twenty.

Of course we had good teams in 1959 and 1960, also. We won the SEC and couldn't go to the College World Series because of segregation. Jimmy Stigler, one of the managers, played baseball, too. Joe Gibbon was in my opinion the best athlete who's ever been through Ole Miss. He played basketball and baseball. He was a great pitcher and a great hitter. He could do it all. And probably the second one I'd put in there would be Don Kessinger. Donnie was a great all-around athlete. He could do anything. Kessinger was just a great guy: very personable.

The basketball team had one person who was the manager. Sprout Simpson would travel with them as a trainer. He took Roland Maddox's place. Sprout and I were in there doing something and he and I got in a fight. We were fraternity brothers, too. He and I still laugh about it. We were Sigma Nus. We went to the meetings and that kind of thing. Went to the parties but that was about it. We just didn't have time to go to all the functions. The Sigma Nus I remember in particular are Guy Hovis and Trent Lott. Roy Williams, the Cossar boys, just a whole bunch of good guys were there then. Tommy Lester was in there. I see him every now and then at high school reunions. You know who Tommy Lester was? You remember Green Acres? Tom Lester was Eb. He was in that class with Hovis and Lott.

Jerilyn Williamson was Miss Ole Miss in 1962. She was from Bastrop, Louisiana. She was a Phi Mu and I dated her some. Doug Elmore was Colonel Rebel at the same time. We drew a lot of students from out of state in those days: east Arkansas, west Tennessee, southeast Missouri and so forth.

On those baseball trips we had to plan our own trips. We would eat in cafeterias along the way and I had to pay for all of the meals. Coach Swayze would give me the money and we'd go to Morrison's Cafeteria and all of those places and I'd pay cash.

Possum Price liked those cigarettes. He and Coach Wobble used to have an in and out relationship all of the time. You could smell cigarette smoke in his room. He never did quit. Larry Grantham smoked. You weren't supposed to smoke or drink beer and all of that but they did.

Some of the football players went over there and stole Bully. We were playing State in basketball at the old gym and so at halftime, Bully comes parading out on the basketball court painted red and blue with a Rebel flag taped to his tail. They turned him back over to State but he died. Coach Vaught interviewed all of the players after that trying to find out who did it.

When they initiated the M Club guys they'd go to Gathwright Reed and get some of those pills. Then they'd feed them to the players and they'd either piss red or blue. One year they got everyone buck naked and painted them red and blue. They had all of them in the back of a van so they'd take them and turn them loose at different places on the campus and they had to run back to the dormitory. At one of those girls' dorms these girls were coming in from home and getting their suitcases and clothes out of the back of the car. We pulled up there and stopped and let out two or three of those guys who were buck naked. Well, this girl was reaching down and getting her suitcases out of the car and she turned around and the guys were blindfolded, so they took the blindfolds off of them and they were standing there and she started screaming. We got in a little trouble over that.

You know before games we'd get a record player and play music to inspire the players. We'd play the Rebel songs and so forth. We'd get a big bucket and fill it with water and put methiolate in it so it looked like urine. We'd put the bucket in the equipment room and Coach Vaught said when they came and got their stuff they had to drink that Tiger piss. Some would drink it and some wouldn't. When we went to the College World Series Carl Coers gave us a Rebel flag with "Ole Miss" printed on it, and we flew that flag over the dugout during the series. I had it hanging in my room up in Mayes Dormitory and someone stole it out of my room. I've always regretted that I lost that flag.

My time at Ole Miss was probably one of the greatest times of my life. I made friends up there. You know, when you're in the military you get real close to your military guys but there is just a fraternity of men who played at Ole Miss and worked there. I probably know some of those guys better than I know my own brothers. There is just a bond there that is hard to describe. To this day I can pick up the phone and call some of them and if I needed something they'd help me get whatever I needed. I was a little old boy from Laurel, Mississippi, when I got there and didn't have a clue what was going on in the world. When I went down to New Orleans with the baseball team I had never had a drink in my life and didn't know what it was all about. We were in the bar and all of those upperclassmen were ordering drinks and everything so this bartender looks at me and says, "One screwdriver coming up without the screw." That was my first time with a bartender in a bar. And it was on Bourbon Street in New Orleans.

WANDA ENGLAND POOLE

Ray coached about twenty years. The first year he was here, they didn't have but two secretaries—Kitty Jones and Faye Parker— and seven coaches and Mr. Hamm the business manager, so they all had second jobs. Ray coached freshman baseball a year or two and football and he and Tom Swayze were the high school recruiters. Ray would leave with Tom on Thursday and scatter out and then come back and report the people they had seen. Alumni really helped recruit in those days and they called and told you who to look at. One time we had this alumnus who had called and called about this boy and Coach Vaught said, "Ray, go down there and see him." So in their meeting Monday morning Coach Vaught said, "Well Ray what about so and so?" And Ray said, "Coach, I turned him down on the National Anthem because he was knock-kneed."

Ray had played professional football eight years, so we were up there in New York five years and spent two years in Montreal and then he came straight back here to coach. When we first moved here to coach, the only place to live was Avent Acres and the Grahams lived directly in front of us. Bonnie was basketball coach but he scouted Mississippi State in football every game for years and years. He saw every game they played and we beat them every year. I'll never forget the first year they beat us. Paul Davis was the coach at State and had played with Ray here, so I had gotten to know the Davises through Ray. The year before we had gone to the Sugar Bowl and the Davises stayed with us. We put the mattress on the floor and they slept on the floor and she slept in Ray's T shirt. Well, after that game when they beat us, she came up and hugged me in a full length mink coat. They had been on a television show and she had won that coat and I said, "You will never sleep in Ray's T shirt again."

We went to a bowl game every year for twenty years. We bought our bowl clothes in the summer. That's how confident we were. The school was small and everybody knew everybody. The town was tiny and there was just nothing negative about it. It was all good.

Ray coached the defensive red shirts so he could leave on Thursday and go scout. Then he would go to the Ole Miss game on Saturday. He would be on the sideline and on the phone to Bruiser who was in the press box. Bruiser would say, "Tell Coach Vaught so and so." Ray would tell him and Coach Vaught would pay no attention. The chemistry on that coaching staff was absolutely perfect. Everywhere they went, they were in an absolute circle together. Coach Vaught played cards with Mrs. Carrier on Wednesday nights. The Carriers gave Coach Vaught that house down there next to the Chancellor's house. John and Johnsie had to go up there on Wednesday night so the rest of us, we'd go out to Buster and Anna's cabin out where the Chadwicks live now. We had the best times you ever saw in your life. Tom Swayze could kick as high as the door and when Bruiser tried it, his toe hit a table. Someone taught us how to do the bop. We kept playing the same record over and over, and Tom Swayze said, "I'm sick of that record," so he took it to the door and sailed it. We never found it. Oh, but they loved each other. All of them loved each other.

I think Anna Poole and some of them went to all of the away games, but I stayed home a lot of the time and kept kids. I never went to Knoxville but I went to LSU and Vanderbilt and most of them. And I never missed one here. It was fun to go to LSU and win, but it was dangerous. I've been in my seat two hours before kickoff many times and those Cajuns would break that whiskey bottle and point it at someone. I tell you it was dangerous in those days. I was on that front row when Billy Cannon ran that silly thing. And while Ray was sick, Charles Walker said, "Ray I have a present for you," and he came out with a signed picture of Billy Cannon running. And when he left, Ray said, "What in the hell did he think I wanted that for?" And I took it out of the frame and threw it over in the basket and used the frame.

Billy Cannon would come up here to Charles' cabin. We had several of the LSU people and Ray would go out there because he liked everyone. And another thing, when our coaches were coaching, after the ballgame the coaching staffs all got together. We knew Bear Bryant well. All of the LSU staff, too. Now, they wouldn't do that. Bear Bryant was a big old gruff easy-going fellow who would do anything to win. He was fun to be around. John and Johnnie Britt Cain lived next door to me over here. John was an All-American at Alabama and he and Mary Harmon Bryant were great friends over there. Bear was John Cain's little brother in the fraternity. We knew them well. The LSU coaches were fun: Paul Dietzel and all of them. We knew them all.

Coach Vaught had exactly the coaches he wanted at Ole Miss and the coaches coached. Each had his part. No one knew who coached what position. See, you were an Ole Miss coach and that's what you did. Eddie Crawford scouted the next week's opponent but before him, Wobble did it. Then we got where they'd send the film.

The games that stand out were all with LSU and Mississippi State. One time the bus was going to Starkville and the highway patrolmen went in front of them. So we got behind the bus and followed it to Starkville. This little policeman stepped out there and stopped us. Johnsie Vaught was driving and her bumper was touching him. We almost ran over him. It was great fun. You'd go down the road and everyone was waving flags and it was just like a miracle. It was just perfect. I couldn't ask for more fun.

When I think about standout players, I think of Jake Gibbs. He was a wonderful player. And Eagle Day. Doug Elmore. He's dead. I couldn't list them all because we were so close to them. See, Ray had just played, so it made you closer to the players.

Archie's folks used to come by here all of the time. They'd stay with us. We were crazy about Archie's mom and dad. Ray said that Archie was a better athlete than all three of his sons. I always thought that Ray was the best judge of football talent of anyone I saw. He could pick them out anywhere. He knew more football and I always thought it was such a shame that the University did not hire Ray to raise money because everyone in the state knew him and liked him. That was during some of those years, but since you're putting this on tape, I won't go there. It was so good there for a long time. And Ray was the golf coach for a long time. He made golf trips. They made the schedule for spring training and it had to accommodate coach Vaught's hunting. Everybody always knew that you set spring training by duck season and turkey season. Billy Mustin went hunting with him. Billy came and he just followed Coach Vaught around. As much as we loved Coach Vaught, he had a big ego. (Laughs) And he could charm a room better than anyone I ever saw. So he got Billy Mustin and Billy lived in the dorm after Wobble and Sara moved out. Billy wasn't nearly as tough as Wobble was. They could trick him but they didn't even try with Wobble. Jim Poole lived out there then and they could pull the wool over Billy's eyes. Wobble taught me when I was a freshman. I had tennis under him. It nearly killed me.

All of that coaching staff played golf. They loved to play gin rummy. See, they had a room downstairs in that old coaches' office and they'd stay down there playing gin. You wouldn't believe it. They all played gin. And then we had the country club and there was a gin room in there and so they'd stop by and play. I used to tell the kids that we left the door open for their daddy while he was playing gin. They just had a good time. They didn't fret over recruiting. You could get anybody you wanted then. Recruiting was easy for them. And then Coach Vaught was a master at drawing up game plans. He met every day with his quarterbacks. Every day. And he never raised his voice. He always dropped his voice when he wanted attention. And you could hear a pin drop. He was really a line coach but he could work with the quarterbacks so well. He was amazing. And Johnsie was a little spitfire. She was a Texas girl. She was working when they met. And they had just one son: Johnny Boy.

HOWARD MCMILLAN

1956-1960

Man, yes, I went to the football games. We had some great years. I think the four years I was here we might have lost maybe four football games and tied one or two. My senior year there were only 21 points scored against that team. It was unbelievable. Nobody knew how good they were until about halfway through the season, and then the press said this is a helluva football team. Everyone had said they were going to be pretty good but no one expected that. I mean all of the big names we played against, they just held them scoreless. Tulane scored on a fumble; Tennessee scored on a blocked punt, and of course, LSU scored on the Cannon run. There was not a true rushing touchdown scored on that team.

I went to Baton Rouge for that game and I swore after that game that I would never again sit through an LSU game in Tiger Stadium. I didn't until the year I was president of the Ole Miss Alumni Association and had to go to that game. The 1959 LSU game was on Halloween and it was misty. The field was wet as it always was. We were outplaying LSU and every time we got the ball Vaught would run three plays and punt. He knew that once we kicked that field goal our defense could stop them cold, and we had. They had never gotten into Ole Miss territory until the Cannon punt return. The ball was wet and on the punt, the ball went toward the sideline and it looked like the ball was going to hit and bounce out of bounds. So everyone from Ole Miss was watching the ball and kind of relaxed. Then the ball bounced opposite of what you would think right into Cannon's chest. I think it surprised him. He grabbed that thing and got a full head of steam going down the sidelines before the Ole Miss players realized what was happening. Now two or three of our players got a glancing blow at him but he was a big guy and he was bow-legged and he was hard to bring down. And he was fast. And he was gone.

Then, after the runback, we were so upset at that point, we took the ball down to the goal line. Everyone has different versions of that drive. Some say we scored, some say we were short. Some say someone missed a blocking assignment I think Doug Elmore was quarter-backing at the time and it looked like we were going to score. But we didn't.

I went to the Sugar Bowl on the following New Year's Day when we beat LSU. They just beat the hell out of Billy Cannon. I'm told that Vaught told two of our guys that no matter where Billy Cannon was on the field hit him and knock him down every play. So when the game was over Cannon couldn't leave the field on his own. Two guys had to walk him off the field.

DAN JORDAN

1956-1960

PITCHERS, FROM LEFT: ALLEN GREEN, BILL SISTRUNK, BOB RAGAN, DAN JORDAN, JIMMIE STIGLER, DENNIS BLOOMQUIST, LARRY WILLIAMS

I grew up in Philadelphia, Mississippi, where my father was a dentist and my mother was active in civic affairs, and entered Ole Miss in the fall of 1956 on a baseball and basketball scholarship. Playing two sports was not unusual back then. I would have come to Ole Miss regardless of the athletic scholarships.

My dad was a gigantic Ole Miss fan and I think the first nursery rhyme I can remember was "Go to Hell, State College, go to Hell." My Dad loved to go up to football games, and it just became addictive to me. I saw Ole Miss play State from Vaught's first year as head coach in 1947 all the way until 1961, and I never saw Ole Miss lose to State. I saw every game and Ole Miss won every game with a couple of ties in there. I was recruited by State and some other schools, but there was never any doubt where I was going to go. I had other family connections to Ole Miss. I think our family went back three or four generations at Ole Miss and at one time, there were thirteen members of the family who went to Ole Miss. That includes Lou's (Schmelzer) family, as well.

When I arrived on campus the freshmen basketball and baseball players were in Vardaman B with the varsity baseball and basketball players, and the freshmen football players were in Vardaman A. After Vardaman my freshman year, the baseball and basketball players stayed in Vardaman and then when Miller Hall opened some of us moved over there. When I was in graduate school I was a dorm manager in George, which was across from Miller Hall, but I stayed mainly in Vardaman. I ate with the athletes and that was an important part of the fraternity of athletes that we did eat together. Prior to the move to Miller Hall, we had our own cafeteria near the Johnson Commons. It was a white World War II temporary building, made of wood and rectangular. The food was amazing. You could have a steak at every meal if you wanted it. Potatoes, ice cream. Great stuff. And then when Miller Hall opened the cafeteria moved over there. The food was not as great at Miller Hall. I think someone decided the food was too expensive and they cut back.

In my class of student athletes were Robert Khayat and Warner Alford, so we met then and became great friends and have remained great friends all these years. Robert was in our wedding, Kay was Lou's big sister, and Coach Swayze was my baseball coach. My freshman year was very exciting. The older athletes made you feel right at home by harassing you as much they could and that's putting it mildly. Most of that stuff would be outlawed now. Still, there was a feeling of being a part of something really special when you were an athlete in that day.

The Cardinal Club shaved our heads out in front of the Student Union when I first arrived and I remember that well. That was the first time I met Frank Crosthwait. He was the head of the Cardinal Club. Everyone was unbelievably friendly. There were signs up that said, "Everybody Speaks," and as far as I could tell, that was absolutely the culture. It was very exciting to be there. Freshmen athletes did not compete in varsity sports then. They were separate, so we had a freshman basketball team and we had our own coach and own schedule. I had been highly recruited in high school and did okay as a freshman but I ended up being a very mediocre college basketball player. I stuck it through and lettered twice. At the end of my junior year, I went to the coach when it was clear I wasn't going to play and told him I'd be happy to be the manager if that would free up part of a scholarship, so I was the manager my senior year.

Bonnie Lee "Country" Graham was the basketball coach and he was operating under very difficult circumstances. He had been very successful as a junior college coach but he never had much success at Ole Miss, where he had been an All-American. Coach Graham didn't have much in the way of resources and he was always a second-class citizen to football. There were some interesting people on those basketball teams. One was Sterling Ainsworth, from Meridian. He was younger and he became an imminent medical doctor and researcher. I think his medical degree was from Harvard. He invented some medical devices. Larry Wagster was on that team and he was a very good golfer also. (Later became Ole Miss women's golf coach.) Bobby Williams became a very successful homebuilder in Memphis. His partner was John Abner Reeves from Yazoo City. They were the biggest homebuilders in Memphis. On the baseball team, John Lee Gainey was outstanding and Buddy Wittichen from Memphis was an all-star pitcher and President of Wittichen Construction or Cement, which was very successful.

The baseball team, unlike the basketball team, was sensational and won the Southeastern Conference my junior and senior years. Coach Swayze was a terrific coach. I've often said that everything I learned about management, I learned from Coach Swayze. He was a great motivator and a great organizer. He had a wonderful competitive spirit but he wanted the game to be fun and took a real interest in his players. Robert Khayat was the catcher and I was a pitcher. The staff was young so I got to play a lot and then, as the staff matured, we had Larry Williams, who was an all-star, and Don Porter, who was a tremendous pitcher. Two or three of those guys were All SEC pitchers so my playing time diminished and I got to be a real good batting practice pitcher my senior year. That year we won the last 17 games in a row. These were terrific teams with a lot of guys who signed pro contracts.

My freshman year, Ole Miss was very small and I think we had only 2,200 students. Through classes, ROTC, sports, fraternities and so forth you knew an awful lot of people. Most of them came from small towns in Mississippi. We knew all of the Delta folks and knew towns that might not even exist anymore, like Drew, which is about gone, and Anguilla and Shaw and places like that. There was kind of a small town community in the student body that was really, really friendly. The second thing I remember very well is that there weren't many big scholars on the faculty but there were some terrific teachers. They were people who probably wouldn't get tenure today but were totally devoted to the students. I never had an auditorium-type class the whole time I was at Ole Miss and I never had a course in which the teacher didn't know my name. My freshman year the Registrar's Office was in the Lyceum and you went to pick up my grades there. So I got my grades for the first semester and was walking down the hall. I had two As, two Bs and two Cs, which I thought was pretty good with playing sports and taking some really tough courses. I remember Miss Harriett Jackson, who was a French teacher, and who I'm sure never published an article in her life, stopped me and said, "Well Dan, how'd you do?" And I told her my grades and I was pretty proud and she said, "Well, Dan, you can do a lot better than this," and my mother basically told me the same thing. Well, that meant something. I had some wonderful teachers and the classes were relatively small. That separated Ole Miss from a lot of schools. I went on and got a Ph.D. at the University of Virginia and was Phi Beta Kappa there and so forth—published a lot of books—but Ole Miss was perfect for me. I couldn't have gone from Philadelphia High School to the University of Virginia or North Carolina or an Ivy League school or anywhere else. And the thing I remember someone saying is, "Your best friend is the one who gives you the most confidence." And there were just a lot of people—in sports, on the faculty and staff, and a lot of friends at Ole Miss—who gave me that sense that I was able to do it. The Ole Miss culture in my day was that way, and I can't emphasize that enough.

Jake Gibbs was an infielder with Ole Miss who was drafted by the Yankees and became a catcher with them. There were not a lot of great players on the 1960 team but there were a lot of contributors. We had about 24 players on the team and half of them played a second sport. There were a lot of football players and there were also some basketball players. That simply would not be possible today but it was the norm back then. Coach Swayze was the head recruiter for Ole Miss football so when he was recruiting football players it was a good thing if they could also play baseball.

Coach Swayze's record speaks for itself but the man was more important than winning and losing. He was a fierce competitor but he had a style about him that almost guaranteed success. He was very encouraging. Coach Swayze liked to make the game fun. He had a nickname for everyone. I was "the Professor" for example and he kidded around about nick-names. He was smart enough to know that the more direct contact with the players in many different ways was good. So he was big on having meetings, but they were all worthwhile—not silly, He would have all of the pitchers, or all of the lettermen, or all of the seniors meet with him from time to time. I've never seen this done anywhere else, but my senior year he had a meeting of all of the lettermen the first day of practice before we went out on the field. He had a big blackboard and he came in there and began scribbling on the blackboard. No one could see what he was writing. And then he stepped away and what he had written was, "If we don't win the Southeastern Conference this year, it's my fault." And he signed it Tom Swayze. He was amazing. Coach Swayze knew the game cold and was a good teacher. He had played professionally himself and was a pitcher so he was especially good about helping the pitchers. He also experimented a lot. Coach Swayze came up with the idea that batters ought to put the bats on their shoulders until the last second. Also, to make sure people didn't hurt their arms if they were in the outfield shagging flies, instead of throwing the ball in over-handed, you threw it underhanded. He was always experimenting. Tom Swayze was just a remarkable man.

In addition to Larry Williams and Jake Gibbs, Robert Khayat was all-conference and just terrific. Don Jobe of Corinth was all-conference. He had been a multi-sport star in Corinth but he focused on baseball here. Don signed a professional contract and was a mainstay on the Ole Miss team. Mule (Billy Ray) Jones, who played football, was a terrific outfielder. He may have been all-conference. Don Porter was a year or two behind me and he was not only a great pitcher but he was also a fantastic hitter. He signed a professional contract and went far. We had a couple of hard-nosed guys. One was Bobby Kilpatrick, who was an all-star at second base. He coached at Memphis with great success for many years. Ken Netherland was from Yazoo City. He had been a tremendous athlete in high school and was just resolute in his determination. In a key game there was a squeeze play and he was the batter and was to bunt the ball. The ball was thrown right at his head and he dropped a perfect bunt. He may be the most successful high school football coach in Tennessee. He coached at a couple of schools. The captain of the team was Al Bullock. He was outstanding.

In basketball I was playing against State and the great Bailey Howell. Once, the ball bounced in my direction and I reached up to grab it and somehow Bailey Howell, who was on the other side of the free throw lane, jumped across and out-jumped me and put out his long arm and his big hands and tipped it back in for two points. He just came out of nowhere and tipped it in. I was playing when we sat on the ball in that low-scoring game. State's Coach McCarthy had recruited me. He did great at State and won a lot of championships. And he was always very nice when we ran into each other at these games. The rivalry is so intense. When we played State in basketball down there the freshmen football players were put behind the Ole Miss bench with cowbells and you cannot imagine how loud and obnoxious they were.

At some point in my baseball era State had wooden dugouts and the State students set the Ole Miss dugout on fire. Everyone ran out and they threw bottles at our players when they came out of the dugout. Frank Halbert was on our team. He was from Aberdeen and his brother Molly was a big football player at State and also played baseball. I pitched against State in relief and got Molly Halbert out. After the game Frank and I went to the dairy bar at State with Molly and had a milk shake or something. But that's the way it is in the rivalry games. During the games the fans and alumni go nuts and the players are very intense but when the games are over the players kind of revert to knowing the guys they went to high school with and have been friends with for years.

Charlie Hall, who was later Commissioner of Agriculture in Mississippi and was from DeKalb, was my age and we played against each other a lot so I knew him really well. State had a lot of out-of-state players and so did we. Most of the guys on my freshmen basketball team were from out of state. Larry Wagster, for example, was from Malden, Missouri. There were three guys from Malden on the basketball team at one time but Larry is the only one who stayed.

I stayed on two extra years to get a graduate degree while Lou was finishing and I managed one of the athletic dorms at that time. I think that's when State had the Red Stroud-Leland Mitchell-Joe Dan Gold teams. I saw them play. Red Stroud from Forrest was great and Mitchell was great and that's when they broke the color line with Loyola of Chicago. I admire Coach McCarthy for that a lot.

My senior year on the baseball team, we had finished so strong and we were ready to go to Omaha but someone had figured out that there was a black player on one of the other teams. The state law was that you couldn't compete against integrated athletic teams so if there was the possibility of playing against an African American, we were not allowed to go forward, even though that was a great team and we could have done well. Coach Swayze had very conservative social values, as everybody else did, and right after our last game he asked me to come over. I was president of the student body. He said, "Dan, would you mind writing Dr. Jobe," who was head of the state college board, "and tell him that the Ole Miss baseball team would like to compete in the NCAA playoffs." I said I would be happy to do it and so I sat down and said that I felt Mississippi boys should be allowed to compete with the best in the country and that we had a great team and could represent the state well. They put it into a telegram and sent it to Dr. Jobe, but whether he ever responded or not, I don't know. Coach Swayze was willing to stand up for the team and if that had happened, the Ole Miss baseball team would have broken the color line instead of the State basketball team.

At that time the SEC was divided into two divisions for baseball and after we won the West Division we played the East Division winner for the SEC championship. My junior year we played Florida and beat them and my senior year we played and defeated Georgia Tech.

I was a Sigma Chi. When I arrived I went to see Coach Graham and asked him about fraternities. He said some of the players were members and some weren't. I said, "What's your preference?" He said, "Well you're a freshman and I would rather you not join a fraternity until you really get settled in." My priorities were academics, the church and basketball so I did not pledge initially. But as the fall semester went along I met a lot of guys who were in fraternities and saw that it was pretty standard for the athletes to be in fraternities. A lot of them were Sigma Chis so I got to know a lot of Sigma Chis. In addition, there was a Corinth group of Worshams and Williams. My grandmother lived in Corinth so I went up there every summer and I knew all of the Worshams and the Williams and Jim Gallion and a bunch of people who were all Sigma Chis. So one thing led to another and I ended up pledging. There were four people in my pledge class second semester. One was Milburn Price. He was a straight-A student and Commander of the Army ROTC and was in the Hall of Fame. Charles Pickering was in that pledge class. He had transferred from a junior college, I think. The two guys who were older than I and had an enormous influence on me were Frank Crosthwait and Sammy Smith, who was also from Corinth. Sammy became a very prominent lawyer and later, a judge. I cherish the memories of being in the Sigma Chi Fraternity.

The feeling I get when I think of Ole Miss and my time there is love and a warm feeling. The memories are all good. That doesn't mean the entire time there was all tranquil and perfect because you make mistakes and some bad things happen to you and disappointments happen to you but the fact is that you learn from everything. The overall feeling is one of intense loyalty to an institution that you learned to love and that helped you in ways that wouldn't have been possible otherwise.

BOB RAGAN

1956-1960

I played baseball starting in the 1958 season through the 1960 season. I was a bench warmer. Tom Swayze didn't let me play very much. I did letter, though, in the spring of 1959 and again in the spring of 1960. My senior year, we had won the SEC title the year before, and we went down to play Tulane in New Orleans. Coach Swayze told me to pitch batting practice, so I threw for about an hour or an hour and a half. Somebody hit a line drive straight into the pitcher's box, and it caught me right in the ribs. I thought I had died, and Coach Swayze came up to me, I will never forget, and he looked down and said, "My goodness, a senior and he doesn't even know how to get out of the way of the ball. Go out in the outfield. Just get out there. I'll throw and finish this last batter myself." The second pitch he threw, the same batter hit the ball straight up the middle and hit him on the leg. It broke his leg. Well, they carried him to the hospital. I went in there and his back was to me and his leg was elevated. I started smiling at him and said, "Some folks will just never learn how to stay out of the way of a ball hit up the middle." I really enjoyed saying that, needless to say. Later on, we had won about ten or twelve games in a row and we went over to Starkville to play the Bullies. They beat us in the first game and broke our streak in a very close game. Then, the next two games, we just killed them, and the last game, they piled score cards around our dugout and set them on fire. That set the dugout on fire and they had to call the fire department to put it out. So we had to sit out in the outfield for most of the third game.

Wobble was the dorm manager for the football players. He lived with his family at one end of the dorm, and the football players were scared to death of him. Heck, we were all scared to death of him, no matter what sport we played. One time Stick Netherland, who was a baseball player, was standing there, and Wobble walked by him. Wobble said, "You've been smoking," and Stick said, "Who, me, Coach?" Wobble said, "If I ever catch you with a cigarette, you are going to have to chew it up with the fire on it and swallow it." Stick said, "You'll never catch me, Coach." And he didn't. You know, back then, they would bring in seventy freshmen football players and by the end of the first season with Wobble they would be lucky to have 35 of them left. If you survived Wobble that first year, you were really something special.

There was a guy named Hugh Poland and he came by and wanted to know where they kept the bulldog down at Mississippi State. I told him they kept it behind the Sigma Chi house, and he said, "Well my car is broken down." He had like a 1939 souped-up Ford that they used to run whiskey in, but it was broken down so he asked if he could use my car because they wanted to go get Bully. He asked me to drive and be the wheel man, but I told him I couldn't do that because I had two damn tests the next day. So I gave him my keys and he took my car and went over there. I really didn't think much about it because I was up studying. Well, about six o'clock in the morning I was still up cramming and here comes Poland with my keys, and he's got that damn dog. He said, "Okay, we got him. You keep him."

The dog was actually pretty well-behaved. He barked a little but what he mainly did is he broke wind all night long. I almost died from gas poisoning. I had to put all the windows up and it was cold. It was during basketball season and it was just terrible. So the next morning we heard that the President of Mississippi State had called the Chancellor and the Chancellor called Chief Tatum. They were going to a room-by-room search of all the dorms, starting with the athletic dorms. We were to be one of the first dorms searched. In the dorm, there was a community shower, a dirty old thing with a concrete floor, so we got the dog and we took him and put him in the corner of the shower and cut on the hot water. It steamed up the room and you couldn't see anything. Chief Tatum came and checked our room and went down to the bathroom. He kind of looked around and couldn't see anything but steam, so he turned around and left. We had treated the dog very humanely: we saw that he ate and had plenty of water.

PITCHERS, FROM LEFT: ALLEN GREEN, BILL SISTRUNK, BOB RAGAN, DAN JORDAN, JIMMIE STIGLER, DENNIS BLOOMQUIST, LARRY WILLIAMS

Well, anyway, we were playing State that night in the old gym and the football players brought him out before the game. They had red and blue stripes painted down his back—it was paint that wouldn't hurt him—and they had a little Confederate battle flag tied to his tail. Bully wagged his tail and the flag was just going all around. They had tied a freshman beanie to his head and the crowd just went berserk. So there were maybe 25 or 30 State students in the gym and they were going to rescue that dog, come hell or high water. Coach Kinard, I think, was there and he went to the freshmen football players and said, "Are you going let them take that dog?" So the freshmen football players went after them and there was an absolute massacre on the gym floor.

Another time, we were playing State and they had Bailey Howell, who was an All-American. State had a fabulous team, and as usual, we didn't have anything. It was long before the shot clock and Country Graham, the coach, told the Ole Miss players to stand out at mid-court and hold the ball. State was probably one of the four or five leading scoring teams in the country, and we were pathetic but we held it the whole game and with maybe three minutes left in the game, we were ahead like 12-11 or something like that. Then State started moving the ball and scored some points and won in a close game. They gym didn't hold but 2000 or so and when you played State or someone good, you had to get there really early to get a seat. A lot of times I can remember sitting on the second level right up where the iron bar was and dangling my legs down under that bar. I can also remember going and there wouldn't be 400 people there.

WARNER ALFORD

1956-1961

W hen I was a senior in McComb, I had never been to Oxford. Actually, I had never been north of Jackson. Getting to Baton Rouge from McComb was easy, and I had gone down and watched LSU play a lot. Tom Swayze was the field recruiter for Coach Vaught and went out in the state and into other states to look for players. He introduced me to Ole Miss after our coach had introduced me to Coach Swayze when he was down there scouting. We had two players at Ole Miss: Jerry Stone and Harry Case, who went on to be a law professor.

My high school coach and I rode the train from McComb to Batesville for the 1955 Ole Miss-Arkansas game. We got off the train in Batesville and Coach Swayze had someone there to pick us up and drive us over to Oxford. We got over here in time to visit with some of the coaches, and after the game, Rogers Brashier took us back to Batesville to catch the train, but there was so much traffic that we were late getting over there and missed the train. The only other hope we had was another train that came through Batesville at ten o'clock at night. They called it a "milk train" because it stopped at every town on the line. We got to McComb at daylight so I said, "I don't know whether I want to go to Ole Miss or not. It's really hard to get up there."

We played Brookhaven on Thanksgiving Day of 1955. Coach Swayze had asked me to come back to Ole Miss and so on Friday a teammate and I drove up to Oxford, spent the day, and watched the team workout. Then on Saturday, we drove over to Starkville where Ole Miss was playing State. We sat on the Ole Miss bench and watched the game, which Ole Miss won. I was real close to going to LSU at that point. Carl Maddox was the assistant coach down there and he recruited the southwest Mississippi area. Coach Paul Dietzel was in his first year at LSU so they invited us to come down and spend the day. My dad and I went down one Sunday because back in those days you worked six days a week and my father wouldn't leave his store on a Saturday. I liked the fact that it was that close. Coach Maddox and I became real good friends, but my buddy Harry Case wouldn't let me go. Harry Case and Jerry Stone said "You ain't going down to LSU." So I decided to come to Ole Miss.

Barbara Jean Hill, my classmate in McComb, had an uncle in Moss Point, and when she went down in the summer to see them, they'd always make sure that she had a date with Robert Khayat, who was the kingpin down in Moss Point. Robert's father and my father had gone to Millsaps together. We were playing the southeast Mississippi basketball tournament in McComb and Robert and I had already signed to go to Ole Miss. Barbara told me, "You and Robert ought to room together. You'd be just right for each other." So I went over and found him sitting in the stands and I said, "Robert, Barbara Jean said you and I ought to room together. What do you think? You got a roommate?"

He said, "Naw. I guess if she says it's all right we probably ought to do it, don't you?" Robert came up to Ole Miss that summer and took that famous chemistry course that he wrote about in his book. I came up one time that summer and visited with him and asked him how it was. He said, "Man, it's tough. These varsity guys will get after you." So we started rooming together that fall. Robert and I roomed together four years.

I had started out in high school playing quarterback but my coach was very diplomatic about it. He said, "Warner, let me tell you what, you're a linebacker." Of course, we played both ways back then, so he said, "Linebacker and center are the way they do it in college. And linebacker is your position to play so I think I want to move you to center so you can learn that position because I think that's going to be your best shot to get a scholarship." And so my junior year he moved me to center. And that's the way it went in college. If you were the center on offense you played linebacker on defense. So that's how it happened that I became a center/linebacker.

In the tenth grade it became evident that I couldn't run real fast so here's what happened. We had a new track coach named Mercer Miller. Mercer wound up being superintendent of the schools in Gulfport but he had run track at Mississippi State. We had hired him as the track coach and a teacher in McComb so he told me, "You come out there and run track with me and I will get you faster." Well, that's all he had to say and I was ready to go. So I ran track and that's what got my speed better. He made me a half-miler. We went to Brookhaven for a district meet. We always ran the district meets in Brookhaven because they had the best track. He said, "Now listen to me. This is what you need to do. When that gun sounds, and y'all take off, you get right in behind that guy who's leading." So I got right in behind this guy. My coach hadn't told me that the guy was All-State so I just did make it across the finish line. But track really did help my speed, and that was important because Coach Swayze and Coach Vaught liked people who could run. Back then speed was really important because you played both ways. I got up here and they moved me from center to guard. Under Coach Vaught, we did a lot of things with our guards: pulling on bootlegs and stuff like that. So Coach Vaught said "I'm putting you at guard." I was delighted because at center there was someone on defense right on my nose.

Our freshman year we had about fifty guys who had signed. A lot of those guys left after the first semester and then the fall of our sophomore year, a lot of us were redshirted. You didn't think anything about it because that's just the way they did it. Most of the freshmen got redshirted. Jake moved right on up after his freshman year because he was a really good player. If you lined up in scrimmage and Jake was on your side, you probably were going to win. We could tell he was good his freshman year. He could run, he was quick and he had the greatest release throwing the football. It was not so much that he was a blazing runner but he had quick feet and he could get outside and throw the football all in one motion. The deal then was who could get down behind the tackle and the end the fastest. That's what Coach Vaught wanted from his quarterbacks. Jake was a great leader, too, and the other thing was, he could punt the football and play defense. It's unbelievable how good he was. About the time that Jake graduated, if the two pro-football leagues had battled over him like they did later, they would have paid him a lot of money.

The year that I entered Ole Miss we had Bobby Ray Franklin at quarterback. Billy Brewer had been redshirted and was a year ahead of us. Bobby Ray could punt it, place-kick it, he could run it and he could throw it. He also played in the secondary and he was fast.

Our freshman year we won two—Vanderbilt and Mississippi State—and we lost to LSU. That's when Paul Dietzel had recruited his first freshman class—Warren Rabb, Billy Cannon and all of those guys—and they beat us pretty good down there. LSU had more people at the freshman game than they had at the varsity game because the varsity wasn't very good. We rode the train to Hammond and then they bused us over to Baton Rouge. After the LSU game, we got the message from Coach Wobble. We were playing Vanderbilt in Nashville and he let us know right quick that we weren't going to lose to Vanderbilt. He said, "Those guys up there are so arrogant. They think they're smarter than everyone else." So we went out there and won the game. Then we played Mississippi State at home and won. The deal with that was the freshmen didn't lose to Mississippi State. If they did, the upperclassmen would shave their heads again.

We had a great group of guys in my class and we formed a bond. Some of those guys left and out of the fifty who signed they probably moved five to seven guys up as true sophomores. Bobby Franklin had moved up and played behind Raymond Brown as a sophomore. There would always be fewer than ten who would move up. So what you had to do was, if you wanted to stay here and get your education, you stayed and took the redshirt. Those who just couldn't handle the redshirt left. Most of them would have played.

Every Friday the redshirts and the freshmen would scrimmage. The varsity wouldn't be there. Some of those redshirts were older because they'd been redshirted more than once. So as a freshman, you'd be going up against some men. You had a redshirt offensive team and a redshirt defensive team and they imitated the team we were getting ready to play. What they would do is when I was a redshirt, I might start off the first half the season on the offensive redshirt team and then we'd flip and I'd be on defense the second half. If we were going to play Tennessee the redshirt defense would be a wide-tackle six because that's what they ran. Coach Wobble was down there with the redshirts because he was probably one of the best scouts around. He could pick up on what the other team was doing. When we were going to play Tennessee he had it all in his head and would put it on blackboard down to a T.

For away games, the varsity had three full teams traveling, plus five to seven more extras. We had the red team, the starters, the blue team, the second team and the green team, the third team. If the red team kicked off, it would go down and play defense. About midway through the first quarter, the blue team would go in as a unit. Then the red team couldn't go back in until the quarter changed. So you had a coach on the sidelines keeping up with who's in, who's out and so forth. Then they had what they called a "wildcard," where one guy could go in at any time. They had an official out on the field and he would scratch off your number when you checked in with him.

Usually, for example, if we received the football, the red team would start most of the time. They'd drive the ball and when they turned it over, the blue team might go in and the red team would go out until the beginning of the second quarter. Or the green team could go in. They were the third team and were trying to move up. But everyone played. The green team didn't play as much as the blue and the red, but they played a good bit.

Coach Vaught ran a 52 defense: five up front, two linebackers and four defensive secondary guys. We ran that defense the whole time—ran it every day—and got after it. He was a great offensive coach, but he could coach defense, too. For example, when we played LSU in the Sugar Bowl he put in a whole new defense for that game. It was an attack-type defense and that's why we won the game. He was attacking. He wanted someone to get across the line of scrimmage every play: gaps or stunts, whatever. The other thing is his defensive ends were going to contain. You had to contain or you weren't going to play. The deal was everyone take care of your position and if you didn't there was another guy behind you trying to get there. The nose guard was the right guard on offense. I was left guard and I was the left inside linebacker. The center was the right inside linebacker. Then the two offensive tackles were the defensive tackles and they were lined up on the outside of the offensive tackles and the two ends outside of them. And by gosh, you didn't get whipped and that's all there was to it. The offensive tackle isn't going to beat you. You're gonna whip him. Buster Poole coached the defensive line and Bruiser the offensive line. Junie Hovius coached the secondary, and John Cain coached the running backs. Coach Vaught coached the quarterbacks. He had been a lineman in college but he was smart and he knew what he wanted the quarterbacks to do. He knew if we did it, good things would happen and that's what we did. He could get it done.

Before we went out to practice every day he would get us all in the team meeting room and get on the blackboard and show us what we were going to do offensively and defensively. At halftime during games we got in with our position coaches, and if there were things not going right, they'd change things up. Fortunately, most of the time we were ahead. Coach Vaught had it in his mind how it was going to work and it usually did.

John Wallace Blaylack was the varsity quarterback my freshman year in 1956 and they were 7-3. The 1957 team beat Texas in the Sugar Bowl, 39-7. I didn't travel with the team that year because I was redshirted. Robert wanted to redshirt that year but they needed him for his place-kicking ability so he didn't redshirt and moved up. The way it happened was we flew out to play Trinity in the first game and George Blair, Allen Green, Robert and I made the trip. Maybe a couple of others. We were all sophomores. Trinity was so small they barely had a dressing room. I don't know why we flew out there and played them. So Coach Vaught said: "Robert, we're not going to hold you out. You've got to be our kicker. Now George, Warner and Allen, we're going to hold you boys out." Well, you didn't say anything other than "Yes sir." That was just the way it was going to be. So maybe six or seven of us made the trip but only one of us—Robert—made the team. The rest of us redshirted. Robert kicked off and kicked some field goals and extra points. Paige Cothren had been the kicker and had graduated. He was a senior our freshman year. They had that system pretty well going by then. They were getting the best players and they just decided who was going to play and held the rest out and the next year they moved on up with three years of eligibility remaining. The key is that he was getting the players.

We had great camaraderie in the group. We lived together and ate together. Miller Hall was not here when we got here. The freshmen lived in Vardaman A and Vardaman B. A few guys got put over in Garland where the varsity was and that wasn't good. You didn't want that. By the spring of our freshman year after we'd gone through spring practice they kind left us alone. The thing about the freshmen with all of us living together is that you became such good friends. That was a big plus for the team. I think Miller opened in the fall of 1959 and we all stayed together, freshmen and upper classmen. A group of us got together and said, "Let's get rid of all of that hazing," so we got rid of that.

Before Miller we ate at a white building right about where Paris Yates is now. It was Mrs. Calhoun's cafeteria. They tore that down when they got Miller going. We had a great dining hall in Miller. They did a great job with it and had a good guy running it. It was cafeteria style. You could get a steak at night and Coach Wobble and Sara were the monitors for the whole thing. They ate in the cafeteria so that kept you on your Ps and Qs. Their children ate there, too. We got to know them. When we were in Garland if they needed a babysitter, we would go downstairs and study while the children went to sleep. Curly (Sara) and Wobble would come in and we'd go back up.

When I was a redshirt sophomore I hoped to be on the green team at least. That was the third team. What you wanted to be sure of is that you didn't go back to the orange team another year. That was the redshirts. So what you wanted to do was move from the orange up to the green team. Ahead of me my redshirt sophomore year was Possum Price. At the end of spring practice, when you knew you had made the green team and you were going to travel, that was a great feeling. And the next year I moved up to the blue team. Possum didn't redshirt. He was too good. We played two years together. He was playing left guard on the red team and I was on the blue team. If two guys were equal, he'd probably play the senior guy over the junior. The camaraderie in the team was good. Everyone thought we were in a good place. The maturity of the team was good because we had a lot of juniors and seniors. It was a system that they had worked out. If you were on the green team you were going to play in the games. What you wanted to do was you wanted to play a lot, so you got out there and played and hoped to get to play some more.

Coach Bruiser coached the ends on offense, too, because they were involved in the blocking. We pulled a lot and trapped a lot. We'd pull out and the quarterback would roll out behind you but you had to be fast enough to get out there in front of the quarterback. If the quarterback rolled out right, our end would go downfield and the quarterback would hit him with a pass or keep it. If I were the right guard I'd try to cut the end down so the quarterback could run or throw without crossing the line of the scrimmage. The timing was critical and Coach Vaught had us running it over and over. Coach Vaught loved his fullbacks. They did a good job: they could run, block and catch. We threw to Charlie Flowers a lot. The linebacker would lose him and they'd just dump it off to him. We had the flanker when I was here and we used the man in motion when I was here. It was a real weapon. I think that was how we scored the first touchdown in the Sugar Bowl against LSU: we put a guy in motion, they got confused, Cowboy Woodruff broke in the middle and Jake hit him for a touchdown. Coach Vaught came up with putting that man in motion and a lot of times the defense would lose him so it became a good weapon. We were one of the early teams to use it. Our guys could run, too, so they'd come across in motion and turn downfield and they'd be open.

In 1959 I was in Baton Rouge for that game. I wasn't in there when Cannon made his run but I was in there when we didn't score from the one. The Red team was in there when Jake punted the ball and Cannon ran 89 yards. They were going to kick off and Coach Vaught put in our blue team. We took the ball on our thirty with about ten minutes to go in the game and moved it down to the seven yard line. We held it ten minutes. They put Doug in and he was the fourth quarterback. I don't know what Coach Vaught was doing but he had Doug in there. So it was first and goal on the seven and then fourth and goal on the one. We had a rule blocking situation. We knew they would be in a gap defense, a man in every gap, and so what you had to do was to keep your man from breaking the seam. You got to put your head in front of your man to keep him from breaking through the gap. But some-one broke the gap and grabbed Doug by the leg as he rolled left. He could have walked in if they hadn't caught his leg and tripped him up. After the game Coach Vaught said, "Don't worry, we're going to get these guys in the Sugar Bowl."

Well the next week we got Tennessee in Memphis. That's when Coach Vaught said, "Don't ever tell anyone, but I want to whip Tennessee worse than anybody because that Neyland was so arrogant." So we beat Tennessee 37-7. They scored when they blocked Charlie Flowers's quick kick. We never had a touchdown scored on us on a drive that began outside of our own twenty that whole season. Tulane scored after we fumbled inside of our own five. Tennessee scored off the blocked kick, which they recovered inside of the twenty. Then, right before the half, Jimmy Hall caught a pass and stepped out of bounds and Robert went in and kicked a field goal so it was 10-7 our way at half. We came back and beat those son of a guns good in the second half. We beat State Thanksgiving weekend 42-0. They had Billy Stacy but we went over there and beat them. And then we got the invitation to go to the Sugar Bowl and that's when he came up with the defense for LSU. It was a particular alignment with stunts that we called a cannonball. We lined up and whipped them. LSU didn't do anything.

My senior year was 1960. We opened with Memphis State in Memphis. They had a little quarterback named James Earl Wright. He was from Columbus and he was good. I re-member they scored twenty or so points. There was a big fight and one of our guys went over there and ran into Spook Murphy and knocked him down. The coaches made adjustments at halftime to shut down whatever it was they were doing. We didn't lose that year. LSU tied us and we had the last second field goal at Arkansas to win that one. The official at Arkansas was named Tommy Bell and what he did was he blew the whistle to stop the play but we went on and kicked it and it was good. So he said, "Naw, do it over again." They always said the second Allen Green's foot hit the football Bell threw his hands up and signaled it good before it ever got up there. Tommy Bell always said, "I didn't say it was good, I was signaling that he missed it this far." I don't think Arkansas fans thought that was very funny. Early in the game, Ralph Smith told Jake, "I can go down here and break inside and I'm going to be wide open, so he did and Jake threw it. Ralph caught it and made a touchdown. And it was 7-7 until Allen kicked the field goal at the end. The 1960 team was a good team but it was not the team we had in 1959.

The next week was LSU and their kicker flubbed an extra point, so Allen Green kicked the field goal that tied the game. I was in the game and we were moving down the field. We got down there with time running out and Allen Green kicked it right through there to tie it. It was a tough physical game. They were good and so were we.

I was a Phi Delta Theta and was vice president my senior year. My freshman year, when we pledged, we had to do so many hours of pledge work and I was pledge of the year. Dickie Kendall from McComb was a close friend of mine and I'd go over there and shine his shoes. But I enjoyed it after football season was over. We'd go over there a lot. Robert was a Phi Delt as was Louis Guy.

Ole Miss had a great impact on my life. The Good Lord must have helped me make that decision. What if I hadn't come here? What if I had gone to LSU? I came here, met my wife, and her daddy was responsible for me coming here. Back then we didn't have but three thousand students and I got to know so many of them. I cherish those bonds of friendship, which have been just unbelievable throughout our whole lives. And then I get to come back here and coach here and work here with our children and grandchildren here. I just don't think all of that would have happened if I hadn't chosen to come here in the first place.

LYMAN HELLUMS
(APRIL 19, 1926 - JULY 4, 2015)

In the 1959 game with LSU, what stands out for me besides Cannon's run was that in the first half we got down there inside the ten yard line four times. We could have kicked a field goal each time but Coach Vaught wanted to put them away. They were able to stop us and keep us from scoring, except for one field goal. It should have been 12 to nothing. Then, when Cannon made his run, it wouldn't have mattered if we had taken the field goals. Right at the end of the game, Doug Elmore was playing and you could only substitute one time in a quarter so the first team was not in at the end of the game. Still, we drove down to the one yard line and Doug tried to quarterback sneak it into the end zone but Billy Cannon and Max Fugler, their center, stopped him. On the bus back to the hotel I said, "Doug, how close did you get?" He said, "If I had just fallen down, I had it but they had me stood up and I couldn't get down and in." It was a great game. Harry Mehre was down there. He was writing for the Atlanta Constitution back then and used to cover the SEC as a writer. We talked before the game and I asked him if the winner could be the national champion. He said, "No doubt about it, these are the two best teams in the country." The next week Tennessee beat LSU and then Ole Miss beat Tennessee 37-7 in Memphis. We were on the south side of Crump stadium. WMC originated the game from the Memphis market and we had the rest. That day we were on Armed Forces Radio and we were packed in like sardines. Ole Miss gave up just three touchdowns that whole year. One of the touchdowns was against Tennessee off of a blocked punt. Then we had a fumble against Tulane right down on the goal that gave them a cheap one. And then Cannon's run. No one sustained any kind of drive on Ole Miss that year. Tennessee scored from about the five and so did Tulane.

Coach Vaught told us before the season started, "I think we're going to have a pretty good team this year because I've got sixteen or seventeen boys who know how to play."

As I look back, the 1959 season stood out the most. The team was so great. You know, back then you expected to win every game. We just had that kind of personnel. You just expected to win. Now you go into a game and you hope you win and the breaks have to go your way to win. But back then we could just out-personnel everyone. And nowadays you go on the road and it's considered tough to win on the road. Coach Vaught didn't care where he played you. An away game meant nothing. He would just line up and beat you, wherever you were playing.

BOBBY RAY "WAXY" FRANKLIN

1956-1960

I got over to Ole Miss for training camp my freshman year but I had been in a wreck and my knee was sore where it had hit the dashboard. So I was in pain a lot but I finally got it back in shape. Wobble was our freshman coach and everybody was scared to death of him but once it was all over and done, everybody loved him. He was the backbone of the Ole Miss football team. He straightened all the freshmen out. Wobble was a very disciplined person and when he finished with the freshmen, they were disciplined, too.

They signed at least two other quarterbacks in my class. One was Ray Cross from Columbus. He left after his freshman year. That year the varsity played Trinity out there. We went out there as sophomores and we didn't know who was going to be redshirted. They took along some of the freshmen and I was one of the ones who went. While we were warming up in the end zone Coach Vaught was walking around and he'd pat you on the shoulder and say, "You're not going to play. You're going to be redshirted this year." Then he'd go on to the next one. He never did tap on my shoulder so I said, "I guess I made it." That's how we knew we were going to be redshirted. We were told in the end zone while we were warming up.

When I was a freshman we scrimmaged against the varsity. They would holler, "Come on down, freshmen!" Mama Hurst would holler at us. He used to try to kill us. Mama had a big gut. That's the reason we called him "Mama." We'd be up there practicing and then, when the varsity got ready to scrimmage, they'd start hollering for us. Coach Vaught would call for us to come down. When we were on defense, there'd be a big hole up the middle and Mama wouldn't try to run around you when he came through that hole. He'd try to run over you.

Bo Ball was a redshirt and we were practicing against the varsity and doing special teams—working on the punt return team. The varsity was working on their punt return team and Bo was on the punt coverage team. Bo had to contain on the outside, so if the punt returner came his way, he had to turn him inside to keep him away from the sideline. We were down in Vaught's valley, and the freshman field was up above us. Gene Hickerson and some of them came downfield and they blocked Bo Ball all the way up the hill to the freshman field. They tried to kill him. We had some uniforms kind of like the ones worn by the college all stars that the company wanted us to try out, so Coach Vaught had Bo in one of those uniforms. He stuck out like a sore thumb. Boy, everybody with the varsity was all over him that day.

They assigned freshmen to upper-classmen and they assigned me to Gene Hickerson for some reason. Gene took care of me. When the freshmen came the first day, they used to beat you with a baseball bat. It was split right down the middle with a hole drilled in it. The first Sunday we reported to school, we lived up in Vardaman dorm. All the varsity was up there with their bats and paddles and stuff and they'd make you bend over and see how tough you were. They'd say, "Bend over freshman and grab your ankles." They wanted to see how much you could take. Then they'd rare back and hit you. You'd better not flinch. If you flinched they would hit you again. When they hit you, you'd have red circles back there where that hole would pop up against your rear end. It was unbelievable what they did to us. All the freshmen used to hide. We'd come back on Sunday after going home on a weekend. The varsity would want something to do so they'd want to whip the freshmen and have a little fun with them. Gene Hickerson told them, "You're not going to hit him. That's terrible. Leave him alone." He was one of the bigger guys on the team. Nobody messed with him anyway so he took care of me and I never did get whipped that much.

Also, there was initiation into the M Club. We'd go down to the field house and they take analgesic balm and rub it all over you, in your rear end and all of that stuff, and they'd take an oyster tied on a string and make you swallow it, then pull it back up and stuff like that. They'd have races with blocks of ice. They'd take two blocks of ice and put an olive on top of each block. You'd be naked and sit on the olive and pick it up, then carry it to the other block where the next guy would pick it up and run back. After the initiation was over they'd put some more of that analgesic balm all over your body—your testicles and your rear end—and you had to go back to Miller Hall right through the campus. So the first place you'd go was to a water fountain out on the baseball field. It looked like a dog sitting on his hind scratching in the grass trying to get that analgesic balm off. Ralph Smith was one of the last ones to leave the field house. He walked straight through the campus, through the library into the Grill, and he didn't have a stitch on. Then he went on over to Miller Hall. That's one of the reasons they stopped it. The main reason they stopped it was when Archie was a freshman. They loaded up all the freshman in one of the old cafeteria vans. It was always in front of Garland dorm and they always left the key in it. The football players used to steal it and go downtown to the movies and then bring it back and put it where it was. They took them down to the Episcopal Church and church was letting out. All the freshmen were in there naked and they put them out and made them run back to the dorm. That's when they stopped all of that stuff. The coaches didn't want them to run Archie off.

I did it all. I punted when I was in the ballgame. All quarterbacks punted. Most of them were pretty good punters. We punted every day. In 1957 we went 8-1-1 and beat Texas in the Sugar Bowl. Here was Coach Vaught's philosophy: he had quarterbacks running out of his ears. He always recruited a lot of quarterbacks. He would always play several quarterbacks. I played a lot as a sophomore, probably played as much as Raymond Brown did. Raymond was a great quarterback, but that's the way Coach Vaught was. He was always getting the younger guys ready to go by their junior or senior year. We were playing Vanderbilt and I was the quarterback. We had Billy Ray Adams and Louis Guy, who were sophomores and I was a senior that year. I could talk to the players and I'd tell the lineman, "We've got to have this play. You've got to block." So we had those sophomores in there and I knew Billy Ray was real tight and nervous from getting to play a little bit. I called something that wasn't even a play. I said, "Wing right, split left, around the chicken coop, on two!" I clapped my hands and they went running out of the huddle up to the line of scrimmage. I said, "Come back here, man. That ain't no damn play." They were so damn nervous they'd didn't even realize what I'd said. I asked, "What were you gonna do when I snapped the ball?" Billy Ray said, "Hell, I don't know. I knew it wasn't a play for me."

I played a lot against Texas in the Sugar Bowl. Gene Hickerson was a senior and I was a sophomore then. We moved the ball down the field to the four or five yard line and Coach Vaught put the seniors back in the ballgame and let them score. So we moved the ball up and down the field all day long. I played a lot my sophomore year and then I started my junior year. My senior year I got hurt in the Kentucky game. We beat them 16-0 and 35 and 36 slant was our bread and butter play. That was the option: the quarterback sprints out and either pulls the ball down and runs or he passes. If the defensive back comes up, he passes, and the receiver should be wide open. If the defensive back stays back, the quarterback tucks it under his arm and runs. So I ran 35 slant right toward our sidelines about the fifty yard line. I kept it and they ran me out of bounds. The stadium wall was real close to where the player's bench was so when they ran me out of bounds, the guy shoved me from behind. I hurdled the player bench and I had to lower my head because I couldn't stop so I ran into the brick wall and it knocked me out. I was lying there on the ground and they all ran over and huddled around me. Doc Knight came over there and had the smelling salts out and under my nose. He was saying, "Waxy, Waxy, are you okay?" Warner Alford swears that I looked up at Doc Knight and said, "I'm fine but how are the fans taking it?" The other thing is that the guy who was behind me stepped on the calf of my leg. It was cut and it was painful as everything. It was right before halftime when it happened and when halftime was over, I could barely walk on that leg. It cut it right in the middle of the calf and it started swelling. So I didn't play the second half. I started back practicing too early on the leg and a blood clot came back in the leg, so I had to go to the hospital. I stayed there for almost a week while they tried to get the blood clot out. So I missed two or three games in a row. Jake had taken over and was doing well so I wasn't playing a whole lot after that. But I started the Sugar Bowl, like Coach Vaught always did. I was a senior so I started and had a great game. I was MVP. Coach Vaught said, "You're always a trophy hound." I had gotten the MVP against Florida in the Gator Bowl the year before so I was MVP of both bowl games.

That '59 team was great. I was the starting quarterback in the LSU game. In the second half I wasn't moving the ball real well, so Jake comes in and he wasn't moving it real well. Then Doug Elmore comes in right at the end of the game and moves it well. We had them 3-0 through the middle of the fourth quarter. I came out and Jake came in and punted and before I could sit down on the bench the crowd roared. Jake had gotten off a good punt and it went over Cannon's head. It had rained the night before so it was a wet field. Instead of hitting and rolling, it hit and bounced right back to Cannon. He catches it with his back to the line of scrimmage and turns around and dodges about three or four players and heads for the sideline. I think six or seven players had a shot at him and Jake was the last shot and glanced right off of him. They had an official running down the sideline with Cannon and we found out later, that was not a real official, that was a guy who didn't have a ticket and dressed up like an official to get into the game. He was running side-by-side with Cannon with both arms up in the air when they crossed the goal line. That was the toughest loss. I don't think they even had a first down all night. We had stopped them cold. That '59 team had only two touchdowns scored from scrimmage against us. One was by Tulane after a turnover down on about our ten yard line and one was by Tennessee following a blocked quick kick right down on our goal line.

On the Friday nights before games during the '59 season, we might go to a movie and then come back to the dorm. We weren't trying to slip out or go have date with some gal or something like that. We were all huddled in somebody's room talking about what we were going to do tomorrow, on Saturday. That was a great football team. All we wanted to do was win. These players are a little different in this day and time. We were very dedicated to winning. We might not have been as big as they are today but we gave 100 percent all the time.

I really don't think Coach Vaught's game plan for the Sugar Bowl against LSU was any different because we knew they couldn't score on us. Larry Grantham did a great job at defensive end. He didn't weigh but about 215 pounds but he was a ferocious guy. Wobble used to check rooms at night, and Richard "Possum" Price and Grantham smoked cigarettes all the time. Well, you better not let Wobble catch you smoking cigarettes. So Wobble was scouting one Friday night and Coach Kinard had to check rooms in Garland dorm. They had a poker game going and Coach Kinard came in Grantham's room. About five of them were sitting around a table with Possum and another guy smoking. So Coach Kinard caught them and said, "Boys, what are you doing smoking in here? Get those damn cigarettes out." So he walked out in the hall and called Coach Vaught because Wobble normally handled the discipline himself. So he called Coach Vaught and told him that he had caught Possum smoking and asked Coach Vaught, "What do you want me to do to him?" Coach Vaught said, "Just tell him don't smoke too many." Possum was a great player, though. He wasn't very big but he was something.

The three years I was on the varsity we went to two Sugar Bowls and the Gator Bowl. I had great games in all three of them. Raymond had a great game and someone told me if Raymond hadn't run that punt back 102 or 3 yards out of the end zone, I would probably have gotten the MVP in that game, too. Against Florida in the Gator Bowl, which we won 7-3, I threw a touchdown pass to Grantham. Man, that was a tough game.

Coach Vaught coached the quarterbacks and loved to work with us. All we did was work on 35 and 36 slant. I remember Frank Broyles over in Little Rock when we beat Arkansas said that there was no way to stop that 35 or 36 slant.

Sam Davis's father was a big Ole Miss fan and Sam told the team that against Arkansas, his dad was going give fifty dollars to every player who scored a touchdown. I scored both of them that day. At the end of the ballgame, Arkansas scored and we were ahead one or two points. They went for two and didn't make it, so they tried an onsides kick with two minutes to go in the game. Coach Vaught had Grantham and me and all of the guys with good hands in there, and I was right in the middle. Well, they kicked it to the smallest man on the team—me—and I caught it but about three of them speared me in the side and cracked a rib. They carried me off the field to the hospital. So when the game was over, Sam comes out of the stands on the sideline and gives Charlie Flowers a hundred dollars to give to me because I scored both touchdowns. Well, on Sunday morning we always reported to the field house to check out injuries so we were down there and Charlie was standing there. Sam comes walking in. He says, "Charlie, did you give Franklin that hundred dollars?" I said, "Hundred dollars? Hell he only gave me fifty." And Flowers said, "Well, hell, I blocked for him. I get half of it." On 35-36 slant, the key block was Flowers's. He had to make the block on the defensive end, so he took him out and instead of throwing the ball, I ran the ball in for a touchdown. So he was right about that.

While I was at Ole Miss, I felt like we could beat anybody, any place, any time. We were a dedicated group of players. Wobble molded us the right way. All we wanted to do was win and we did what we had to do to win. It was a great group of players and they all loved Ole Miss.

JOHN "BONES" COSSAR

1956-1961

There was an economics professor we called Pops Ewell. All of the freshman football players were in Economics 101—Bobby Ray Franklin and all of us sitting on the back row—and Pops would open his book and ask a question: the gross national product is the difference between the gross sales and the cost of products available or something like that. Then, he'd ask, "Mr. Franklin, is that true or not true?" And Bobby Ray would be back there reading the sports section and he'd look up and say, "It's true." He didn't even know what the question was. He made a damn A in the course. That freshman football class in 1956 was the team of the decade in 1959. It started out that it was about a hundred freshmen and by the time Wobble got through with them it was down to about fifty and then they'd get it down to about thirty. We'd sign everybody in the state because it didn't matter how many you signed back then. Ninety percent of them got redshirted, so by the time you were in your third year you were just a sophomore for football and you didn't get to play a lot until your junior or senior year. So you ended up with Charlie Flowers as first team fullback and an All-American in 1959 and Hoss Anderson behind him and Billy Ray Adams, another All-American, behind him. That was the way Coach Vaught did it. By the time you got to be a fifth year senior you were likely starting. I told my parents that was the reason I needed to stay for my fifth year: because I would be graduating with my class. When we were all graduating—me, Buster Bailey, Warner Alford and Bo Ball—we were all sitting there in our caps and gowns. We'd entered in 1956 and were graduating in 1961 because of that redshirt year. Well, Chancellor Williams walked by, looked down there at us and said, "I'll have to say this about this class of 1961, y'all are the dumbest class that ever graduated from Ole Miss." But I'll tell you what else, we also had the best football record of any class: we were here five years and didn't lose but three games and played in five major bowl games and had two Miss Americas.

VAN EAST

1956-1960

I didn't miss a football game. I looked in the post office at the bulletin board and they had the tryouts for freshman cheerleaders. Since Johnny Vaught didn't need a slow 155-pound end, I didn't think I had much chance of getting on the football team, so I tried out for freshman cheerleader. Paul Frank and I were selected and there were six girls. Thad Cochran and Buena Lee English were among the varsity cheerleaders who selected us from our tryouts. Jerry Hornsby was also a varsity cheerleader. We didn't do all that pyramid building and stuff, but I had a loud voice and the reason I did it is I thought, "Well, there're some cute girls on that team," so that was my motivation.

We went up to Vanderbilt with the freshman team, and Daddy had bought me a 1955 tan four-door Ford, very plain. He bought ugly cars because they were cheap. So I took my car and the cheerleaders rode up with me—they didn't have transportation at that time—and we went up and of course, we beat Vanderbilt. After the game, Bo Ball had been to Nashville before and he said, "We need to go down to Printer's Alley," and I said, "Okay, let's go." So we loaded the car and went down to Printer's Alley. We got upstairs at some dive and some gal was dancing on the stage and Bo started to get rambunctious. I thought we might need to get out of there before we got in trouble so I walked down the stairs. Jimmy Hall was talking to two policemen down there in the Alley. The policemen were getting ready to corral this wino and hall him off to the drunk tank and Jimmy tells them, "He's with us." So the policemen said, "Boy, you better take care of him then." So we get in the car and Jimmy shoved the wino in the center, and I'm driving. Jimmy's on the right with the wino between us. And the wino says, "You want a drink, buddy?" And he hands me a bottle of Mogen David wine. I said, "I don't believe I do." Well, Shed Roberson and Bo Ball and Paul Frank, the other male cheerleader, were in the backseat so we started driving down Broadway toward Vanderbilt with the police car following us. So Shed gets mad. He says "Let me out. I'm going to whip those policemen." I said, "Y'all keep cool." And finally the police turned off and we let the drunk out and went on back to Vanderbilt. We got back to the dormitory around one o'clock in the morning, I guess. Jimmy falls down in the hallway and instead of getting up he rolls around on his back because the floor was real slick. And he slides across the floor down the hall and back and forth to his room. The people who lived there were looking out the doors at us like we were idiots.

Johnny Brewer was a Kappa Sig. He was a nice guy and a heck of a football player. Bill Basham was a guard and a Kappa Sig. He had not made the traveling squad and the team went down to Houston. Bill went on his own. He was sitting up in the stands and two or three guards got hurt in the first half. One of the coaches looked up there in the stands and saw him and said "Hey, come on down here, Basham." He dressed out and played and started every game for the rest of the year.

On that Texas Sugar Bowl game I worked at Gathright Reed and made fifty cents an hour. I saved enough money to buy a game ticket and a train ticket to New Orleans. So Mama drove me over to Batesville and I got on the train. I had on a car coat and had a change of underwear in one pocket and a toothbrush in the other and went to the game. I had to catch the train coming back around seven in the morning and about midnight I ran into Gene Hickerson. He said I could come stay in his room. So I went up there and he wasn't in so I knocked around in the hotel. WNOE's radio station was there on the mezzanine and I got to talking to the disc jockey and explained my plight. He said just lie down there on the couch. I'll wake you up in time to catch your train and he did, so I got back on the train and got off in Batesville. I had an empty Hurricane glass, some dirty underwear, a toothbrush and no money. Gene Hickerson was a heck of a football player. I used to take binoculars to games just to watch him.

JAKE GIBBS

1957-1961

Istarted first grade in Grenada and went there twelve years. I didn't start football until my freshman year. In the eighth grade I told my parents that I wanted to play football. I had my own pants and my own shoulder pads so I went out one day to practice. They had already started and they said, "Aw, naw you go on home." I said okay so I waited until I was a freshman. Bud Gerrard was our head coach in football and had been a center on the Ole Miss football team. He had married a pretty lady named Eleanor Green from Grenada. I went out for quarterback and I played a little bit as a freshman. We went over to play Starkville and they were kind of the top dogs in the Little Ten. They had a good ball club. State had a quarterback named Jackie Parker who went on and had a tremendous career in Canadian football. Coach Gerrard was talking to a guy who was taping my ankles before the Starkville game and said, "You see this kid right here. He's going to be another Jackie Parker." I really didn't know much about Jackie Parker but it stuck with me what that fellow said. I hadn't played hardly any at that point.

We were the blue-and-white Bulldogs but we weren't Grenada at that time. We were

John Rundle High School, not Grenada. Grenada had a good school system back in those days. It was tough, and you had to study. I started playing baseball in the seventh grade as a second baseman. My brother Bobby Gibbs is three years older than I am and he played short-stop. He's a retired full bird Colonel and lives in Petal. My first cousin Paul Gibbs played third base. We had a Gibbs infield. We were better known as the Highway Eight boys. I lived on Highway Eight East two or three miles from Grenada Lake. In that neighborhood we had our own ballclub. We had enough boys out there to make up a team. If I ever write a book, the name of it will be "The Highway Eight Boys." We had our own team and our own field that we made out of a pasture. We also built our own grass tennis courts. I started six years in baseball. I think the smallest pants they had were like a 28" waist so Mama had to take them up. I had a double kneepad because we had to take them up so much. I played baseball from then on and started every year. We faced two good pitchers. One was from Sardis named Butler Jones, a big tall left-handed pitcher and God could he throw. He threw hard and he was like 6' 4" or 6' 5" and I'm a left-handed hitter so when he started winding up and letting the ball go you didn't see anything but legs and arms. That was pretty hairy for a guy who was just a seventh grader. Then the other one pitched at Batesville. He was from around Polk and Enid and was named Gowan. He had great control and I had pretty good luck against him. He threw strikes and I knew it wasn't going to hit me. I had a 36" bat and I choked up about four inches. I remember those days as if it happened yesterday. We had a pretty good baseball team back then. The Highway Eight boys had five positions on the high school team: the three of us and then Thomas Freeman and Ray Freeman, so five positions were from the Highway Eight boys. Anyway, we'd get in the District and you'd have to play Sardis. Well, Butler Jones pitched and he was tough. Olive Branch was also very good. They weren't in the Little Ten, which was Grenada, Oxford, Okolona, Aberdeen, Amory, and Sardis. Winona, Batesville, and Indianola were in the Delta Valley, but we played some of them. We had good baseball teams. Basketball: so-so.

I didn't start at quarterback until my junior year in high school. I played quite a bit as a sophomore and I think Bud Gerrard left after my freshman year, and then Bob Ellard came in. We ran a wing-T and did a lot of faking up the middle and sprinting out. It was a good offense. The best year we had was 7-3 when I was a senior. We were always around 6-4 or 5-5. Starkville was by far the best team. Oxford was about like we were. Oxford had a big fullback named Angelo Mistilis—he cooks those hamburger steaks—but he was the big boy in the Little Ten. He was big. He probably weighed over 200 pounds and he got people's attention. That was big back then. Aberdeen was pretty good. Amory was pretty good in those days. They had a guy named Kiger Adams. He played over there and came to Ole Miss and married Maye Wick Coers. Kiger hit a guy (Bobby Holcomb) one night and the guy died. He never got over that.

I broke my nose my sophomore year and I had double vision for six weeks. I had a class in English upstairs and she put me on the front row to start with but the only way I could see her was to tuck my head and it worried the fire out of her. So she said, "Jake, you need to go on to the back of the class." It cut my nose open and I had two black eyes and I left the field throwing up blood. I was sick as a dog and they operated about 25 minutes on my nose and then Daddy, when he heard about it, said "I don't care if you play football anymore. Play baseball."

I was recruited by both Ole Miss and State and in fact, State recruited me harder. At Ole Miss, the coaches were assigned areas and Buster Poole had my area, Bruiser had Jackson, Ray Poole had Natchez and so on. Buster came to Grenada to scout a boy from Indianola and saw me. He went back and said to Vaught, "We need to take a look at this little quarter-back from Grenada. He can run." So when Paul Gregory, the State baseball coach, offered me a full baseball scholarship, Daddy looked at me and I think he wanted me to take it. But I said, "Coach Gregory, I'm going to Ole Miss. If I'm going to play football, I'm going to play for Coach Vaught. And that's it. I'm going to play baseball for Coach Swayze but I'm going to play football for Coach Vaught. So I'm going to Ole Miss."

When the State coach left, Coach Buster met him in the front yard. So when Coach Buster came in, I said, "Coach Buster, I'm signing with you." Ole Miss was offering me a football scholarship. But I said "Now, Coach Buster, you know I've got to play baseball so if I get hurt in football, I got to get y'all to keep me on scholarship so I can play baseball." Swayze told the story that he goes back from recruiting me and tells Vaught that he wants to sign me as a quarterback and Vaught says, "You just want to sign a baseball player."

Tennessee called me one night and said, "We hear you could be a triple threat tailback: run, pass, catch." They ran the single wing back in those days. And I said, "I don't know much about you. Who are you?" And he said, "We're the University of Tennessee." And I said, "Where are you?" And he said, "Knoxville." I said, "How far is that from Mississippi?" and he said, "400 miles." I said, "You don't need to call me anymore. That's too far."

Now the way they did it with the Ole Miss freshmen was they divvied up the freshmen into an offensive team and a defensive team to scrimmage the first team and the second team. So they put me on the defensive unit and the first day we went down to the band field, I was the safety. And you got Billy Lott, Mama Hurst, those guys running the football. I was about 5'10", about 160, and Mama Hurst weighed about 225 or 230, low to the ground. But anyway after about three or four plays, you get hit and you settle down. And then they happened to run 48 trap and I'm looking at Mama coming through the hole. I said, "Where's my linebackers? Ain't no linebackers. It's me and Mama." And I said, "Lord, let him fall. Let him do something." But I had to hit him, so I hit up around his waist and when I ended up, I was down around his ankles. So I said, "You know what, you just got to get with it." And after that I was okay. So on that one day, I got all of that nervousness out of me. We scrimmaged quite a bit against the varsity my freshman year. But we had enough redshirts my second year that the incoming freshmen didn't have to do that.

Coach Wobble was great with fundamentals, even with the quarterbacks. We ran the same system—the same plays—that the varsity ran and he taught us the fundamentals necessary to run Coach Vaught's system, from the linemen to the running backs to the receivers and the quarterbacks. The basketball coach, Country Graham, helped him and by the time we got to the varsity, everyone pretty much knew what to do.

My freshman year the varsity went 8-1-1. That was the team that went to the Sugar Bowl and beat Texas. Ray Brown was the quarterback. He made a long run off of a punt. The story about that is he's through everybody on the Texas team and Jackie Simpson is right behind him, running with him. So Jackie Simpson is hollering: "Lateral it to me; lateral it to me." And of course, Ray Brown kept running. Jackie wanted to get a touchdown.

They put all of the freshmen in Vardaman A and Vardaman B. All of the varsity was in Garland. And right down below Garland was a little white building that was our athletic cafeteria. And Mrs. Calhoun ran it. Her son was Bill Calhoun and his son—Mrs. Calhoun's grandson—runs Oby's now. That's where we had all of our meals: that little white building there. It was probably a World War II type building and they tore it down when they opened up Miller Hall. It was in the vicinity of where the bell tower is now.

So that spring Ray was gone so we had Waxy Franklin and Billy Brewer. I came out of spring as the third team quarterback. That was the spring of 1958. That fall we lost to LSU 14-0. It was hot, sweaty, and misty, a slow field, typical Baton Rouge weather in late October. We played good. It was a hard fought game. They scored right at the end of the game to make it 14-0. Bull Churchwell hit an LSU running back around the line of scrimmage and knocked him over the goal line. They always got on old Bull for knocking him over. But they were a good football team. They had all of those guys already in there: Cannon and Rabb and Johnny Robinson. J. W. Broadnax played fullback. I didn't play a lot in that ballgame. Coach Vaught played mostly first team, second team boys. They matched up with us about as good as anyone then. They weren't any bigger than we were and we weren't any faster than they were. LSU had pretty good personnel in 1958 and 1959. Whoever got the breaks won. They got a couple of breaks against us and were national champions that year.

We lost to Tennessee 18-16 in 1958. I played in that game a little bit. George Blair and I went in and played and did pretty well and then didn't go back in. That's just the way it was. We had a chance to win. Robert had a chip shot field goal and he missed it. Robert was an excellent field goal kicker, but it happens. He was in position to kick it and it just went right or left, I can't remember. And they won by two points. And it was like Tennessee people thought they had a jinx over us. This was their jinx. Ole Miss can't win up here. They can't win at Shields-Watkins field. We went up there my senior year—we had beat them 38-7 my junior year in Memphis––and beat them 24-6. People never left. They said this can't be true. That's where they cut my hand. They would try to get to your eyes. Dirty football. I didn't have much love for Tennessee back in those days. They were still running the single wing. So I was playing defense against the single wing. What you did on defense was you keyed on the fullback. Coach Wobble was responsible for this. He had scouted Tennessee. Being from Tennessee this was the team that he saw a lot so he had everything down that they did. What they ran back then was a little like what they try to run out here now except this is more spread open.

Now like I said, in the single wing their fullback was the key. He was going to lead you where the play was going. So you keyed off of him and boom, you stopped it. You worked on it in practice and worked on it so if they didn't make any adjustments then you stopped it. Coach Vaught loved to play defense against the single wing. Yeah, he loved it. We had a thing called "We've got to stop the kitchen sink." Tennessee had a play called "the kitchen sink." It was where the tailback spins and does this and fakes to the fullback and then goes up one side. We stopped that pretty good. That was the first year Ole Miss ever beat them at Shields-Watkins. Hoss Anderson had a big game. He was concerned going into the season that he couldn't jump over the line. So we get down on the goal line and we run 48 power. Turn around and give him the ball and let him jump over the line. And we did that quite a bit with Charlie Flowers and of course, he could jump. And it was pretty easy back in those days. Hoss was concerned that when we got to be seniors that I wasn't going to let him jump like Charlie. Word got back to me. So I said, "Hoss, don't you worry about that. We get down there I'm going to let you jump. Just be ready." So we got down there and I called 48 power and he took it and jumped over. But he was concerned whether I was going to call that.

My junior year was 1959. Waxy and I played a lot in 1959. In fact, I was second-team at Ole Miss and second team All SEC behind Tarkenton from Georgia that year. I think that year I led the SEC in total offense and was second-team behind Waxy. But Waxy was hurt a lot so I played a good bit. We go into Houston and I'm on the second team and the first team doesn't do anything so Coach Vaught puts us in and we get the ball and swish, we go down there and score. And it's 7-0. We ended up beating them 16-0. It was all passing. But in that game, I played quite a bit. The next game was at Kentucky, and Waxy got hit and the stadium is not too far from the field. They hit him and carried his little ass and ran him into the wall. And hurt him. So I had to go in there and I played most of the game. Then, that Monday Waxy was starting practice as the number one quarterback. So Coach Vaught called me over there and said I was running with the first unit. But I never started a game that year. Waxy always started. That was Coach Vaught's leadership. That's just the way it was. He started a senior. And then after a series, he'd put you in.

We called passes a lot because we ran bootlegs, sprint outs, and you had the option to run or throw. So we would probably call it forty times a game and the quarterback would end up throwing maybe twenty passes and running 15 or twenty. It wasn't like now, when you drop back and pass, pass, pass. It's not much option out there now. But Coach Vaught wanted you to run first and pass second. So you'd call roll-out right, roll-out left, swing pass right, swing pass left, 36 slant, 35 slant, 36-0, 35-0 so you'd probably call it 35 times a game. Between roll out, slant and 34 F bootleg, 33 F bootleg, Charlie Flowers caught a bunch of passes that year. And we had 26 and 25 and we had bootlegs off of them. So if you'd take 25 and 26 bootlegs and 33 and 34—34 is running off tackle, 33 running off tackle, bootleg off those two, that's two bootlegs, then you have swing pass right and swing pass left—that's kind of a bootleg, so that's three bootlegs. Archie wasn't much of a bootleg but I told him, Archie, when I was coaching the quarterbacks later on, "That bootleg's open anytime you want to run it. Because anytime you have misdirection somebody on defense is going to be out of position. You've just got to find it." So you fake the handoff and get everyone going one way and put the ball on your hip and roll the opposite direction. In the Arkansas game where we beat them 10-7, 25 bootleg was what got us down the field right toward the end of the game. I told Flowers that I wished I had called that in 1959 more, because it was open. It's open right now if they'd ever call it. You get them confused.

Crespino was one of my favorite targets. In one game we would throw 35-over and 36-over. You make it look like 36 slant. You got the ball and you ran the five yards like hell, but you got to the tackle and you pulled up. You have four people running out. So Crespino is running short, and the tight end is going straight down the field. This left end—you have rolled right—is going to come across and this wingback is right in the gap. If I called 35-over, so boom! So I called it against LSU in the Sugar Bowl right before halftime—thirty seconds left in the half and Cowboy (Woodruff) is my wingback; Crespino is my right half, and that play he goes out the back door down the sidelines. Man, it worked, worked, worked, worked. Because you got nobody on him. If that end doesn't drop back to cover him, man he's wide open. With a three deep secondary—and so this is the way it actually happened: I called 35-0, which means Warren Rabb is playing safety. And I pull up and Crespino is going out the back door and I looked at Warren Rabb and he takes the line going toward Crespino, and he leaves this gap open, and that's where Cowboy is and he's wide-ass open. Now Warner has missed his block. It was one of those lookout blocks. He says, "Lookout!" And this guy was coming down on me so about the time I got hit I threw it and I thought I had overshot him. Cowboy didn't have the hands that Crespino did. But he had to go up and I saw him catch it and by this time I was on my back. He went 43 yards for a touchdown and we go in leading 7-0 at halftime. And that play worked because Warren Rabb left his position to go to Crespino. Lot of people don't know that. I cued in on him because if he had stayed there, then I go to Crespino. If he leaves I hit Woodruff. Now the line had to stay home on those rollouts because they didn't know whether I was going to run it or pass it. The line always got down in a three-point stance. So if you were on the line, you didn't know whether we were going to run it or throw it. Coach Vaught wouldn't let the quarterback go straight back. You had to turn this way or this way. So I asked him once, "Coach, how come we don't just back up?" He said, "When you back up from the center, you have told the defense that you are going to pass it or you are going to run a draw." So he never did that until way down the line. You always turned this way or turned that way. The linemen always got in the three point stance and they would butt that guy in front of them. So the defensive linemen didn't know whether it was a run or a throw because they got butted. They didn't drop into pass protection. Our linemen butt you and stay with you. So this defense just didn't know whether it was a run or a slant pass or something.

For the first LSU game in 1959 Coach Vaught put in a play where there was a straight drop back pass, either 58 or 57. On 58 you turned left and then dropped back five or six steps into the pocket. They had noticed that this end sort of charged to the outside, so I would set up and Flowers was supposed to take that end and kick him out and that tackle would block down and there would be a gap. Coach Vaught thought with me running the ball we could get some yards. So it was a new play. Well, the first time that we ran it, hell I barely got back to the line of scrimmage. That end was hitting Charlie Flowers. So I called it again because if Coach Vaught puts it in, he thinks it's going to work. And the same thing happened. And I said about the third time I called it, I said, "Charlie, dammit you gotta block that end." He said, "I'm doing everything I can but that SOB is wearing my ass out." He said, "Don't call it anymore." So a series later, I dropped back to pass, straight back in the pocket—I always kick myself for not running more 25 and 26 bootlegs. We got away from that some way. So I called another pocket pass. And I said, "Guys, I've got to have a little more time." And Richard Price is our left guard, and he looks at me and says, "Jake, I got my hands full. It's every man for himself." And that's the God's truth. So I knew damn well that I was going to have to call something else. First time we got the ball we drove down there and had a chance for a field goal and I ran rollout right and what happened was it was noisy down there near their student section at the north end zone. So I called rollout right. It was a run all the way. We were on their one or two yard line, fourth and goal. And what happened is Dewey Partridge is my right half. Quail. Good defender. And I kick myself a hundred times every time I think about it. The ref told us to go back in the huddle because of crowd noise. I've thought about this I don't know how many times. I should have brought my team back to the huddle and let the refs get 'em quiet. But what happened is I called the signal, called the cadence, and when the ball was snapped, Dewey was supposed to block the end but the end beat him across the line. So by the time I got rolled out, he had hit me a little bit and I started running but the flow of the traffic caught up with me and knocked me out on the one yard line. And it was because Dewey couldn't hear the snap signal. I should have let the ref get 'em quiet. They were supposed to get 'em quiet in those days. That was the first time we ever got the football and we could have ended up with three points. Coach Vaught admitted later on that he wished he had kicked the ball a little bit more. He had opportunities.

I punted, too. It's in Robert's book. That night, I punted I think nine times and Cannon punted nine times. Robert says I averaged 52 yards and I think Cannon averaged about fifty. The punt he ran back I kicked it like 47 yards and it wasn't a very good kick. I was trying to kick it out of bounds because we had run down there and run down there and our team was getting a little bit tired. That ball was hit. And LSU had a rule that you do not touch anything ten yards going in. You don't field it. Paul Dietzel has this in his book. He saw the ball going on over there. And he knew it was going to be down there around the ten. And he was hollering, "Don't catch it! Don't catch it!" And all of a sudden Cannon's catching it and Dietzel hollers, "Run, go ahead, run!" In his book he admits you don't field it but after Cannon fielded Dietzel is hollering "Run! Run!" It bounced as high as this ceiling. It was end-over-end. I usually kicked spirals but this one was end-over-end. The ground was soft. You'd think that ball would hit and scoot. But it bounced straight up in the air. Cannon told Charlie—they played in the Hula Bowl that year—he said "I had no thought about fielding that ball until that ball bounced high." He said when that ball went up there he said, "Yeah, I'll take a chance." And that's how it happened. He wasn't going to field it until the ball got that big bounce. About the time he caught it, two of them hit him. He shook them off, took another step, and someone else hit him. I kept telling people a long time ago: "I'm the last one who missed him—what happened to those other ten?" And Cannon says he put a little fake on me and I missed him. He didn't know what a fake was. He was a straight-line runner. A big old strong boy. We talked about this. I went down in August for an SEC beach fest and they had about ten ex-SEC coaches.

I don't know if I had a real breakout game. I know over here against Mississippi State (21-0) as a sophomore, the first time I went in I called rollout right and I made the turn and tripped and lost four or five yards. So I called either a slant pass and completed it and got all of those yards back and more and that's when I started getting better. I got a lot of confidence against State. And then I played in the Gator Bowl. Coach Vaught was like this. I was playing number three quarterback against Florida in the Gator Bowl. That was when Flowers got hit by Kent Lovelace in the head and he didn't know where the hell he was. Dr. Ferrell Varner was in the dressing room with Charlie. Anyway, I go in the game about the third quarter. So we got the ball on about our 20 or 25 yard line and we make a first down and then make another and then another and we get down to about their 35 yard line. Then Coach Vaught takes me out and puts in another quarterback. That's just the way he was. You didn't question him. Naw, man. It might have been Brewer coming in. Or Waxy. But that's the only time I played in that game. I did pretty good but didn't go back in. We won the game, though.

John Cain was our backfield coach but Coach Vaught was the quarterback coach. He was a guard in college and he was the valedictorian of his class. He was smart and he knew offense. I don't know whether he picked it up when he was up at North Carolina or not. There was another coach that he coached for who ran this type of offense, speed wise. Roll-outs and bootlegs, that kind of thing. So when Coach Vaught came to Ole Miss he kept that system in his mind, and he recruited quarterbacks who could run. You had to be able to run to play quarterback here. That's why Crespino went to right half. He wasn't quick from the time he got that ball. Now you let him get on down the field and he could get those long legs going and he could run. But he wasn't quick the first few steps and Coach Vaught wanted quarterbacks who could run. He wanted you to take that ball and get from Point A to Point B in no time. So if you ran 36-slant, you had to get out to where that tackle or end was and he wanted five yards depth and so you had to be flying to get to the corner. And by that time, you were putting pressure on this guy and what was he going to do? All you needed was one block from the fullback on that end and then you would either run or pass. Thirty six slant you rolled out to the right and 35 slant you rolled out to the left. Everything even numbered went to the right and odd-numbers went to the left. 36, 38, 42 to the right and 45, 43, 41 to the left. Didn't matter whether you went right or left, you still had your depth. You had to get five yards depth. So when I turned away from center I was going at an angle to get five yards depth. I learned back in those days looking at defenses and where they were. When I got the ball I knew where Crespino was and I knew where my right end was so I would kind of pick up where they were. You came out looking

What I read depended on what defense they were in. If they were in a five man defense, the linebacker is sitting in front of that guard and it's hard for him to get to the outside so then you're looking at your right defensive halfback. So if you're going right, this guy—the right defensive halfback—has got to come up and get you or take Crespino. So if the full-back blocks that end, it puts the right defensive halfback in a hell of position. This tight end was going down and out so the safety had to come over to cover him so this guy—the defensive halfback was your key. If he came up, you threw it and if he stayed back you ran it. Now Coach Vaught had this rule on the option: if you got a chance to run it and make ten or twelve yards, you run it first. That was the choice: run first, throw second. If you can get ten yards running you get it. That was his fundamental strategy.

I hit Crespino up at Vanderbilt for a swing pass and it went for 78 yards. That was my senior year. We beat them 26-0. We should have beat them 33-0 and Coach Vaught got a little mad at me. Art Doty was running the ball good and we were on about the one or two yard line and Coach Vaught sends in a quarterback sneak. And I said, "Dammit, I'm not quarterback sneaking." I said, "Art, you ran this football down here," and I said, "By damn you need to score." So we ran Doty and we fumbled. They recovered and we didn't score. Coach Vaught didn't say anything. I said, "Coach, Art Doty needed to score. He'd run the ball down there." But he didn't say anything. He didn't get on me too much. It was the one bad thing that could happen—fumble and they recover it—and it happened.

The spring of 1959 was my sophomore year in baseball. I hit .404 and was All SEC. We were SEC champions. First time. Ever. Coach Swayze had taken the 1954 and 1956 teams to Omaha but he had not won the SEC. Ole Miss went as an at-large team. I didn't realize this until someone pointed it out to me, and I don't know of any other school that's ever done this. I think Ole Miss ought to publicize it more than they have, because this is something that not many people know. That was the first year we won the SEC in baseball—in 1959 first ever—and I'm a sophomore. Then the 1959 football team goes 10-1, is Team of the Decade, the Sugar Bowl champs, and wins a couple of national championships. In 1960, we win the SEC baseball championship again—back to back years—and the 1960 football team is SEC Champ, Sugar Bowl Champ, and national champs. Now you tell me what school in the SEC has ever won SEC baseball championships back-to-back, SEC football championships back-to-back, back-to-back Sugar Bowls and back-to-back national championships. Tell me one other team that's done that. It hardly ever gets mentioned.

In 1959 we were 18-6 overall and SEC champs. In 1960 we were 22-3 and won 17 in a row. We went down to Louisiana and lost one game down there for sure. I think it was Southeast Louisiana. We had a good team but we couldn't go anywhere. In fact, in 1959 we beat Georgia Tech for the SEC Championship and Georgia Tech represented us. In 1960 we won the SEC but Florida represented the SEC. We sat at home. We had a pretty good ball club. I hit .424 in 1960.

I had played second and short in high school. I'd never played third. But when I got here as a sophomore, we had a second baseman—Hugh Poland—who was a good ballplayer and Coach Swayze needed a third baseman and he said, "Jake, you got to play third," and I said "Okay." Al Bullock played shortstop. Stick Netherland played first. A lot of football players played. I hit .333 as a senior. Every time I played a ballgame there were about ten scouts in the stands. And I got to thinking, I got to do good. So I kind of got out of my character of just having a good time and I guess I felt a little pressure with those guys being up in the stands.

Nobody ever knew it, but after my junior year when I hit .424, the Milwaukee Braves head man came to my house in the summer and offered me a hundred thousand dollars if

I would sign a baseball contract with them. He didn't say that first. He said, "We'd like to sign you now." And I said, "What kind of money are you talking about?" And he said, "I'm talking around a hundred thousand dollars." John McHale was the guy's name. He was president of the Braves. And I said, "John, I can't sign it. I've committed to Ole Miss. I gave Ole Miss my word. We got a chance to have a good football team and I can't leave 'em. I got loyalty there. They gave me a scholarship when I needed a scholarship. I can't cut 'em loose now. I can't leave 'em." And he looked at me and he said, "Well, okay. We'll try you next year." I said, "I know I'm taking a chance."

That was more money than we've ever seen in our lives but we turned it down. And he probably thought we were crazy as hell. I said that I wanted to get an education and I'm going to play football and if I don't get hurt, I've got another year, "Y'all look at me then. I'm going to get my education and I'm going to help the football team out." And that was it. I'm not bragging or anything. That's just the way it was. Coach Vaught found out that I'd turned down a lot of money that summer and I think he appreciated it. Back in those days, it was different. You had some values about you. I just couldn't turn my back on Ole Miss. I wasn't going to do it. My mother kept saying, "You got to get an education, you got to get an education," and I said, "I know, I know." So that's the way it went. But I tell you, it was hard money to turn down after my junior year because I did have a good junior year. I had scouts calling. It was something.

Then, my senior year, after I turned down that money, we played Tulane in football. It was homecoming at Tulane and there were 72,000 people there for homecoming. Now the Milwaukee Braves had a scout at every football game I played as a senior. A lot of people don't know this, but one was there at every game I played. So we're 6-0, number one team in the nation, picked to win by 12 points, so about the second quarter, I called a slant pass and our right tackle didn't block and their tackle came through and hit me and drove me down into the ground with force. When he did, it was just like a ball of fire came out of my right shoulder. I said, "God Almighty, he's torn my shoulder up." So I got up and went off the field. It was like a bone pointer or something like that and it was just on fire and hurting bad. When I was running off the field, I could see those dollar bills going out of the stadium and I could hear John McHale saying, "I tried to give it to you but you wouldn't take it." And those dollar bills were flying away. I went over there and took my jersey and shoulder pads off and I said, "Doc, put some of that atomic balm on my shoulder. It's fiery. I don't know what's wrong with it." So he rubbed me real good with that atomic balm. I put my pads back on and some of the feeling started coming back and I said, "Coach, I'm ready." I wanted to get in that game to see if I could throw. So the first play I called was a pass play. I think Johnny Brewer caught it. He always asked me, "Why don't you ever throw it to me?" I never saw those dollar bills again, though. I never thought about those dollar bills again. I threw that pass and there was no problem. And from that time on there was no problem. But I thought that night I had torn my shoulder up.

I feel that I was happy to be at Ole Miss. They gave me a chance and I tried to make the best of it. I left here loving the place. It was good to me and I made a lot of good friends, not only in sports but other people. So you take a lot away with you. The experience you had up here. The fun you had up here. The love you had for your teammates and the University and the coaching staff. Trish came up here and stayed two years and we got married in 1961. It was just good times. That's how I remember it. We didn't have much adversity in football or baseball. We never got in trouble. I had some problems in academics. Once, I was walking through the Student Union and I ran into my English teacher. She said, "Jake, I want to talk to you about your punting." I said, "Yes ma'am, what about it?" She said, "I don't like the way you are kicking it." And it was something about not kicking it high enough or kicking it end-over-end. I don't remember exactly what, so I said, "Ma'am, if you'll give me a D in English, I'll kick it anyway you want."

LYMAN HELLUMS

I've always said that the best passing quarterback we had was Glynn Griffing, that the best running quarterback was Archie Manning but the best quarterback overall we had was Jake Gibbs. I'm pretty sure that Jake scored every time he got us inside the 20 yard line. Jake was some kind of a good athlete and he turned out to be one of my best friends. He was telling us about the time down at Tulane when the defensive tackle came through and hit him and drove him into the ground on his right shoulder. Jake said he couldn't move his arm. He'd been offered 100K to sign a baseball contract with the Braves but he had turned it down and came on back to play his senior year. Jake said, "I looked up in the stands and you know what I saw? I saw 100,000 dollars just flying out of the stadium." So I went to the sideline and I told Doc Knight, "You got to fix me up." Well, it turned out to be a stinger so Jake went back in and said, "I'm fixin' to find out if there's anything wrong with my shoulder." He called a pass play to Johnny Brewer, the tight end, and it was about thirty yards. Jake threw it for a touchdown and he said, "I looked up and I saw that 100,000 dollars come flying back in the stadium." He was a good 'un. Bobby Franklin was a good one, too.

KAY SWAYZE ALFORD

1957-1961

When we were thirteen all of us took swimming lessons in the morning and sunbathed in the afternoons. Then Judy Trott, George Roy and Shirley Godbold—several of us—started teaching swimming lessons in the summer. The University pool was an Olympic-sized pool. We got our water safety instructor's qualifications there and were big into it. I took lifesaving one summer and nearly got killed. I had to save some football player, maybe Gene Hickerson, and he almost drowned me. But I got out of it by pinching him real hard. We had to swim a mile to graduate and by the grace of God, my strap broke and I had to get out of the water and go find a pin. That saved my life.

We had moved here from Moss Point. Dad was everything down there. It was World War II and Dad was 4F because he had gotten malaria working on the levee over on the Mississippi River. It had ruined his pitching arm and ended his pitching career with the Memphis Chicks. Then he went into coaching and was in Moss Point. He was principal, Spanish teacher, English teacher and the football coach. We were in the Methodist Church yard playing Red Rover and we called a little boy to come over. He ran over and broke through the line but busted his nose wide open on the fence right behind us. Well, it turned out that the little boy was Robert Khayat. Then Robert and his family came up here (to Oxford) in the summer. His dad was in education and had been the football coach at Moss Point just before Daddy.

Daddy had gone to Ole Miss and played football and baseball. He met mother when he was playing summer baseball in Cleveland, where Mother had grown up. The first time he ever saw Mother, he said, "I'm marrying her." And he did. They got married when she was seventeen. Daddy was hired to recruit but Coach Vaught said when he hired him, "Do this for a couple of years until we can get a team put together and then you can coach." But that never happened because Coach Vaught would always say that he needed Daddy out there recruiting. He started coaching baseball when he got here. I don't think he was even salaried to coach baseball; he just wanted to do it because he loved baseball. Recruiting kept him on the road a lot, especially during high school football season.

I knew all of the coaches, all of the Pooles, the Kinards, Coach Vaught's family. Everyone in those days ate Sunday lunch at the University Cafeteria and everyone wanted their preacher to get through first so you could beat the crowd to the cafeteria. Dr. Eickhorst thought my mother was wonderful and every time we would see him in the cafeteria he would say, "Ahhh Mrs. Swayze, you are such a flower of southern womanhood. Ahhh you are so beautiful." Lee McCarty (founder of McCarty Pottery in Merigold, Mississippi) was my ninth grade biology teacher. He always wore brown penny-loafers and would rare back and cross his legs and swing his foot. His loafer would be dangling off the end of his foot. Somebody ran up and grabbed his loafer and made the rounds of the room and got everyone all excited. Lee couldn't have cared less.

The coaches were close socially. They played penny poker, ate out, ate together, we did lots with them. Mother played Mah Jonng and Bridge with the ladies and the wives integrated into the community real well. Claire Smith—Tad Smith's daughter—was two years older than I was but we were close friends. She had a horse named Major that we rode. The Kinard boys—Frank and Johnny—were here and Johnnie Britt Cain, John Cain's daughter, was behind me. The Gates family was close with that group. The Hovius boys were right in there with us. I had great respect for Coach Vaught. He was gossiped about but never dropped to that level. Coach Vaught hunted over in the Delta with the Hamm family.

I had gone to camp in Colorado and told mother and daddy I wanted to go to school out there but Daddy said, "How can I ask people to send their children to Ole Miss and send my own child to Colorado?" So that didn't happen and I came to Ole Miss in 1957 and lived in Ward Hall, which was just a big party.

I was in Art School first and had a date with an art student, so later on Daddy said, "Why don't you date a man?" And I said, "Well who do you have in mind?" He said, "Someone like Warner Alford," and I said, "Well Warner Alford hasn't asked me out." And he didn't until the next spring and I always wondered whether Daddy put him up to it. Daddy and Warner's mom had gone to school together. She was a Phi Mu up here when Daddy was here. Daddy loved the Alford family and of course, he recruited Warner. I met Warner, Robert and Ken Kirk at lunch at Mistilis.

I went with Bones Cossar on the train to LSU and certain wild and unmentionable things happened to some of them on the train, not to us, thank goodness. I was so green and so shy and Bones was such a wild man. He was just living it up. Of course, I didn't drink and still don't. I just never have. My friends did, and Mother and Daddy drank socially with their friends. It was funny: all of my friends who had the hard-shell Baptist parents just jumped right into drinking. They had never seen it and wanted to try it. I'm sure I was the biggest bore of a date that Bones Cossar ever had.

Robert Khayat's father was a great patriot. When we were freshmen at Ole Miss, Warner and I were dating, and Robert was dating Lynda Mead, Jimmy Hall was dating Pat McRaney, and we all went to Robert's for the spring break. Mr. Khayat called us in to the living room and talked to us about what a great thing it was to be an American and what a great thing it was to be a Mississippian. I think he was the only person who ever said anything substantive to us up to that point. He was so thankful and grateful to be an American.

I feel blessed about my time at Ole Miss. And the same for having grown up in Oxford. Warner and I were blessed to raise our family here, too. I remember that the University of Texas recruited Daddy to come out there once but he said, "I'm not going to go out there. I'm not going to leave Ole Miss." And he didn't.

DON SHEFFIELD

1958-1963

I was born and raised in Dorsey, Mississippi, 12 miles east of Tupelo and six miles west of Fulton. My daddy was a farmer. I went to high school in Fulton at Itawamba Agricultural High School. I've only been to three schools in my life: Dorsey, IAHS and Ole Miss. I wound up at Ole Miss because my brother Robert was teaching there. Robert was in the National Guard and got mobilized and went to Korea. He had gone to Itawamba Junior College out of high school so when he came back from Korea he went to Ole Miss. Robert got his undergraduate and masters degrees in Chemistry. When I graduated high school I was kind of looking at options and Robert said, "I can probably help you get on with the football program as a manager." He played golf with Coach Vaught and Ray Poole and all of the other coaches.

I went over to the coaches' office and met Coach Vaught and all of the assistant coaches and they invited me to walk on as a manager the fall of 1958. They didn't give me any aid that first year. I had to pay my own way through school then but if you proved yourself that first year, they would put you on full scholarship like an athlete. The first year—in 1958—I lived in a regular dorm because I was paying my own way. I went right to work, reported to the field house and got my instructions. Nub Sanders was my boss; Doc Knight handled the trainers. Nub was the head equipment manager and I worked for him in the equipment section. It was me, Tippy Milner, Billy Keyes and a Jenkins boy from Clarksdale. There were like two people who helped Doc in the training room: Roland Maddox was one of them and a Stigler boy who pitched on the baseball team helped us some.

So we just fell right in and went to work. I didn't travel the first year. I went to the Memphis games and maybe the Jackson games with Nub. He would just haul us, but I wasn't traveling with the team. Then, in 1960, I began traveling with the team. The only difference between me and the scholarship athletes was I didn't get the $15 a month laundry money but otherwise, it was a free ride.

I lived in some pretty unique places. I lived in the back of the old gymnasium one semester. I lived in the field house three years. The old gym had a big room and I guess there were about a half dozen of us living back there. Some of them were baseball players. In those days, you didn't question. If they said that's where you're going to live, then that's where you lived. After that, I moved into the field house. When you went in the front door of the old field house there were two little rooms, one on each side, and they were very small. In the one on the right we kept our desk and hung our clothes; in the other we had two beds. You used the regular showers that were there for the players. Billy Keyes was living in Miller Hall; he was a floor manager for the freshman wing in Miller. Billy holds the record for the longest manager in Ole Miss history: seven years. He went to Law School and worked all seven years. When he graduated in the spring of 1962 I moved up to Miller and took his slot as freshman wing floor manager. I ate with the players. Like I said, I had the same thing they had except the $15 a month.

In 1959 I was like a redshirt freshman athlete and then in 1960 I made the varsity. We worked with both the freshmen and the varsity. On a day-to-day basis, we had to give out practice jerseys, personal items, pick up stuff after practice and put it in the laundry basket. The local laundry came in every day and picked up our dirty stuff after practice and took it and laundered it and brought it back the next day. We would then sort it and give it out again. Now they have mesh bags with their names on them so they can just throw it in the washing machine and then match it to the lockers. But in those days the players had to pick it up each day. They didn't have names on them; we just sorted by size and handed them out by size. We had shoulder pads, hip pads, thigh pads, knee pads and helmets. And a few of them might have special pieces that would attach to certain pads, but they kept those in their lockers. They had a pair of practice shoes and a pair of game shoes. Their shoes stayed in their lockers. The game shoes were a little lighter and a little higher quality. Most of the linemen wore high top shoes. It was up to the coaches, I think, what kind of shoes they wore. The managers had to clean the shoes and re-polish them to get them ready for the next game. I spent many Sunday afternoons at the field house cleaning and polishing shoes, getting them ready for the next Saturday, especially if it had been a muddy game. They had face masks by the time I got here. We had trouble keeping up with chin straps. The players would give them away after games. We just kept an adequate supply. It wasn't up to us to try to stop that. Nub would fuss at them about it. Some of them used elbow pads and they'd toss those things to the kids.

When we went on the road, each player had a plastic box that would hold all of their equipment. So we would have to pack their boxes on the Thursday after practice and each box would have the name of the player written on a piece of tape. The individual player boxes would then fit into a big trunk that would house maybe sixteen boxes. Back in those days, we traveled with only 39 players. So we would load the trunks onto a truck that would leave Thursday night going to the game site and when we arrived on Friday the equipment boxes were already placed out at the lockers where the players would be. There were two guys who drove the truck who would put the boxes out. Sometimes a manager would go with them. I never did. As soon as we arrived the managers would get in there and get everything placed out for the team when they came in to do their work out the day before the game. The team would generally get to the stadium a day before the game and have a walk-through in the stadium in pants and jerseys. It was laid out right to the minute what they would be doing.

Nub was our boss. He was a great guy. Nub had a speech impediment and until you got to know him, it was difficult to understand him. And if he got excited and started talking fast you would have to slow him down to get what he was saying. He was from Oxford and went to Northwest Community College then came over here and was a manager. Coach Vaught and the assistant coaches liked him so they kept him on in a full time job. He was married and his wife taught school here in town. They had five or six children. Nub loved Ole Miss and Ole Miss sports.

Coach Vaught had a great coaching staff. Bruiser Kinard was the offensive line coach. Johnny Cain coached the running backs. Coach Vaught was the quarterbacks coach. Ray Poole worked with the tight ends and receivers. Coach Buster Poole coached the defensive line and linebackers and Junie Hovius coached the defensive backs. Roland Dale came a little later on, and of course, Wobble Davidson coached the freshmen. Those coachers were good people. They were good disciplinarians. They commanded respect from the players. Coach Wobble was the driving force behind team discipline. He was in charge of the athletic dorm and everyone respected him. They'd sneak around and do things but if they got caught, they'd pay for it. There were many of them who'd be in the stadium at five-thirty in the morning running the stadium steps. Coach Wobble was a Marine and he functioned a whole lot like a Marine. Coach Swayze was the primary scout/recruiter. He didn't have any football coaching responsibilities other than recruiting. Coach Country Graham scouted Mississippi State every game they played. The only time he saw Ole Miss play was when we played Mississippi State or in a bowl game. That was one of the secrets to how we were able to handle State so well. He knew them backwards and forward, knew everything they were going to do.

Back in those days there wasn't but one practice field. The varsity practiced there and the freshmen practiced in the outfield area of the baseball field. We had a freshman manager who would stay up there with them. During practice we did whatever we were told to do.

About the second year I was here Coach Vaught asked me to keep stats for him on the quarterbacks and receivers so I became Coach Vaught's personal computer before there was such a thing as a personal computer. I would take a clipboard and a piece of paper and I would put every quarterback's name down and every receiver's name down and every pass that was thrown during a drill I had to record how many they threw, how many were completed, and how many the receivers caught. Since I had to do it every day, I developed a little form and showed it to Coach Vaught. He said he liked it and his secretary took it and typed it out on a piece of paper. She mimeographed a number of copies of it, so during practice I stood with Coach Vaught most of the practice and was his personal secretary on the field. If it was a catchable pass and the receiver didn't catch it I marked that. Those receivers, every time something happened, they'd come back and look over my shoulder to see what was on that form. So when practice was over I'd give Coach Vaught that form and he would study what his quarterbacks and receivers were doing. My sophomore year we had Franklin, Gibbs, and Elmore. Griffing was redshirted that year. Later on, we had Perry Lee Dunn and Jimmy Weatherly. Comparing the 1959 quarterbacks—Franklin, Gibbs and Elmore—they were all good in their own way. Doug wasn't as accurate a passer as Jake and Bobby, and in those days you didn't throw that many passes. Fifteen passes in a game was a large number. So you'd have guys completing eight or nine passes. Passing wasn't as big of an art as it is now. I thought Bobby Ray was a very good passer and so was Jake, especially in the short passing game. He didn't throw long much. Bobby was a senior, Jake was a junior and Doug had been redshirted so he was a sophomore. Coach Vaught saw to it that all of them played.

Coach Vaught was basically a relatively quiet individual. On the field he was talking but he wasn't a rah rah type guy. He was like E. F. Hutton, when Coach Vaught spoke, everyone listened. He just commanded that sort of respect. Privately, though, he was kind of shy. He didn't say a whole lot. It was not that he was being rude; he was by nature just a quiet kind of guy.

Although Coach Vaught had been a lineman, he could coach the quarterbacks. He taught them technique: fundamentals, footwork, eye-placement and everything that involved quarterback decisions. Faking, all aspects of what a quarterback is responsible for doing. I don't know how he learned that. I wish I had had an opportunity to sit down and talk about that stuff. But back then, I didn't have the nerve to do that. He and his assistant coaches got together and formulated the game plans. Coach Bruiser Kinard and Coach Buster Poole weren't called coordinators then but today that's what they were. At halftime of games, on the offensive side, Coach Kinard had a great deal of influence on Coach Vaught as far as making changes at halftime. Coach Buster was the same way on defensive adjustments.

The staff worked extremely well together. They were a unique coaching staff. You don't see coaching staffs with their kind of knowledge and ability who stay together like they did. All of them except Johnny Cain and Coach Vaught had been players at Ole Miss and they were all highly regarded in their fields.

Coach Wobble was a one-man gang with the freshmen. He was the weed-eater of coaches. He weeded out the ones he believed wouldn't be successful varsity players at Ole Miss. They would bring in as many as sixty freshmen in those days. Scholarships were basically unlimited. They'd sign fifty or sixty and then have another 15 walk-ons. So it was Coach Wobble's job to weed them out and find out which ones really wanted to play football at Ole Miss and which ones really didn't. He worked them hard and demanded that they learn the proper way of doing things and how to execute. If they didn't do those things they were invited to turn in their equipment. And that was it. If a varsity player got in trouble Coach Wobble consulted with the varsity coaches to see what punishment was appropriate. Coach Wobble was responsible for carrying out the punishment. If they had to run the steps at 5:30 in the morning he'd be there watching.

The 1958 season doesn't stand out because I wasn't working all of the games. There were a couple of games where I sat in the stands with the students. I don't remember much about the two losses: LSU 14-0 and Tennessee when Robert missed the field goal that he wrote about in his book. But in 1959 I was more involved. I went to all of the games in Memphis and Jackson. For that Tennessee game in Memphis, I had to go be the spotter for the Tennessee radio broadcast. The Tennessee SID came to Billy Gates and said they needed someone to spot Ole Miss players in the game. I don't know how I got selected but I was sent to the press box. That formulated my interest in becoming a radio sportscaster, too. It was cold but I was inside, so I didn't feel it. I didn't go to Baton Rouge; I heard it on a car radio. Coach Vaught was very intense about preparation for that game and we were very disappointed after the game. The 1959 team was the best team Ole Miss ever put on the field. When you give up only 21 points for the entire season, it's incredible. One of the touchdowns was a blocked punt inside the ten-yard line and one was a pass interception down on our goal and then Cannon's run. They really could have gone through the entire season without being scored upon. No one ever sustained any kind of drive on them. Some people think that was the best college football team of all time.

The practice uniforms were colored. The red team was the first team, the blue team was the second team, green was third, yellow was fourth, and everybody else wore white. So that's the way they were known during the game. Every day the coaches would post on the bulletin board the list of players for each team and the players would come pick up their jerseys. We had a copy of it, too, so we gave out jerseys based on which team they were assigned to. The practice jerseys had no numbers on them, only "UMAA," so Coach Vaught called them out by color to substitute. There was limited substitution in those days. You could substitute like one time a quarter, so coaches had to be real sure what they did when they made changes. Of course, if a player got hurt you could substitute for him. You didn't run people in and out. They had to check in with the refs. They had some kind of piece of paper and they checked them in when they came on the field.

The 1960 year, I traveled with them. We opened the season in Houston and it was the first time I ever flew on an airplane. The team flew out from the Oxford airport. We took three DC-3s from right here and flew to Houston, Texas. The team flew back on Sunday morning. We played Houston in Rice's stadium. Jake was the starting quarterback and Elmore and Griffing backed him up. I almost got arrested at Arkansas before the game. Nub was in charge of selling player's excess tickets. They were given like four tickets to the game. So it was Nub's job to dispose of the tickets. He sent me out to sell tickets and I was selling tickets through the fence. They were like $6 tickets and I was selling them for $15. Somebody complained to the cops that I was scalping tickets. And here comes the cop. So I took off and headed for the dressing room and went inside and handed Nub the tickets. I said, "Look, these cops know me. Someone else is going to have to go out there and sell these tickets."

Jake got hurt sometime in the first half. Arkansas almost killed him; they just beat him to death. At halftime, Doc Knight was giving him leg massage so he could get back to where he could play. I wasn't a trainer but Doc showed me what he wanted to do—it was probably his hamstring—so I was rubbing it and putting some kind of salve on it and I did that most of the third quarter. Jake finally came back out in the fourth quarter and Coach Vaught put him back in. Then he led us to that game-winning field goal.   The first field goal: no question it was good. But Tommy Bell, who was the official, thought he heard someone call time out. In those days, couldn't just anybody call time out. So he made a mistake by signaling for a time out just as we kicked the ball. It seemed like the second Allan Green's foot hit the ball, Bell's arms went up in the air. Again, from my angle on the sideline, it looked good. I think it curved around the goal post but Arkansas fans will never admit it. Folks came down on the field and I had to work to get equipment off the field. It was a nightmare. I was told after the game that my seat on the plane flying back to Oxford had been taken and I was going to have to spend the night and ride back the next day with Coach Swayze. He had been over there recruiting, watching high school football games of Friday night. So I had to spend the night in Little Rock. I have been told—I don't know whether it's true or not—that it was Tom Turner from Belzoni.

I think Nub reported to Coach Vaught, as did Doc Knight. Doc Knight was just a wonderful human being, a prince of a man. You couldn't help but like him. He was from the northeast and had that Yankee brogue. He was quick-witted and sharp-tongued. Doc loved to play spades and hearts. When there was nothing going on, Doc always had a card game going on. Since I lived in the field house, I played many a game of cards with Doc. I thought the world of the man. After the 1960 Sugar Bowl, all of the coaches were given a new color television, which was a big deal. No one had color televisions back then. Doc Knight and his wife invited me to come over to his house one night and we watched "Bonanza" in color. That was a unique experience. The players loved him, too. He was the one who did all of the motivational stuff for the team. He would make up these sayings for each game and put things in players' lockers. He would give the pre-game motivational speech and the pre-game prayer. He used acronyms, like MSU and a motivational sentence out beside each letter. He was a unique individual and was very gifted as a trainer in his day. And he was gifted as a motivator and a communicator. He was a prince of a human being.

Doc had two assistant trainers. Things were not as sophisticated as they are now. He had a whirlpool tub that players would use some. And he had a few little stimulant machines he'd use on pulled muscles. The biggest thing they did was tape players before games and practices. They used what they called an "atomic balm," which was a heat treatment to help stimulate blood flow through a muscle to heal a strained or pulled muscle.

The beatings Jake took that year actually started at Memphis in the first game of the 1960 season. They tried their best to put him out of the game. They got several 15 yard penalties for roughing him up. That Memphis game was a tough game. Jake was hurt a good portion of that season because people just beat on him so much. We came back home the next week after Arkansas to play LSU and Jake was still beat up. Jake played very little that day. Arkansas had beat him half to death. The LSU game was on national TV and we were down 6-3 late in the game. So in the last minute and some seconds of the game he drove us down to the LSU thirty and Allan Green kicked another field goal. The next year we played LSU in Baton Rouge. I remember going out to warm up and I was standing next to some players screaming and they couldn't hear me and I couldn't hear them.

There were a lot of golden handshakes. I even got one, one time. It was $20, which was a heck of a lot of money back then. From then on, I went out of my way to speak to that individual every time I got a chance. But I only got the one golden handshake from him.

We played Tennessee up there in 1960, and it was the first time we beat Tennessee in Knoxville. Hoss Anderson had a big game. Coach Vaught was so happy and so excited to win up there, as were the players. We went to the Cotton Bowl the next year—after the 1961 season—and flew out to Dallas about five days before the game. When we got off the plane, they gave us our cowboy hats. They had things planned for us. They took us to the national rodeo finals. That was interesting to me because I was a country boy who had grown up on a dairy farm. They took us to the big First Baptist Church on Sunday morning. It was a first class affair. They fed us well. I like my steaks well-done so people were seated at tables according to how they liked their steaks done. There weren't any like me who liked it well-done and there weren't many who liked their steaks rare so Doc Knight put me with Jim Dunaway who liked his steaks rare. I had to sit there eating my well-done steak watching Jim eat his rare. It was blood red and looked like it had been just passed over the fire.

Jim was the biggest guy we had ever gotten at that time. He was about 6'5" and weighed about 300 pounds. When he was a senior in high school I walked out of the equipment room and you turned right to go to the varsity room and training room. I turned right and Jim was walking down the hall toward me. I had never seen anyone in my life as big as Jim Dunaway. He was a prince of an individual, just a gentle giant. You had to make him mad in a game to really get him to put out.

When I got here during the year I had lost 35 pounds and so about the last month of school, Doc Knight went to Coach Vaught and asked him if he could put me on the training table. That was my first experience with the training table. When they opened Miller Hall in the fall of 1959 I ate over there. The food was as good as you could get: all you wanted, well prepared, and plenty of variety. You didn't leave the training table hungry and if you did, it was your fault, not theirs. It was just really good food. A guy named Chief Kisner was in charge. He did a great job with it. The players could get a steak anytime they wanted it.

In the 1962 season I missed the homecoming game with Houston that was played in Jackson. I was with the National Guard out in Brown's pasture and listened to it on the radio. I went to Knoxville with the team. That was when Louis Guy intercepted a pass and ran it back 103 yards for a touchdown. That was the play that broke their backs. I didn't see the play. Managers usually didn't get to see most of the game because you were working on someone's equipment, getting something for someone, or just being busy. I just didn't get to stand around and watch the game, so all I saw was Louis running up the field and everyone running down the sideline with him.

When the game was over we had to get the equipment off the sideline and get it into the training room. We asked the players to put their equipment in their boxes but it was a half-hearted effort, and then we put the boxes in the big trunks so we could get it on the bus for the ride back home. The players would leave together as a team. I didn't get to go out and socialize.

HARDY STENNIS

1958-1962

After the Marine Corps I came back in 1958 and finished undergraduate in 1959 then went on to law school. I went down to Baton Rouge when Billy Cannon made his run in 1959. They chartered a train that came from Memphis to Oxford and picked up everyone who had bought a ticket to go on the train. There were about ten cars full of nothing but students. I took Barbara Hardin to that game. She was a Macon girl. We stopped in Jackson so I said to the conductor, "How long are we going to be here?" He said, "A couple of minutes," so I said, "I'm just going to run across the road here and get some of these lawyers some beer before they run out." He said, "That's fine but I can't hold the train up for you."

So I ran across the road where I saw a beer joint with a Miller sign and bought four cases of beer. There were two little black boys there and I said, "You boys want to make yourselves 50 cents apiece?" and they said, "Yessuh," so I said "Each one of y'all grab a case of beer and let's go. We're gonna put it on the train." Well, I looked out there and the train had left so I said, "Oh my goodness. I'm gonna have to get a cab and catch that sucker down in McComb." And there I was fiddling around with that problem and lo and behold here comes the train. Another train had passed it. My train had gotten off on a side track and let this other train go through. And then here it comes but it's not gonna stop. It's going right on by and I'm standing there with four cases of beer but they hadn't built up too much speed so I grabbed those cases of beer. They had a box car and my roommate Spec Wilkinson and some other law students had gotten in the box car to sell hamburgers and hot dogs. They had those big doors swung open so I threw the cases of beer on. By that time it was going pretty fast and I said, "Someone's gonna have to grab my arm and pull me in." So I jumped up and two of the biggest guys there each grabbed an arm and jerked me inside that box car. Barbara was there and she was almost in tears. She said, "I don't care if he never comes back but he's got our tickets." So we walked down the aisle back to our seats and I had that beer in sacks and ran into the chief of police of the campus—Chief Tatum—and he knew me well. And he says, "Hardy, we thought you were gonna miss this train," and I began telling him and he said, "By the way, what you got in them sacks?" I said, "Just a case of beer," and he said, "You don't have any beer," and he walked on by. I went back there and I got a huge welcome by the whole law school. And now, every time I see someone who was on that train they say, "Tell us about the time you jumped on that train."

GLYNN "SQUIRREL" GRIFFING

1958-1963

I redshirted my sophomore year and played varsity in 1960, 1961, and 1962. Kenny Dill, Billy Ray Adams, Jim Roberts, Ralph "Catfish" Smith, Woody Dabbs and Chuck Morris were in my recruiting class. And Richard Ross was there, among others. Richard Ross was a really smart guy. He was in Engineering and developed a software program that college coaches could use to analyze what the opponents were going to be doing in certain circumstances. Like third and long from their twenty yard line or third and six at your twenty. It would tell you their tendencies on certain downs and distances so you had a pretty good idea what they were going to do. You could also do it for defense: when they were going to blitz and so forth. Richard and his brother were the first people I know of to develop something like that, and I think Coach Vaught used that computer a couple of years before other people caught on and started using a program like that. Richard was a good guy. He was killed in a plane crash shortly after they developed that software.

I was from Culkin, a public county school right outside of Vicksburg. A lot of people thought it was private but it wasn't. The school had about 400 students in grades one through twelve. Junie Hovius, Kayo Dottley and Crawford Mims recruited me. Coach Hovius was from Vicksburg so he was down there quite a bit to see me. Kayo and Crawford lived in Vicksburg. They married two of the Nosser sisters. Coach Vaught also came to the school. The principal didn't go to Ole Miss but he was a huge Ole Miss fan and he would tell Coach Hovius, "If you want to take him out, go ahead, just have him back at so and so time." If LSU or State showed up, he wouldn't let them talk to me. He'd tell them they would have to see me after school, that he couldn't disturb me during class. Coach Hovius would get us tickets and the principal and I would go up together to see Ole Miss games. Coach Vaught showed up in Culkin one day and said, "Glynn, if you'll sign with us, I won't offer any other quarterback in Mississippi a scholarship." I thought that was pretty powerful but what he didn't tell me was that Ole Miss had signed fourteen quarterbacks the year before. And the year I signed he signed the number one quarterback out of Arkansas and one of the top quarterbacks out of Tennessee but he didn't sign another quarterback out of Mississippi. So he didn't lie about it but he didn't tell me the whole truth either. He loved to sign quarterbacks and fullbacks because they were usually the best athletes on a high school team. They'd end up playing guard and linebacker. I was about five ten-and-a-half and weighed about 165 pounds and today you wouldn't even be looked at, being that size. So it was a great time to come along.

My freshman team played three games and won one, lost one and tied one. We beat Vanderbilt, tied LSU and State beat us. State usually beat our freshmen back in those years and then after that, they didn't win against the varsity. I think we went 25 or so years where we either won or tied so State had a long draught there. The next year I was redshirted which was a pretty awesome year. We had to scrimmage the first unit, which was the best team in America at that time. That was the 1959 team, which should have been the number one team that year. They were pretty brutal on us and at times, they almost killed us, but we made it through. Scrimmaging them definitely made you better. We always had to learn some of the plays for the opponent the next week. So if it was Tennessee Coach Vaught took us down to Vaught Hemingway—it was Hemingway in those days—and we'd learn the single wing. We had to learn all the plays off that stuff. By the time we came back up, we'd have learned the plays pretty good. I'd be the tailback and that first day I think the number one team thought they were going to push us around but we got after them pretty good. We moved the ball pretty well on them and Coach Vaught really got after them. The next day they almost killed us. They made sure we knew what our place was. It was fun learning the other offenses and being the quarterback on the other team. Then, when we got through with that, the redshirts had to scrimmage the freshmen on Friday, because the varsity was getting ready to go wherever they were going to play on Saturday so we'd have a big scrimmage with the freshmen. That was always a fun thing because it was the redshirts' opportunity after getting beat up by the varsity all week, to beat up on someone else. It was a good time.

When you were a freshman, Wobble let you know where things stood when you first came in. There were no scholarship limitations so we started with about sixty guys and it was Coach Wobble's job to see who wanted to play and to get rid of the rest. It was a pretty tough deal to go through it with him. He was trying to run off people by making it hard on everybody. He didn't play favorites. If you didn't run sprints out then he'd make the whole team run them. Everyone stayed on each other to make sure that we ran them out so we wouldn't have to run extra sprints. You went out and loosened up on your own. If practice started at three then you had to be ready to go at three. Then you'd go through the practice session and scrimmage and after scrimmage you'd run sprints. Coach Wobble did all of the conditioning at the end of practice. So after everything, we'd have to run twenty fifty-yard sprints. Coach Wobble would be screaming at us and telling us to run, run, run and if he didn't think you were running fast enough then the whole team would run it again. He was a tough guy and got rid of a lot of people.

We were scrimmaging one day and the end— Rick Bush —was supposed to block down on the defensive tackle. He was a tough guy and had been in the Marine Corps. Rick was about six two or three and weighed about 220 pounds. He didn't carry out the block and made just a halfhearted effort so Coach Wobble called him over after the play. Coach Wobble chewed him out pretty good and then said, "I want you to get over there." Then he called out all the big linemen on the team and said, "I want you to run over him and anybody that doesn't try to run over him, I'll have you over there." They'd knock him down and he'd get up on his knees and another one would run over him. So the next day Bush was gone.

Coach Wobble and Sara were at Miller Hall when I was at Ole Miss. Coach Wobble was a strict disciplinarian, of course. First semester of my freshman year the freshmen were in another dorm but second semester they dumped us over into Miller Hall. We thought we were in a luxury palace over there. Coach Wobble would come through every night and hold bed check. We had to be in at 10:30 and he would come through and check. It didn't matter who you were, you better be there because he'd put you in the stadium if you didn't. It didn't matter if you smoked or didn't smoke, if a regular student came in and smoked a cigarette in your room and Coach Wobble came down there checking to make sure you were in, if he could smell smoke you'd be at the stadium running the next day. When you went down to the stadium he'd make you light up a cigarette and he'd tell you to run to the top of the stadium with the cigarette and then back down. He'd make them smoke that pack of cigarettes while they were running. Larry Grantham was notorious for smoking and he had to run that stadium a bunch of times. And Coach Wobble could smell chewing tobacco, too. Some of the guys chewed tobacco and spit it into their garbage cans and he didn't like that at all.

He demanded that everybody dress properly. You didn't go in the cafeteria to eat not properly dressed, because his wife and children were going to be in there. That meant you didn't wear flip flops to dinner or cutoffs or any of that. You had to dress properly to go in and have dinner. He demanded discipline and demanded that you do it the right way. Everybody loved Sara because she was just like a housemother to us and she'd come over and talk to us. When you're up at Ole Miss by yourself sometimes it got pretty lonely and she was just a really sweet person to come by and visit the players and talk to them and get to know them. It was great having a family in the dorm.

Back in those days, everyone liked to hunt so most everybody had a gun on campus. So when the Meredith thing first happened Coach Wobble said, "Bring your guns to my apartment. I'm taking all the guns and I'm going to keep them." And so everybody had to take their guns down there and he said he'd make sure they were taken care of. Coach Wobble got those things out and the Army 101st came through to check all rooms to make sure there weren't any guns so he was ahead of them on that. He really took care of us and made sure that everybody was all right. Because of Coach Wobble, we just didn't have any of the problems they have now.

Now when he wasn't there, it was a different story. We had tile floors on the second floor, and I came in one night and these big guys had put water going down the hall and they had soaped themselves up. They'd get a running start and see how far down the hall they could slide. It was pretty hysterical to see those big dudes. I mean they didn't have a stitch of clothes on sliding down the hall. Wobble would have killed them if he had caught them doing stuff like that.

At Coach Wobble's funeral Sara stood up and said she'd never heard Coach Wobble say a cuss word. We looked at other and said, "Man, she wasn't at practice." We thought that was funny because he could come out with some of the most god-awful things you ever heard. I think he learned that in the Marine Corps. Coach Wobble had been a drill instructor at Parris Island. He was tough but he was fair, and if you really tried, he was going to take care of you. But if he thought you were loafing, you were in trouble.

You got a grade for playing for football. It was like taking a college course and you got one hour credit for each semester. So Coach Vaught got the grades for all the freshmen and Wobble had flunked some of the guys because he said they didn't try. He never coached the quarterbacks but we had some graduate assistants like Ray Brown, who was with the Colts, and he came back one spring and worked with me my freshman year. Coach Wobble knew what Coach Vaught was looking for though. Speed was Coach Vaught's thing. He wanted the quarterbacks to have the speed to get outside that end. Coach Wobble was looking at who could run and who could throw the ball and that was about it.

It was the fullback's responsibility on a rollout to get contact with the defensive end so the quarterback could get by him. He didn't have to make a perfect block, just make contact. Coach Vaught felt like if the fullback could make contact of any sort, the quarterback would be quick enough to get around him. He would put a helmet on the ground outside and take a stopwatch and time us taking the snap from center and getting around that helmet. One day we were out there and he said, "Glynn, you need to change your steps. It'll make you quicker." So I tried it his way two or three times and turned around and said, "Coach, I swear I'm not any quicker," and he said, "Yeah, but you look better." You had to do it his way. He would make us take the ball and raise up and throw the ball and see how quick we could get the ball out of hand. He did a lot of that stuff: quick movements; quickness getting the ball out of your hand and getting outside of the end. We worked on that all the time. There were a lot of guys when I was there who couldn't do it fast enough.

They decided to redshirt me my sophomore year because they had Bobby Franklin as the number one quarterback, Billy Brewer was behind Bobby and played a little bit, then Jake was behind Billy and they had Doug Elmore behind Jake. He told me, "You may be able to play some defense, but you're not going to play any offense." So I told him, "I didn't come up here to just sit around. I came up here to play, so if I can redshirt and get to play more then that's what I want to do." Of course, Billy didn't get to play that much. Jake became the number two quarterback and Billy got on the field every once in a while. There was just a bunch of good quarterbacks ahead of me and I knew I wasn't going to get to play very much.

We had Jake and Doug and then me. Then Doug and I and Perry Lee Dunn. Then, my senior year, they switched Perry Lee to fullback but he alternated at fullback and the number three quarterback if they needed him. Jimmy Weatherly was number two and Bobby Boyd was number four after Perry Lee.

The Sunday night of the Meredith riot, when we got in from Jackson, I went over and the Marshalls were loaded for bear and were in riot gear all around the Lyceum. We knew Meredith was coming up the next day but why were they bringing all of these marshals in? I thought that was probably a mistake on the government's part to do that because I think that incited the whole deal. All those guys in riot gear. I was reading something the other day by some guy who said that students and some of the people were throwing acid but I never heard that. There were only about 4000 students at Ole Miss then and when all of that stuff started a lot of them left campus—especially all the girls. I was dating my wife and she's from Ohio. Her roommate was from Vicksburg and so her roommate's boyfriend took them down to Vicksburg to get them out of all that mess. It was a lot of people who had left campus at that time so there weren't a lot of students there in the Circle during the riot. Most of them were from outside.

One of the guys in the National Guard said that when they and the 101st Airborne started clearing the Circle and the Grove, there were very few of the rioters who peeled off and went to the sides to stay on campus. Most of them went running across that bridge and up University Avenue. That tells you right there that if they were students they would have been trying to get back to the dorms. It was all these people from outside who had come in there who were trying to get out of there and get back to their cars.

When I was a freshman the upperclassmen beat us like a drum. They'd beat you then pull your underwear down to see if you were bruised and if you weren't they'd give you some more. Then you had to go and polish their shoes and all of their brass for ROTC. They hazed us pretty good. Freshmen tried to stay away from anything connected with the varsity. They would call special freshmen meetings and then give you three licks. Some freshmen would try to be smart and wear two or three pair of underwear. Well, when they hit him and heard that thud, they'd make him drop his pants and pull off those underwear and they'd give him two or three licks on his bare rear end. It was pretty tough sometimes. We lost some guys because of the hazing. We lost an All-American fullback from Missouri. He just left and said they weren't going to whip his butt anymore. I saw him later and he said leaving Ole Miss was the worst mistake he ever made in his life. He wound up at Southeast Missouri State and was a little All-American there. He said he really regretted it, that it was a terrible mistake. When he left, he was running ahead of Billy Ray Adams, so he was a good football player. Billy Ray turned out to be a great football player. An All-American.

The Memphis State game my sophomore year was tough. They had a linebacker named John Bramlett who jumped offsides and hit Jake on a straight drop back and hurt him. Our folks didn't like that so it was a pretty tough game after that. And then the Memphis State players got out on the field and started a fight at the end of the game. Bramlett turned out to be a preacher. He was one of the toughest guys I ever played against. He started preaching and he's been around the country speaking at schools for a good while. He was a tough, tough dude, I'll tell you.

I didn't play against Arkansas. Jake got hurt but he came back. I was standing there when Allen kicked the field goals. The first one was perfect but I couldn't tell about the second. All I saw was when the ball cleared the goal post, the official, Tommy Bell, raised his arms to signal good. He was an official for the NFL for years after that. At that time they didn't have anyone under the goal post and he was back with the kicker and put those arms up to call it good. Arkansas people and Ole Miss people have been debating that field goal ever since. They thought we just stole that game.

The next week we had LSU here on national TV. They almost had us there at the end but Allen Green kicked a field goal after a great drive by Jake. I didn't play a whole lot of offense my sophomore year but I did play some defense. Coach Vaught was good about getting you in to play. If you were a sophomore he'd start you playing a little bit. Then as a junior he'd play you a little bit more and by the time you were a senior you were ready. He brought them along. Today, they want to get these guys all of the big numbers and big statistics and all that kind of stuff and as a result they're not getting the younger guys ready to play. They need to be a little more forward-looking rather than just looking at the moment.

The '61 season we had Doug Elmore, then me and then Perry Lee Dunn as the three quarterbacks. We had a good ball club that year. We were nine and one with five or six shutouts and some huge offensive games. LSU beat us in Baton Rouge and it was a hell of a game. I was in the ballgame and we were moving the ball down into their territory right at the end of the game and I went back to throw the ball. I threw it but I got hit just as I did. The ball went over the line of scrimmage and hit the ground and the refs called it a fumble. I couldn't believe it because I thought we were going to go down and score. That was the only game we lost that year. If we had that film I'd love to see what actually happened. The ball went forward just across the line of scrimmage and I think Duck Dickson tried to jump on it but he missed it and the LSU guy jumped on it and they called it a fumble. That was a bad deal. I don't think it was a fumble because the ball got over the line of scrimmage.

The Cotton Bowl was a heartbreaking loss. We should have won that ballgame. If we had had a fullback we would have won it. Billy Ray was the fullback that year and he came down to Jackson to pick up the Jackson Touchdown Club's Most Valuable Player Award for the most valuable player at Ole Miss. They had a steak dinner and gave the award to the most valuable player from each school. Billy Ray tried to get everyone on the team to ride down to Jackson with him but nobody wanted to ride all the way down to Jackson for that and then come back home. So he came by himself and on the way back he had a bad wreck and of course he never played football again. And then in the first quarter against Texas out there, Buck Randall tore up his knee and was out, so Freddy Roberts was the number three fullback and went in. We were at a party one night and someone asked Freddy, "Freddy, what did you think when you had to go in? You had to play both ways the rest of the game." He said, "I thought, this ain't no place for an eighteen year old." But he did a great job, did the best he could, and he was worn out playing both ways.

The last drive we were moving and going in for a touchdown. I usually didn't like for Coach Vaught to call plays for me. I would talk to the linemen and receivers to see what was working. If I wanted to do something they could tell me whether it would work or not. Coach Vaught sent in a rollout pass so as I took the ball and was rolling out, the Texas defensive tackle came in and hit me. He landed on top of me and wouldn't get off. All I could see was the scoreboard and I knew I had been there before and had seen that scoreboard and I knew we were losing. It was a weird feeling. That was on fourth down and we did lose it. We killed them except for the score, had way more yardage than they did. Moved the ball all day long. I took the ball down just before halftime. They had a little linebacker you couldn't see. He had intercepted Doug once and just before halftime I drove it down to the goal line and Wes Sullivan was wide open. This durn little guy tipped the ball up in the air and someone caught it. I mean Wes was wide open and if he had caught it we'd have won the game. That's the way it goes. They had had a lot of high school playoffs on that field so there was no grass on the field. They had painted it green for TV and it was cold that day and those spike marks would cut you like a razor. Everyone's arms were bleeding. They had Jimmy Sexton, a little running back and he was their big star. I was ashamed we lost that game because we won it every way but the score. We had our 50th reunion of the '62 team in 2012 and were playing Texas here. A Texas guy named Culpepper came over and visited with us at our tent in the Grove and was very complimentary of our '61 team. We had a really good ballclub that '61 season and probably should have won the national championship.

My senior year, after the riot, it was really confusing because at first we were going to try to keep the Houston game on campus. Then they said we couldn't play it at home because the soldiers had taken over the practice fields and everything except Hemingway Stadium. So Coach Vaught said, "Well, we'll just play it out at Houston." Then they said we were going to play it in Jackson. The only practice field we had was inside the stadium because the Army had everything else. It was really interesting because we had 20,000 troops watching us every day. Coach Vaught wanted us to go down there and play well in Jackson. I was really surprised that we played that well because the whole week before had been so confusing. One thing about it, Coach Vaught didn't like mental mistakes and he would practice the same things day after day to avoid any kind of mental mistakes. Against Houston, we just went out and did the things that our coaches had taught us to do (40-7). After the riot Coach Vaught said, "In the state of Mississippi we should be number one and do our best and help everything. We can't do anything about the riot. We can't do anything about what's happened, but we can play football and we can hold our heads up and do something good for the state." He did a great job of holding everyone together.

That year, we had some good road wins. Louis Guy had that great interception return against Tennessee (19-6). I wasn't on the field at that time but I played the whole game on offense. That was the first year they allowed more substitution so I didn't play much defense that year. I had my knees messed up so Coach Vaught kept me out on defense and I was just playing on offense most of the time.

Then we went to LSU and had a great win (15-7). We were behind but went down and scored just before halftime and the thing about that drive that was really impressive to me was A. J. Holloway, the former mayor of Biloxi. I hit him with a little dump pass right across the middle and he caught the ball on about the five or six yard line and he broke down to the goal line where it looked like they were going to stop him. Then this big dude comes through there and hits him and knocks him in the end zone. There was no way A. J. was going to get in that end zone except for that big dude knocking him in. I usually held on extra points. I had the whole time I had been at Ole Miss so I was going to hold the extra point on that touchdown and I fumbled the ball. We should have been tied 7-7 at halftime but were down 7-6 when we went in at halftime. I ran the ball more that night than I had in the past. I don't know why. Coach Vaught just decided that I needed to run the ball more. We ran a couple of new plays that he had put in and it worked so I think I had a good night running the ball that night.

At the beginning of the game he had put in a special play for the first play we ran. Coach

Vaught liked to put in special plays for the first play so he had a play where I'd take the ball and throw it to Louis Guy down the sideline. He was open but I overthrew him by a hair. It would have been about an 80 yard touchdown pass on the first play of the game. We really dominated the second half. In fact we had the ball down there getting close to another score when the game ended. We could probably have scored again.

State played a really close, tough game (13-6). We weren't expecting State to be that tough. They had this guy named Johnny Baker who played defensive end and he had the most wicked forearm I ever saw. He could really hurt you with that thing. They also had a defensive tackle who ate me up the whole game. The first series we had the ball we took it down and scored and everything was great and then all of a sudden, we couldn't do anything. It was tough, really tough. It was hard to understand exactly what was going on but then Jimmy Weatherly just missed a handoff and bootlegged. He went in untouched. That play won the game for us.

Student support was a very important factor. We could hear them cheering and doing "Hotty Toddies," but we had only about 4000 students. A number of them would show up at say Kentucky, which was unheard of. That's a long way to go. They would be there and especially after the ballgames we'd hear them and see them, so we knew they were there. During the ballgames, you really don't hear a lot of that stuff. LSU was probably the worst place because of the way that stadium was set up, it was pretty noisy there. The first time I was there, the first play I was in the game, the field shook and it got so loud I couldn't believe that noise could shake that field, but it did when they got going. They intercepted a pass on us one time and Doug and I were standing right next to each other—it was my junior year—and we were yelling to each other and couldn't hear.

I have great feelings about being at Ole Miss, especially about the guys I played with and all. It's a bond you have, especially when you go through all the stuff we had to go through, especially that last year with the riot and all of that stuff. You know, when you got to go through something that traumatic and that bad it really pulls you together and I think most of the guys on that '62 team really love each other because we can see each other twenty or thirty years later and still have the same feelings for them you always have. It is just an unbelievable thing how those things stick with you. That bond you develop in having to go through all of the mess we had to go through during that time, is really strong. It's a great feeling.

CURTIS WILKIE

1958-1963

During the five years I was here I think I went to almost every game. I missed the Tennessee game in Knoxville where Robert missed the chip shot field goal and we lost 18-16 my freshman year. I missed Arkansas in Little Rock my freshman year. I think I went to most everything else. I drove to Lexington with Jack Turner to go to the Kentucky game and went to Vanderbilt in Nashville. We played a lot of games in Memphis and played Tulane in New Orleans. We didn't play that many games on campus. LSU we played every year in Baton Rouge except 1960. I had been going to Ole Miss-LSU games since 1951. My freshman year both teams were undefeated and LSU beat us 14-0 in a game much closer than the score. Right before halftime, LSU was down on our goal and Warren Rabb, their quarterback, ran an option on fourth down. We had him stopped on about the one and Bull Churchwell, one of our linemen, came roaring in from behind and knocked everyone, including Rabb, into the end zone. Everyone started cheering and Bull thought everyone was cheering for him so he was waving to the crowd. The Ole Miss players wanted to kill him because he had given them a touchdown. It was 7-0 from then until the very end when they scored another touchdown. They won the national championship that year. I remember all of the games we lost when I was in school: that 1958 LSU and Tennessee games; the '59 game on Cannon's run; the '61 LSU game on Stovall's run; the Cotton Bowl to Texas when Billy Ray Adams had a car wreck and couldn't play and Buck Randall got hurt early in the first quarter. We lost that one 12-7. An then, my last year, 1962, we were undefeated. So that's five losses in five years, and only four of the losses were regular season games in those five years.

I took the train down to the 1959 LSU game. Joe Finley and I were in the dorm together and we were afraid we were going to sleep too late and miss the train, which was leaving at about six, so we stayed up all night drinking and made the train, drunk as owls. Somewhere around Grenada or Winona I passed out and the train was making stops. It made a stop in McComb and my mother and stepfather were going to be there to say hi to me because I rarely got home. So my friends started trying to wake me up around Brookhaven and they got me up so that I was able to go out and greet my parents. I'm sure they were appalled because I was obviously groggy and disheveled and reeking of whatever I'd been drinking. One of the versions of the story—told by Robert Khayat—is that the train never stopped in McComb and they held me up in the window and waved my arm as we went through. The good thing was that by the time we got to Baton Rouge I was stone cold sober and didn't have anything else to drink. I went over to the LSU SAE house and went to sleep under a chair. I remember the game vividly. There was a big fight before the game. They had that mezzanine right over the Ole Miss student section in those days where people could get on others' shoulders and attack people in the mezzanine. That took place with huge fights with hundreds of students and LSU people. The LSU people were dumping stuff on us. Semmes Luckett was a freshman and had an umbrella. He was on someone's shoulders pummeling people with his umbrella. Semmes was holding the peak and hitting people with the handle. The cops finally got up there and pulled these Ole Miss students off the shoulders. They hauled them up into the mezzanine and arrested them then put them in some kind of cage the rest of the game. One of my best friends from Summit days was a guy named Lew Barnes, who had gone to LSU and had gotten married and dropped out. He got in the stadium and came and sat with me in the student section. He had a bottle of whiskey and as soon as Cannon made the run, he drank what was left in the bottle and threw the thing. It went sailing down and hit someone in the back. There was a penalty on the play and while the LSU stadium went crazy there was still this apprehension it was going to be called back. Today, if you have a false start, that negates the play. And it may have been a false start but it wouldn't negate the play back then. The penalty was against us, so the play stood and the place went crazy again. The other thing is that when we punted that time, I think it was on first down. Robert Khayat looked at the play-by-play and thinks it was first down. Vaught was punting because he didn't think anyone could score on us. It was a wet field that night and Robert thinks that they had watered the field down heavily because it had not rained. If you look at the old black-and-white film you can see it was a very muddy game. It was a pretty day and Robert is convinced they got fire hoses out and watered the field because we were faster than they were so they made it in to a quagmire.

It was 9:59 left in the game when Cannon crossed the goal line. Doug Elmore was the third team quarterback and he went in and moved the team. People who were on the team say that Vaught should have brought in the number one team when they got down to the goal line. Our third team had moved the ball on the Chinese Bandits and Dietzel then brought in the White Team, which was their first team. I think because Elmore had succeeded in moving the team, Vaught didn't substitute. But people on the team say that he should have brought in Jake or Bobby Ray Franklin and Charlie Flowers and we would have scored and would have won the game. Of course, we didn't do it. Fred Lentjes blew the blocking assignment and we came up short. I blame Vaught also because we should have kicked a field goal at the end of the first half. We were already ahead 3-0; we were down in easy field goal range and Vaught decided to for it and failed to get the touchdown. If Robert had kicked the field goal then he could have kicked a field goal right there at the end to win it 9-7. The other thing that most people don't realize is that on that option, 4th down play, with less than a minute to go, Billy Cannon made the tackle.

My senior year, Ferrell Varner and I reserved a car on the regular train from Memphis to Knoxville. We thought we'd make a lot of money but nearly lost our hats. We rode up and it poured rain that game, like a monsoon. They had a huge brawl among the players and there's a picture of a guy named Mike Lucci who had been a linebacker there the year before hitting one of the Ole Miss players with an umbrella on the sidelines. It was a tense game. Louis Guy, who I grew up with, intercepted a pass and ran it back 108 yards for the touchdown that sealed the 19-6 victory. Then, as we were leaving the stadium—there were three couples of us who were there together. Two of the couples were Ferrell and his future wife, Tony Roberson and me and my future wife, Jane Pelegrin, who was on crutches because she had torn up her knee doing the twist earlier in the fall. It was a dorm stadium and we were all soaking wet anyway but these hillbilly students threw a bucket of water out the window on us as we were leaving the stadium. So I got what I think was a Coke bottle—some people say it was a whiskey bottle—and I threw the Coke bottle through their second floor window and knocked their window out. There were about five or six guys and they came running down to beat the crap out of me. I looked around and all my friends had disappeared. Ferrell and whoever else it was had run off so I was there by myself with Jane. I grabbed one of her crutches to fend them off. Fortuitously, the Ole Miss team was going to their bus and Louis Guy, Sam Owen and Bobby Robinson, who was a lineman from McComb, came running. It was like a western movie in which the cavalry comes to the rescue. Several others then came over and the UT students scattered so I escaped unscathed.

ERNEST "LIP" LIPSCOMB

1959-1963

TENNIS TEAM, FRONT ROW: DONNIE WALKER AND SIDNEY SMITH.
BACK ROW: JERRY MASON, FRED SANDIFER, ERNEST "LIP" LIPSCOMB, AND MIKE MILLS

I was on the Ole Miss tennis team. You had a freshman tennis team, and started on the varsity your sophomore year. At one point, five of the six starters were Phi Delta Thetas and the grade point average was somewhere north of 3.6. Number one was Sidney Smith, who graduated with one B, and Fred Sandifer, now a doctor, who was in the 3.8 range. Jerry Mason was up there; he went to law school and became a judge. And Jo Jo Saloum. The two who held the average down were myself—I was in Chemical Engineering—and Johnny Walker, from Laurel, who was a PE major. Mike Mills was on that team. He was a Phi Delt. He was my doubles partner for two years. Mike was born with a deformed left hand, which was kind of a nub, and he used it to beat the crap out of me when he drove on tennis trips. All of us were great friends and all of us were coached by Coach John

"HurriCane." He was the backfield coach for the football team and a wonderful guy. We didn't have tennis scholarships like they do now and we all spoke English quite well and were all from Mississippi. The kind of coaching we got was—I was left-handed and Coach Cain used to coach me by saying, "Goddammit Lefty, hit the ball." One day I was slipping and sliding on the court and he said, "Come here boy. Let me see the bottoms of those shoes." He looked and said, "You don't have any grippers on those shoes. Go on down to the field house and get a new pair." While we didn't have scholarships, we did have privileges to eat at Miller Hall in the athletic cafeteria during tennis season. We had a real good time. Like Coach Cain said, "My boys may not win a lot but they have a lot of fun." One time we were coming back from a match at Alabama and we stopped at a little roadside place that sold hamburgers. There was an old woman in there who was taking orders and she was getting them all mixed up so we were fussing at her as college boys would do. Coach Cain called us all aside and said, "Boys, if she had sense enough to get those orders straight, she wouldn't be back there taking them in the first place." He gave us a lot of good coaching about life itself. He was just a wonderful, wonderful man in terms of how he treated us. Coach Cain hated smoking and he would really get on people for smoking but he didn't mind if we went out after a tough match and had a few beers. He said, "I can run that beer out of you in two or three days but I can't run that smoke out of you in two or three days. It'll take me two or three weeks to do that."

One time we were playing the SEC tournament down in Florida and he came in the motel room. There was a can of beer sitting on the TV. He picked the beer and called us all in the room and said, "I don't want ever to hear about someone leaving half of can of beer. If you're not going to drink the whole can of beer, bring me the rest of it." The only time he got peeved with me was my senior year when we played the SEC up in Vanderbilt. I was playing number three singles and I had the good fortune of upsetting the guy from Alabama who was seeded and had beat me during the regular season. Everyone else lost so they were ready to go home but we had to stay up an extra day so it cost him an extra day of travel. I had to play the number one seed from Tulane the next day and I knew he was going to beat the you know what out of me, and he did. So that was the only time Coach Cain got peeved with me.

We travelled in two cars. There were eight or nine of us. We never got to go on spring break because all of the northern schools would come down here to play at that time. One year we were playing Western Michigan and there really weren't that many restaurants in Oxford so they let them eat in the athletic cafeteria in Miller Hall. One of their guys asked me, "Well, where's the rest of your campus?" I said, "This is it." He asked, "Well how big is Ole Miss?" And I said, "About 3500." He said, "My God. We have about 35,000." We had most of our matches on campus and when we travelled, it was to four or five SEC schools, and to Memphis and Jackson. We would generally finish the year about seven and 22. I lettered as a sophomore and Trent Lott borrowed my letterman's sweater to wear as a cheerleader.

We went through M-Club initiation. It was one night and wasn't that bad; just kind of bad. I got maybe one or two licks with the paddle, but some of the football players got a lot more. Charles Merkle and I went through together. He had lettered in baseball. They made us take our clothes off and leave them at the field house. Then they put us in the back of pickup trucks and took us way out in Lafayette County and put us out on a country road, spaced about a half mile apart. So Merkle and I and somebody else caught up with each other. We found a farmer's house with the light on and rang the doorbell. We stood out in the bushes and he died laughing then wrapped us in some old blankets and took us back to campus. It wasn't all that bad but it was kind of cool out there.

We didn't do much training for tennis. We practiced a lot and ran some wind sprints on the tennis court. We practiced or played seven days a week. With tennis, stopping and starting are the most important part. My junior year I won 23 of 25 matches, most of which were doubles matches. We finished the SEC tournament and I weighed 135 pounds. Coach Cain said I wasn't starting the next year unless I got my weight up to 150 pounds. I got it up to 145 but I still played.

DON KESSINGER

1960-1964

I grew up in Forrest City, Arkansas. When I grew up you played just about everything if you were a decent athlete, so that's what I did. When I was growing up, Arkansas had very little baseball in high school. People ran track in the spring. Football coaches pushed that track, so most schools didn't have high school baseball. I played football, basketball and ran track during the school year and then played baseball all summer with the American Legion, so we got it in.

I was blessed to have a chance to go quite a few places in basketball and I narrowed it down. I didn't want to go to Purdue or to UCLA. I wanted to stay around where my parents could see me. You grow up in Arkansas, you have to consider the University of Arkansas or else you'll get run out of town on a rail, but Arkansas didn't have much baseball either and I wanted to come play basketball and baseball somewhere. I thought if given a chance, I would have the opportunity to play professional baseball when I got out of school, so that kind of ruled out Arkansas. It got down to Ole Miss and Mississippi State. They were two excellent baseball schools but I thought Ole Miss was the best baseball school in the south. Coach Swayze was a great coach and a great person and when I visited here I just thought it was the friendliest place I'd ever been. When you walked around, everyone spoke and I just felt like I was in school here. So it was just the right place to me and I entered Ole Miss in the fall of 1960.

When I entered Ole Miss my focus was on both basketball and baseball but I knew that eventually I wanted to play professional baseball if I could. If you wanted to play both sports, you had to sign a basketball scholarship because the rules read that if you sign a spring sport scholarship, like baseball, you could only play that sport. It was to prevent football coaches from signing a lot of people to baseball scholarships for them to play football. So if I signed a basketball scholarship, I could play anything but football.

Freshmen didn't play varsity sports in those days, so I played on the freshman teams for both basketball and baseball. We played a lot of junior colleges in both sports, and played Mississippi State and Memphis State freshman teams. I played basketball with Mel and El Edmonds, Bill Bolton, Marshall Criss from Memphis and Larry Higginbottom from Memphis. Sterling "Tree" Ainsworth was on a couple of those teams. The football team lived in Miller Hall and basketball players stayed across the street in George "B". Then we moved over to Miller eventually but even at George, we had the athletic cafeteria in Miller, right across the street. That was great, not just because the food was good but that's how I got to know all of the football players and now, some of my greatest friends are football players from that day. You'd go sit over there and get to know them and they'd come to our ballgames and we'd go to theirs. It was a great deal. Mel and El were good athletes. They ran track and played backcourt on the basketball team. We played three in the backcourt most of the time.

I had Coach Graham two years. I loved him. He recruited me to Ole Miss. Coach Graham had lots of knowledge about basketball. He really knew the game. Coach Graham wasn't the greatest communicator I've known but his knowledge was unbelievable and you learned a lot of basketball from him. He wasn't a strong motivator and didn't always communicate that well, but he had some basketball knowledge and we all loved him as a person. As a team we were always kind of in the middle, were about a .500 team. Eddie Crawford came my junior year and coached me two years. Then, after I went to play pro baseball, I came back to Oxford a couple of years and helped Eddie coach basketball. I coached the freshman team when I came back. Eddie is quite a person and has been a great friend through the years. There are no better Ole Miss fans than Shirley and Eddie Crawford.

In baseball, I hit .402 as a sophomore but didn't think much about it. It was just what I did, how I played. Coach Swayze had a marvelous way of making you believe that he believed you were going to get a hit every time you went to the plate. It was quite a trait for a coach. Coach Swayze was a tough fundamental coach. He really believed in fundamentals but there was never a day that someone played for Coach Swayze that he didn't know that he loved them. He was hard; he was tough. He demanded that you do what you're supposed to do. He was a good, strong disciplinarian. He knew the game, demanded that when you went on the field you were dressed right, looked right and all of that. He loved the Yankees and he wanted you to look like the Yankees. And in his mind, he thought we played like them sometimes. But I found out later that we didn't. He was a good strong guy to play for and a good, strong coach and was fundamentally very sound.

When I got into pro baseball, I had some people tell me that fundamentally, I was as prepared as anyone they had ever seen. That was a great compliment not to me, because I didn't teach me the fundamentals, but to Coach Swayze. I played shortstop my entire career. Coach Swayze did it all: hitting, fielding, pitching, whatever. And he recruited for football. My junior year I hit .371 and my senior year I hit .432. Now, I don't fathom that. I don't know how that happened. It was just one of those remarkable years that an individual has. We were really a good team that year. That team went to Omaha and unfortunately didn't get to stay long enough but we went, so it was a great thrill: a great group of guys, great coaching, a fun time. We won the SEC that year and went to Gastonia, North Carolina, for the regional. The way it was then you had an east and west in the SEC and at the end of the year, the winners of the east and the west played each other for the SEC championship best two out of three. We played Auburn both my junior and senior years, and they beat us one year and we won the next so we went to Gastonia and won the regional there and then went to Omaha. We played Southern Cal and Arizona State, two great baseball programs at that time, but we played with them. The first game was really unfortunate for us. It was a close game and we were either ahead or behind 2-1 and about the fourth or fifth inning it rained the game out and then poured for about four days, so we didn't play. Then they started the game from that point and of course our best pitcher couldn't come back so we ended up losing 3-2. Then Arizona State had an All-American pitcher who just beat us. We didn't score and it's hard to win if you don't score. We had some really good players on that team, some that went on and had professional careers, not always in the big leagues, but good careers.

Tommy Keyes was a great player, played first base for us and signed maybe with the Phillies and did well. Did very well. Unfortunately, Tommy died not too long after he quit playing. Glenn Lusk was an outstanding player. Played outfield for us. Chet Bertolowski was from Laurel with Tommy Keyes and he played pro ball. We had a pitcher named Richie Prine, who was our ace that year. He hurt his arm his senior year and unfortunately, didn't get to go on.

In basketball, there were two nights that stand out. I scored 48 points against Tennessee at Tennessee my junior year and then had 49 against Tulane here. If you play sports, you know that some nights you have it and if you're a scorer and if you shoot enough, you'll score. I was never too bashful about shooting, and some nights you just feel that you can throw it in from everywhere. I think I shot 28 times and hit 22 of them or something like that. I'm the same guy who hit one for nineteen against Kentucky one night so let's don't get too carried away with it. I think until they closed Stokley Arena up there I held the scoring record up there. It was just one of those nights that everything felt right.

I went through M Club initiation my sophomore year. That is another one of those things you remember. It was (pause) different. They put us out with no clothes on and we had to run back to the dorm. I was glad I was pretty quick. We probably embellish it as the years go on. It probably wasn't as bad as we remember. (Laughs) The worst part was on initiation night, when you were blindfolded the whole time and you're walking through the old clubhouse and don't know what's coming next. I think the fear factor kicks in at some point, but we all got through it. The football players were all involved in my initiation, but fortunately, some of them were good friends and they protected me.

I have nothing but great memories about my time at Ole Miss. I love Ole Miss and I made great friends who are great friends today. It's great when they come back to Oxford and we get to visit. Ole Miss was and is the friendliest place that I've ever been. Certainly we've had our issues at Ole Miss. We've had our problems. But it's a great university and my memories of it are I came here from out of state and made great friends and never wanted to leave. I'm blessed to have been able to come here and I'm glad to still be around Oxford.

JIMMY HEIDEL

1961-1966

In high school I was a quarterback and a defensive safety. My first two years up here I played safety and then my senior year they switched me to quarterback. That's when Joanna told her daddy, "You are going to ruin us in the pro draft, because you are making Jimmy play quarterback."

When I was a young boy, my daddy loved football. He'd take my brother Roy and me to the Yazoo City high school football games on Friday nights. I can still remember when they hit a kid out of bounds and up against a steel pole and it broke his neck and he died. It scared me to death, so I was never going to play football. My older brother, Ray, started calling me "chicken," and "yellow," and all of that stuff. So my daddy came to me one day and said, "If you'll go out for one week and try it and don't like it, then I'll get your brother off your back." I thought, "Well, I can dodge them for a week to get my brother off my back." I went out and loved it. That was in the tenth grade and so I ended up playing here at Ole Miss and then professionally.

I was recruited by Ray Poole. I really thought I was being taken because of my brother Roy. I was just a tag-along. They did sign a couple of guys—family members—to get people to go to Ole Miss. We signed with Ole Miss and we never went to these other schools that wanted to sign us: LSU, Tulane and so forth.

On Wobble's freshman team they had me playing both quarterback and defensive back. But we had Jimmy Weatherly and a few others so they decided to start me as a defensive back. I played free safety for my first two years on the varsity and led the SEC in interceptions with five my sophomore year. The next year I played defensive back, then all of a sudden, I was quarterback my senior year. According to the coaches, we just ran out of quarterbacks so they just moved me over. Weatherly had graduated and Jody Graves was coming on but he hadn't been here that long, so they decided to switch me. The spring before my senior year, I had worked out at both positions, so it wasn't a hard transition, also because I had played quarterback in high school.

I dressed out my redshirt year for the first five games. I was on the sidelines at one of those five games, and Coach Vaught started yelling: "Heidel! Heidel!" So I ran up there and said, "Sir?" He said, "Get in there." I said, "Coach you don't want me. You want Jimmy Weatherly." I would have lost a whole year of eligibility.

The upperclassmen put us out on the road and whipped us with paddles and all of this other stuff. They put me way out in the country on a road, naked, and cars would come by and I'd jump in the bushes just trying to walk all the way home. That's just what they did. They quit that after awhile, but they did it when we were there. They got on us like crazy and loved doing it. M Club wasn't as bad as being a freshman. There was a lot of dunking you in water and stuff like that and pouring water over your head with a mask on and your eyes blindfolded. Like water boarding.

I loved Wobble Davidson. He was in the dorm with us, he and his sweet wife, Sara. One night Mama Robinson and Jerry Brown came in the Miller Hall and came down the hall singing. They had had a couple of beers and Wobble came out and met them in the hall. They said, "We're going to whup your ass." So he said, "Well is it going to be one of you at a time or both of you at the same time? Either way, I'm going to whip both of you and then you're going to run the stadium." And the next day, sure enough, they were out there running up and down the stadium. He was something else. But Sara was the sweetest thing in the world. She took care of the boys in there. Wobble, overall, was a real good guy. He had to be a hard taskmaster coach. We were a bunch of young guys who didn't know how to behave ourselves. We were in college and away from home without our mamas and daddies to tell us what to do, so he became our disciplinarian and kept up pretty straight. Wobble kept up with our academics. He'd walk outside and look in the windows to see if you were studying, and if you weren't he would come in and tell you to start. He wanted us to study and would check our grades to make sure we were doing good. The ones who weren't doing good, he'd put them in the stadium running up and down those stadium steps and make them go to a study hall. He was like a good father to us and Sara was like a real good mama to us.

We probably had about 45 or 46 freshmen that year and some of them transferred out, like Billy Fletcher, a quarterback, who went to Memphis State. A lot of guys tried out and some of them made it and some of them didn't. They were always having people try out. We probably lost 13 or 14 scholarship guys that freshman year. Either they thought it was too hard on them or something else. The good thing was that even if they quit they could stay in school another year. Eddie Touchberry transferred to Delta State. A bunch of them went to smaller schools and to junior colleges. Nobody ever went to another SEC school.

Wobble was our freshman coach and he had assistants who were graduate students there and they'd work with us. Eddie Crawford helped a little bit, and some others helped, but it was mostly Wobble and it was hard at times—he scared you to death—but looking back on it you really appreciate the discipline he gave us because it made you a better person. My redshirt year was 1962 and that was an undefeated team. Glynn Griffing was the quarterback, and it was the Meredith year. Wobble told us not to leave the dorm that night, and of course, several of them did, but they didn't do anything. They just wanted to see what was going on. My brother Roy was one of them. He and Touchberry and Don Windham and a few others sneaked over there but Wobble never caught them. They sneaked back in.

I remember being out at one point after the riot and some guys showed up. They said, "Where is the Ole Miss campus? We came to kill that so-and-so." I was standing right in front of Miller Hall and I pointed away from the campus and said, "It's over on the other side of town." We could smell the tear gas for about a week. Buck Randall went out there that night, but most of the people out there weren't students. There were rednecks in there from all over.

We opened in '63 with Memphis State in Memphis and I played defensive back. Billy Fletcher, our former teammate, played quarterback for them and it was a zero-zero tie. We beat LSU in Baton Rouge that year. I was a defensive back and think I intercepted a pass. That was the game in which Stan Hindman, a tackle, ran down Joe Labruzzo, a running back, from behind.

Roy, my older brother, and I were up here together, then Ray, who is five years younger, came along with Archie and Jim Poole and that bunch. Roy quit either his sophomore or junior year and got married and went home. In '64 we were so close to being 9-1. We lost a couple of one-point games. In '65 we lost to Alabama 17-16. We had them beat with one minute, thirty seconds to go. They drove all the way and scored. So here comes the Bear across the field. I dodged a highway patrolman, trying to get out of Bear's way. He says, "You!" I said, "Sir? Me?" He said, "Yes, son. You're one hell of a football player." Well I floated off the field. I had completed eight or nine passes in the first half and we were beating the dickens out of them. And then they came back and beat us.

Now Doc Knight was a super guy. He was very quiet, didn't say a whole lot, but he really cared about the players. He'd make sure they were okay and he'd take care of us. He'd wrap you up and of course, we had Nub there, too. Nub was taking care of us, also, but Doc Knight was always saying "What are you doing? Are you studying like you should? Are you doing what you need to do? You're not slipping out at night, are you?" He was a great motivator and I just loved him to death.

Coach Vaught really coached overall. He let his position coaches coach. Coach Vaught was a quiet man for the most part. He let his coaches do what they needed to do, discipline-wise and coaching-wise. He came up with most of the plays for us and developed the game plans. He already had everything he wanted us to do down pat. Each game plan was mostly his. His strength was using what was the best asset of each player. For example, I wasn't a great passer, but I could roll out and run, so he did little short passes for me, hitting a back out in the flat, or the tight end. Most everything I did was roll out and either run or throw. He adjusted each person to what they did best and did an excellent job of doing that. I'm sure the other coaches helped him with it, but I think overall, he knew the talent of each individual. Weatherly, for example, was more of a drop back passer than a roll out passer. He could run but he couldn't run that fast. I ran the hurdles in high school. There's a picture of me hurdling this kid from Chattanooga in a football game here. I hurdled over him and then went on for another ten or 15 yards. I tried that against Houston and a guy came up between my legs. I didn't do that again.

Playing Houston was like playing the Quantico Marines. That's where all my teeth got knocked out. A fist came through and hit me square in the mouth. I had one bar guarding my face and that fist came right through. It was two thirty in the morning and I was back in Oxford sitting in Dr. Abernathy's chair and he's cutting my teeth out. All of those Houston guys, it seemed like they were Marines. They were men and they used their fists. Memphis State did that, too.

I was drafted number nine by the St. Louis Cardinals and number three by the New York Jets. I told Coach Buster, "Coach, you need to come and help me. You need to help me negotiate this contract." So we flew to St. Louis and met with the Bidwell brothers who owned the Cardinals. They gave me a two-year, no-cut contract, a car, a honeymoon, and a bonus. So we came back, and I said, "Now Coach, we need to go talk to the Jets. They had drafted me number three. The Cardinals had drafted me number nine."

Here was an eight-year player, three years all-pro, and he said, "Son, let me just tell you something. First of all, the AFL will never amount to anything. Second of all, it's more money than you're worth. Sign the contract." I said, "Yes sir," and I signed it.

MIKE DENNIS

1962-1966

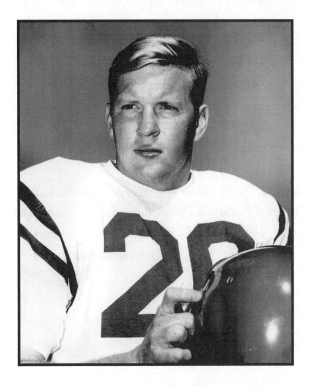

I was a freshman in 1962 and of course, in that era freshmen didn't play on the varsity but played on the freshman team. That was the season that the varsity went
undefeated. Of course, the freshmen were coached then by Wobble Davidson. The
Meredith riot was also my freshman year. I was in Miller Hall and three or four of us went
over to the Lyceum just to see what was going on. I saw someone throw a Coca Cola bottle
and hit one of the marshals on the shoulder. The marshals popped their headgear down and
gas masks and started shooting tear gas. We took off. I had no opposition to James Meredith
coming to Ole Miss. A lot of the people there that night whom I could see were not students.
There were a lot of people around the Lyceum involved in all of the fighting and whatever
who were not students. My understanding is there were a lot of out-of-state tags on the cars
parked around the Circle. It's hard for me to say, but it's certainly not one of our brightest
moments. I had never experienced tear gas before but boy, it burned my eyes something

terrible so we got back over at Miller Hall. I went to my room and sat down. My eyes were burning for the next two or three hours. Of course, a lot more went on after that. Everyone responded really good and the football team had an undefeated season with Glynn Griffing at the helm. He and Buddy Crosby roomed together and they were my big brothers on the football team. Each freshman was assigned to two older players and they were my two. I went to their room, I shined their shoes and both of them were so nice to me. They never hit me or abused me in any way. I ran some errands for them. I was living in the freshman wing of Miller Hall with my high school friend John Turner, who was a linebacker. Later in the fall, Coach Vaught called me in and said, "Mike, I want you to room with Stan Hindman." I said, "Well, Coach, I've already got a roommate." And he said, "Yeah, but I want you to room with Stan because he's coming back from West Point." Stan had signed originally with Ole Miss and went up there when Paul Dietzel went to West Point. Stan stayed through the summer and decided he didn't like it and wanted to come back to Ole Miss. Coach told me I was going to room with Stan and I ended up rooming with him the rest of my career. Stan and Steve were from Newton, and Steve came our senior year and was a freshman in the fall of 1965. On Monday after the Meredith riot, we went right back to practice. There was no break. Everybody just kind of said, "We have our own agenda and we know what we're going for," and so it continued, with success. It held everything together through a sad time. But some good things came out of it. We had a great team that year and then I played on the varsity in '63, '64 and '65.

Coach Wobble and Sarah were still living in Miller Hall with us and did, I think, for two more years. Then Coach Mustin and his wife moved in. Wobble ran a tight ship at Miller. He was tough, but he and I got along great. I was gung ho football and I did everything he wanted me to do—or tried to, anyway—so I never had any hang-up with him. The guys who had trouble with him were the guys who liked to go out a little more or didn't like to run as much or whatever. He just tried to straighten them out and they needed that. We all needed that. We were 18 and 19 year olds and we needed discipline. He had some assistant coaches—graduate assistants—who helped him but mostly it was just Wobble and that was enough. Jake Gibbs came back and coached some after baseball season with the Yankees ended.

Wobble made you pay for any mistakes you made. I mean, you paid big time. The biggest thing was to run the bleachers at the stadium, for a long time. People would get so tired they'd fall down and skin their knees and elbows. He had a way with words. He was tough and you knew it and he could get to you emotionally. He had a nickname for everyone. He called me Lordosis, which is swayback. I'm kind of swayback and have been all of my life.

He'd say, "All right, Lordosis, get in there." We had a good bond and in later years, he and Coach Buster Poole came to Jackson to come see me as a dentist. I took care of them every year. We had a great relationship. We saw a lot of Sara, that sweet thing. You got to have a bad cop and a good cop, and she was the good cop. You definitely knew which one Coach Wobble was. Sara was really pretty and sweet and always glad to see you. Just a real lady.

Doc Knight was a good cop. I ran track for Doc for three years on the varsity. He was a great guy. He really helped us physically and was concerned about everybody's health. If you had injuries he'd check on you and if he couldn't help you he'd get you to someone who could. We had some great doctors: Dr. Hopkins here in Oxford, Dr. Varner in Memphis, and Dr. Campbell, of Campbell's Clinic in Memphis. They came in at least once a week and Dr. Hopkins was here all the time. We had a lot of fun with Doc Knight on the track team. Now granted, track was not a priority at Ole Miss at that time, and it was very relaxed and we had maybe one guy a year get a track scholarship. The rest were football players. I ran the 400 and 800 meter relays and I ran the 200 meter several times. I also did the long jump. Doc and I had a great time with me trying to get the javelin down. He needed a javelin thrower and I had done fairly well with it in practice. So the first big meet was coming up to qualify for the SEC meet and I went out there at practice and lined up and threw it as hard as I could. I tore three muscles in my ribs. That ended my javelin career.

Doc took us to all the track meets. We went to Louisiana and Texas and all around and had the best time. Some of the other football players on the track team were Jimmy Heidel, Billy Clay and David Wells. J. W. Jones was a track guy from Macon and he ran on our relays. They called Larry Smith "The Stallion." We had run several track meets one year and Larry did not run in any of those meets. But he stepped onto the track over there in Georgia at the SEC meet and ran a 48-someting and got second in the 400 meters against a lot of SEC track guys who had been running all season. Larry almost won the thing after not working with the team that much. He went on to be a dermatologist on the coast. Some others who really helped us on the track team were the Edmonds twins, Mel and El. They both played basketball with Donnie Kessinger. When we had those three, we had three of the best basketball guards in the SEC. We just didn't have a big man. Mel and El were our assistant coaches on the track team. They had run track and were a lot of fun. Their relay team in Brookhaven when they were in high school was them, Lance Alworth, and Catfish Smith. They had some real good races with Murrah.

I don't think I would have made it as easy under Wobble if it hadn't been for Coach Jack Carlisle at Murrah. He got me ready. He was tough. I loved my high school football coach before him, Jim Merritt, a super guy, but he was a little easier on us than Jack was. Jack just demanded a whole lot more. When Jack came in my senior year at Murrah, we had about a hundred out the first day. We were a big school. There were like 500 in my class. So we had all of those guys out there and when we finished the season, I think we had 36. He played about sixteen of us. We were in great shape, no question about it. And that was the difference maker in the games. We were in such great shape that at the end, we pulled out a lot of games. That was the first year that Murrah ever won the North Big Eight. We played in the state championship against Laurel and they won, 17-10.

Our freshman team at Ole Miss did pretty good. We lost to Mississippi State, which was not good. We had some good players, though. I think Coach Vaught had signed fifteen fullbacks. I had been a fullback in high school and I was concerned a little bit after seeing how many fullbacks he had brought in there. A couple of them were pretty good players whom I knew from different teams. But that was what Coach Vaught did. He and I talked about it and he told me that since I was a sprinter, he wanted me to play tailback, so I moved to halfback. Joe Malone from Provine was our starting fullback. He left Ole Miss because he wasn't going to get to play as much as he wanted. Lee Garner was a linebacker-fullback on that team. We had a Womack signed as a fullback out of Magee and they moved him to guard. A lot of those guys went to different positions. There were four of us who didn't get redshirted: Stan Hindman, Billy Clay, David Wells and myself. Everyone else got redshirted.

We played two ways on into my junior year. My senior year was the only year we really played two platoon. It was easier for me when we finally went to two platoon because I was running the ball fifteen or twenty times a game. I can remember one game my junior year down in Jackson. We were playing Kentucky in 1964 and I was still playing both ways. I was on the punt team, the punt return team, the kickoff team, the kickoff return team, and I don't think I came out of the game but maybe one or two plays the whole game. They made some substitutions but I didn't get substituted for and after the game, I went into the dressing room and had cramps in almost every muscle. They had to take me over to the University Hospital and get me a drip to bring me out of it, but it was a very scary feeling when everything cramped up. I lost twelve pounds in that game.

When Bear Bryant was recruiting he was very personable. No question he was a great recruiter with his style and his success, too. Coach Vaught ended up coming down to Jackson on signing day. I'd always speak to Coach Bryant after that and he was upset with me for not signing with Alabama but he was a class guy like Coach Vaught. They were just above the rest. I played against Coach Bryant twice: the Sugar Bowl and my senior year when we played them in Birmingham. He was very cordial and came up and shook my hand.

Jake Gibbs was one of my heroes and I was elated when he came back and worked with us. Later on, I saw him in 1968 out in California when he was playing with the Yankees. I played for the Rams and our team doctor was also the team doctor for the California Angels. He told me he was going to the game that night and did I want to go with him. I said, "Man, yes," and we walked out and went down in the dressing room. I got out to the dugout and looked down there and there was Jake in the Yankees dugout, so he looked up and saw me. Of course he had just coached me two years before, so I sat down with him and visited.

We finished up strong in 1965. We lost some games early—close—like that 17-16 loss to Alabama, and of course, they won the national championship that year. They were the best team in the nation and they beat us one point on a missed extra point by Jimmy Keyes. We were up 16-0 and we missed the extra point—it was either blocked or bad ball positioning—and then they came back and at the end of the game they scored. I had two games like that in college: that one and that 11-10 loss to LSU. Against Alabama, we had the game and the refs gave them two pass interference calls. There were also two or three fourth and ones where they went for it and got great spots. Our coaches were just yelling from the sidelines and I really want to look at the film of that game. I've never gotten to do that but I'd like to see how bad those spots were. We ended that season by beating LSU in Jackson and Tennessee in Memphis.

Against LSU in 1965, Joe LaBruzzo was involved. He got the opening kickoff and ran it back for a touchdown and they called it back for clipping. And then we held them and beat the stew out of them. Had that stood, who knows what the situation would have been. But we went on to beat them 23-0. That was one of my best games. Coach Purvis, one of the assistants at LSU, came up to me after the game and said, "I can't believe you ran like that. We were stacked to get you." So they were prepared for what we were going to do but we just lined up and did it: blocked them and ran the ball. Jimmy Heidel played quarterback that game. He had a great game. He ran it well. We ran a little counter play where he would start off in one direction then hand it off to me and I'd cut back in the other direction. We got a bunch of yards that day. Then we beat Tennessee and went over there and pounded State, which we needed to after losing that game to them the year before. We beat them 21-0 and just pounded the ball. We didn't throw much that game. We played Auburn in the Liberty Bowl, so in a row, we beat LSU, Tennessee, Mississippi State and Auburn. Those were good teams. We weren't where we wanted to be but we lost some close games right off the bat. The Florida game wasn't close, 17-0, but that was really the only bad loss we had. Tennessee, whom we beat, was a close score, 14-13, but it wasn't as close as the score indicated. We pretty much dominated the game but they had a couple of breaks in the game and stayed close. They were after us, too, because of that 30 to nothing game that we had put on them the year before up in Knoxville. They were ready, but we were too and we played hard that day.

I wouldn't say that M Club initiation was a lot of fun. It was pretty rough. They put us out without any clothes on and we had to run back to the dorm. But that was the easy part. It was what was going on before that was rough. We had to do some things that were pretty tough. It was humiliating. We won't go into that. But it was worth it. All of these great guys. We have M Club meetings in the summer and a lot of the guys come. It's a great fraternity. I got to know guys like Kayo Dottley. He comes to M Club meetings and we just have the biggest time. I see Jimmy Lear at baseball games. He is one of my heroes. Eagle Day was another one. I was Eagle's dentist down in Jackson. I got to know him. He started an NFL alumni chapter and I got to know some guys who are still my friends twenty years after. When Eagle passed away, our chapter went down. He was the leader of that. I still hunt with Eddie Payton and talk once a month. I got to know him. Eddie Payton held the record for the Detroit Lions for running a punt and a kickoff back in the same game. Nolen Smith was in the club; he ran back punts for the KC Chiefs. He works with kids down there. They called him Super Gnat. Willie Richardson was also in it. He played for the Colts. Willie Daniels played for State and the Pittsburgh Steelers for nine years, then two years for the Rams along with me.

My wife Jane's maiden name was Jane Key. She was from Hartsville, Tennessee and was a Delta Gamma. I was a Phi Delt. We couldn't go through rush time-wise, but I did a limited rush and they accepted that. Louis Guy was one of my friends and he was a Phi Delt already and an awful lot of my friends from high school were going Phi Delt so we all kind of did it together.

Bruiser was a great man. I loved Bruiser. Buster Poole was super. Ray Poole was so nice. All of them had played football and they knew the game. Junie Hovius coached defensive backs and Johnny Cain coached offensive backfield. Roland Dale was the man with the plan. He was the guy who got the information on the teams we were playing and helped Coach Vaught develop the game plan. He was sharp, probably next to Coach Vaught in terms of making the plans. He did most of the scouting and decision making in terms of what to go with. I think he passed away a couple of years ago.

I played high school ball for Jack Carlisle, college for John Vaught, and professional for

George Allen and Vince Lombardi. George Allen was probably the most intense. He hardly ever went home. I don't know how he had a married life. So I played for great coaches and what they had in common was intensity and brilliance. They were all smart men and they were intense. They weren't the same but they had that in common. Not many guys get to play for one of those guys but I got to play for all four. I really had some great coaches.

At Ole Miss, the students were absolutely a motivating factor. Back then Ole Miss was so small that we knew half the students. Knowing a lot of them and getting the encouragement they gave us, you go out on that field and hear them hollering, you wanted to play for them as well as yourself, your teammates and your coaches. Knowing a lot of them, having personal contact with a lot of the students, it was really important. We were close to them and we could hear them. It was a big factor. Our students were great. They were fond of the Rebels. They got into the ball games and let us know it. It mattered. When we failed, we felt like we were failing them. Besides our coaches and our families and our teammates, it was a big factor. I run into people I remember and I light up because I remember how enthusiastic they were and how much they loved Rebel football.

I was All SEC two years. How I found out was it was in the paper. My junior year I was kind of shocked. I thought Tucker Frederickson from Auburn was going to get it. He was an All-American player but he played offense and defense and they put him on the first team defense. I was certainly happy because that 1964 season had not been the best year for Ole Miss. There were some guys my senior year I thought might get it: Joe Labruzo from LSU, Roger Byrd from Kentucky and some others. But I got it unanimously my senior year. They had UPI and AP and I got all of the votes. That really made me feel good and I felt that I had accomplished something.

I just love Ole Miss and the people. I have had so many great experiences with people who love Ole Miss. I just have great memories. The support I got from the students and people even in the troubled times. They followed us. Some of them, like Mr. Turner from Belzoni, rode on the plane with us. In my dental practice in Jackson, a lot of Ole Miss people came to me. I would ask who referred them and they would say, "I knew you from Ole Miss." I also had a lot of State people. I loved Ole Miss, and I loved my time, and I'm loving living here in Oxford now.

LYMAN HELLUMS

The difference between Coach Vaught's early teams and the era that followed was that later, he really didn't have the number of players. In the early years, you played one platoon football so each player played both offense and defense. If you had 22 men who could play football you were really something. Later, you had to be two and three deep and everyone was a specialist so that was the big difference. We went to two-platoon football in 1964, played Kentucky down in Jackson and they beat us. But Vaught eventually adjusted to it and he remained successful all the way up until his heart attack.

JAKE GIBBS

Quarterback Coach

1965-1970

In 1965, I was up on the hill looking at a passing drill, and Coach Vaught hollered up at me and said, "Come on down here." Jimmy Heidel was a senior quarterback and Coach Vaught introduced me to the group and said, "Get up under the center and show these guys how to run 36 slant." And then he said to the quarterbacks, "Now guys, y'all watch this." I said, "Coach"—I had on a white shirt and cufflinks and had just gotten home from the Yankees—"I haven't thrown a football in five years" and he said, "I don't give a damn. Get under that center and show these guys how to do it." Well, I felt a little embarrassed, but you couldn't argue with him so I've got street shoes on and I sprint out and throw the ball and hit the receiver. So he says, "Run it again." Well, we could run it in our sleep, we did it so much. He liked repetition. So I did it again, and swish, I hit him. So I ran it seven times. I had worked up a sweat. That was on a Wednesday and on Friday I got a call from Coach Vaught's secretary, Faye Parker, and she says, "Jake, are you coming to the game?" I said, "Yeah, I'm coming," and she said, "Coach Vaught wants to see you at eleven o'clock in his office." So I walked in at eleven o'clock and we spoke and he said, "Sit down." And he says, "What are you doing the rest of the fall?" I said, "Well Coach, I'm really not doing anything." Most baseball players had to get a job when you got out of baseball because you didn't make enough. I said, "Coach, I'm looking for a job." So he said, "Would you come up here and work with our quarterbacks?" I said, "Coach I'll do anything I can for you, you know that." He said, "I'll pay you $500 a month," and I said, "Coach I've got to commute from Grenada to Oxford." So he said "Well I'll give you $35 a month for gas money." And that's how I got started coaching. I saw what the quarterbacks were doing wrong. They were running seven or eight steps before they picked up any of the receivers. And that's what I saw, so I told the first one, you've got to come out looking. You've got to come out running but you've got to come out looking. Head up. You've got to see what's going on out there and that'll tell you who you're going to hit.

Jimmy Heidel was the number one quarterback that year and the team was two and three when I started work. We beat Vanderbilt that first weekend then the next, we beat LSU 23-0 in Jackson. We ended up winning five of the last six and went to the Liberty Bowl, where we beat Auburn.

I kept coaching quarterbacks until Coach Vaught had a heart attack and retired. Archie came along in 1967 and I coached him in '68, '69 and '70. We could tell from the beginning that he was going to be a Jim Dandy. And of course, he was.

BOB BOOTH

1965-1970

I went to every football game I could. I loved it. I was there when Spurrier came up here with Florida in 1965 and they beat us at Homecoming. It was the first Homecoming game Ole Miss had ever lost (under Johnny Vaught). I've hated Spurrier ever since. He gives you a wealth of material to hate him for. We would sit out at games and if it was raining, we'd wrap ourselves in visqueen. Weather didn't bother us at all. We went to Jackson and saw the hee-haw Kiner game. I had watched Archie in freshman games, knowing he was a pretty good quarterback. Then he started his sophomore year and it was just incredible how he could run with those floppy legs. He was such a competitor. At the Tennessee game down in Jackson (1969) we never sat down. The deal was that when they asked Kiner about the hosses at Ole Miss, he said we had donkeys or jackasses or something. So we never sat down and Ole Miss beat them 38-0. I was also there when Archie broke his arm. We were playing Houston and Warren McVay was their big ticket guy, their running back. I remember Archie was lying there after the play and the air just went out of the stadium. Shug Chumbler was the quarterback who replaced him and we ended up winning that game (24-13). I think we all had a good bit of trepidation about the rest of the season when Archie got hurt. He was such an integral part of the team. Later, he competed, even with a cast on. Not successfully, but he did compete. LSU just ran all over us, 61-17 and then he played against Auburn in the Gator Bowl.

BOB NUNNERY

1965-1971

One night I came into the dorm. I had been out partying and had a couple of adult beverages and my roommate was over in the corner being real quiet. He said, "Buck Randall has moved in next door to us." Buck was considered one of the toughest football players that there was and he loved to fight. They had kicked Buck out of Miller Hall. It was probably after he was supposed to graduate and was no longer playing. Buck was from Greenwood, and so I was being loud and about to scare my roommate to death. He thought Buck was going to come in there and kill us.

MIKE HEDGES

1966-1970

I don't know how we came up with the idea for the circulars before the 1969 Tennessee game. The guy who did it was from Batesville and we remembered the "mule" statement that Steve Kiner made, so this guy came up with the leaflet about the Ole Miss mules. We dumped them out over campus, then we had a crowd gather later that day around Meek Hall—kind of an impromptu thing. The next night it was twice that many and by the third or fourth night we had a pep rally every night that week. Then the cheerleaders showed up and it was an electric atmosphere and the excitement was building. No one could think of anything else but that game.

Back then, there were no reserved seats in the student section. We walked in about two hours before kickoff and there was not a seat to be had in the student section so we sat on the grass down in the end zone. Then the Tennessee team came out to walk around the field with their orange jerseys on and when they got over to the Ole Miss side, they got bombarded with oranges. We had all of the dads on the field for the team to run through when they came out onto the field, so it just built and built. Bo Bowen was on that team and he ran all over them. Of course, Archie had one of his greatest days, so we went from 0-31 the year before to 38-0. Tennessee was undefeated and number three in the nation when they came in and we had already lost three games, but we finished out the year and beat number three Arkansas in the Sugar Bowl. I was back for the Alabama game a few weeks ago (2014) and it was pretty special, too, but I still couldn't put it up there with that Tennessee game in 1969.

BO BOWEN

1966-1970

I went to Ole Miss in the fall of 1966 and graduated in 1970. I was the son of a football player at Ole Miss, who was my hero: Buddy Bowen. My mother, Mary Ann Bowen, is still in Oxford, and my dad and my mother were big influences on me. My father was a big Ole Miss fan and I grew up being an Ole Miss fan and then had the dream come true of having a football scholarship at Ole Miss. Back in those days we had an athletic dormitory and cafeteria. Few of us had cars so we walked everywhere and it was just great to be right there on campus with everything provided by that scholarship.

Alabama with Bear Bryant was one school I considered. I also had offers from State, Southern, Texas and Georgia Tech. But Alabama was the only one I considered seriously.

Then I went over there to a game. At the game I was thinking if Alabama were playing Ole Miss how could I play against Ole Miss, so that was a day of reckoning. I knew I couldn't play against Ole Miss, so that was the end of my recruiting. Shortly after that I committed to Ole Miss and was glad and happy to get that scholarship. Coach Bruiser recruited the Jackson area and he was the one who recruited me. Coach Vaught was there, of course, with Coach Bruiser and Buster Poole and Ray Poole as coaches. Billy Mustin was there and also Eddie Crawford, who is the only coach still working for Ole Miss. They were great coaches and great guys, men who did the right thing and always encouraged us to do the right thing. We had a great time while I was at Ole Miss.

Recruiting was a lot simpler than it is today. We came up and visited the campus and enjoyed being there. Coach Wobble Davidson was coaching the freshmen. He was a great guy and a great inspiration and having been a Marine himself, he was disciplined and he inspired us to be disciplined. I miss all of them. One day we were walking across campus, a group of us walking back from practice. We were freshmen and we heard this voice and didn't even know where it came from: "Bowen, tuck your shirttail in." It was Coach Davidson, so from then on we knew he might be looking at you anywhere you were. It was a great encouragement to do the right thing, to have someone who cared so much about you and who was also going to see that you did the right thing. He and Miss Sara were still in the dormitory and the first couple of years I was there he would come by at night and do bed check during the season. He came by at 10:30 to make sure we were in our rooms. Miss Sara is a great lady.

Our freshman team was a big disappointment. We didn't do well. We were supposed to do well because we had most of the best prospects but we just didn't do well. I don't know why. I guess the other teams did better. LSU beat us a whole bunch. Alabama beat us, and also, State beat us, which caused us to have our heads shaved again. In those days they shaved your head if you lost to State so we got shaved twice that year. And deserved it.

I went up to the varsity as a sophomore in 1967. I played a good bit. I actually ran the second half kickoff for a touchdown against Memphis State. We lost that game but we came back and beat Georgia in Jackson 29-20. That was a great game. We had such a good offensive line. There were lots of holes open and I ran through those holes and scored a couple of touchdowns. We went to the Sun Bowl that year and lost that game, so that put a damper on the trip to El Paso.

Archie was a freshman my sophomore year, but we had no idea how good he would turn out to be. We had four really good prospects for quarterback on his freshman team. And that spring, when Archie was a freshman, and I was a sophomore, Archie, Shug Chumbler and Don Farrah were all playing quarterback and there really wasn't much difference between them. But Archie was a game day player. You really can't tell from practice how people are going to be at the game. When it came to the game, that's when Archie shined. I don't know if they would admit this now, but the coaching staff weren't that sure who was going to be the quarterback but from the first game, it was clear who that was going to be.

My junior year we beat Alabama in Jackson 10-8. Steve Hindman was a running back and I was a running back. Our defense played real well. We played LSU down there and beat them. We were down a couple of touchdowns or more at halftime and came back and beat them. What I remember most about that game is the noise. It worked in our favor, because when we came out to warm up and also when we came back out to start the game, the noise level was so great, the only thing we could distinguish was a faint "Hotty Toddy." The students were in that end zone section where we came out so it seemed to us we had a lot of fan support. The noise didn't affect us in a bad way. It was actually an encouragement. Archie had a good night against LSU. Then Tennessee beat us pretty bad (31-0). We fumbled and got intercepted and just couldn't get it together. We tied State 17-17 but I don't remember anything about it.

In 1969 we lost to Kentucky 10-9 and again, it was one of those games where we should have won. We had many opportunities to score and we fumbled and dropped passes so it was a game of a lot of mistakes. Then we played Alabama in Birmingham, and it was the same type of game. Coach Vaught sent a play in and the running back told Archie: All of the receivers go to the left, I'm going out to the right. Archie then threw it right into his hands and he dropped it. Coach Vaught had told him, "Go in and you're going to get that ball in the end zone." And that's what happened except he dropped it in the end zone. That would have won the game. They had a good team and a good quarterback and we had a great team and a great quarterback and so that was a disappointment.

We played LSU in Jackson, a big win and then the "Mule" game against Tennessee (38-0). That game was so awesome. We had been so disappointed with some of those losses and then we started to win so we had some momentum going. The coaches did a lot of different things: dropping leaflets on the field, supposedly from Tennessee, about Archie Who and the quote that Steve Kiner had in the paper. He said, "People say that Ole Miss has a bunch of horses but I think they're a bunch of mules." Dropping those leaflets over the campus and all of the signs, it was something. When we came to the stadium it seemed to us that the stadium was already full of Ole Miss people doing Ole Miss cheers. So when we went out to warm up we were about two feet off the ground. Everything went well for us and the Lord blessed us and it was just a great day. The defense made two goal line stands. With Hap Farber and Frank Trapp and all of those guys, they stopped Tennessee twice and kept them from scoring at all. I ran the ball a good bit that day and everything we did was working—running and passing. The line was blocking. Skipper Jernigan, Wimpy Winther, Buddy Mitchell, Jim Poole and Billy Coker did a great job. Archie kept them from stacking the line on us because he would hurt you either running the ball outside or passing. So the defense had to defend both the pass and the run.

We played Arkansas in the Sugar Bowl. It was another good day. I had a long run in the second quarter. It was an option give. Archie made a great fake and a couple of guys tackled him after he handed the ball off to me, and the offensive line blocked—Skipper and Wimpy Winther—then, when I got downfield, I picked up more blocks. Jim Poole was down there blocking, Vernon Studdard had a big block and Buddy Mitchell had a block downfield. It was just a team play, a perfectly executed option play. Archie's fake drew people away from me so I was downfield ten yards before they even knew I had the ball. It was a 69-yard run for a touchdown, a memorable moment for sure.

Coach Vaught was a gentleman. He delegated to his assistants very well, let the position coaches do their job and didn't interfere with them. He would go around and see how the assistant coaches were doing but he spent most of his time with the quarterbacks and wide receivers. We would practice by position, then we'd come together and the first and second team offenses would scrimmage against the third team defense. He was very organized. Coach Vaught was probably a little ahead of his time. Jake came back each year after baseball with the Yankees to work with the quarterbacks and he worked with the running backs, too. One day, he told me to keep my head up a little more when I was running the ball. "You got to watch where you're going. You need to be low but you need to see where you're going."

I was initiated into M Club after my sophomore season. I had actually lettered in track my freshman year but they didn't initiate me then. That was the first year freshmen could participate in varsity track. It was a few years later for football. So they let the freshmen run on the track team that year. I ran on the mile relay and lettered as a freshman but the M Club initiation was after my sophomore season was over, probably in early January. I don't remember exactly when. I just remember how bad it was.

Doc Knight was the track coach and the trainer. Doc was great. He was a great spiritual inspiration to all of us. He's the guy Coach Vaught asked to lead us in the Lord's Prayer before every game. He would also give the pep talk. Other coaches would give it from time to time and Coach Vaught always had the last word but Doc Knight always gave a pep talk and led us in the prayer.

I was a Phi Delta Theta. They didn't require us to participate at the same level that they required other actives. I was initiated and enjoyed the associations and still do with Phi Delta Thetas.

A number of the business professors stood out. Papa Joe Cerney was the accounting professor and I had a great economics professor. Business School prepared me well for later life. Lots of students stand out to me. The guys I was freshmen with are close. My roommate was Bernard Deaton, who was called "Penny" at that time and is a successful real estate guy in Dallas. Bill Jones is an outstanding lawyer down here in Jackson. And Hap Farber, who was a defensive end at Ole Miss and played professionally with Minnesota and the Saints, I think. We stay in touch and that's been so important. And the class under me: Archie, Billy Van Devender and George Lotterhos and those guys: Randy Reed—they were a great group of folks.

I feel a real blessing for having been at Ole Miss at that time. So many things happened and relationships formed that have been important to me all my life. I sell life and health insurance so my business degree helps and I met my wife—Marty Black, from Hammond, Louisiana—at Ole Miss and my first child, Taylor, was born at Ole Miss. Most importantly, I met the Lord there. The Campus Crusade for Christ missionary, Mike McNames, who had played football at Georgia Tech, was assigned to Ole Miss and two or three other campuses. He came and talked to us two or three times and that planted the seeds that eventually grew into a plant, so that was a great thing. We had a very active Fellowship of Christian Athletes then. We prayed and had huddle groups in the dormitory and the coaches supported it but didn't lead it. Tommy McKibbens and Julian Fagan were the leaders of that.

The opportunity with a four-year athletic scholarship was great. The environment we had at that time with the coaches we had and the way it was on campus—the girls' dorms and the guys' dorms and all, it was just a great environment in which to grow and grow up and be the man God wants us to be. It was a great place to do that because of the coaches and because of people like Doc Knight and the spiritual influence.

SKIPPER JERNIGAN

1967-1971

I grew up in Jackson, graduated from Murrah High School in 1967 and entered Ole Miss that fall. Bruiser Kinard was responsible for the Jackson area and recruited me. My mother had gone to Arkansas for a year or two and my father didn't go to college so we really didn't have much of an allegiance to any particular school. We went to the Jackson games, depending on who was playing. My sophomore year one of our seniors signed a scholarship with Ole Miss and my junior year Bo Bowen, Penny Deaton, Bill Jones and Hap Farber, who were good friends of mine, went to Ole Miss. So my senior year there were three of us who went to Ole Miss: me, George Lotterhos and Billy Van Devender. The next year Ole Miss signed five from Murrah. Jack Carlisle who coached at Murrah was kind of a pipeline for Bruiser back then. He sent a lot of players to Ole Miss. Mike Dennis had played at Murrah and a few more had gone up there in the sixties. I played several positions in high school: guard, tackle, defensive end, nose guard, linebacker, just kind of what they needed me to play. We were undefeated my sophomore year. My junior year we beat Gulfport for the overall Big Eight championship and my senior year we were ten and two with a couple of hiccups along the way, but we had great teams and Coach Carlisle was one of the best.

I got recruited hard by LSU and Texas but at the end of my junior year I tore my knee up and had to have major reconstructive surgery. I wasn't sure whether I was going to play again so every school but Ole Miss kind of backed off. I went to Campbell's Clinic and had surgery. Bruiser came by to check on me and then Nub came by to check on me. I rehabbed my knee, got back to playing that fall and never had any more trouble with it. Because Ole Miss never backed off, I didn't take many trips my senior year—just LSU, Alabama and Ole Miss. By that point, I pretty much knew I wanted to go to Ole Miss.

I went up in the fall of '67, in the same class with a lot of guys who started all three years of varsity at Ole Miss. Coach Vaught signed eight quarterbacks that year and there were about 45 of us on scholarship, with about 25 walk-ons so we had a total of about seventy. Some of the walk-ons didn't stay very long, but some of them did, at least for awhile. I don't think any of them survived that first fall with Wobble. He coached the freshmen and he had some graduate assistants. The senior graduate assistant was David Wells. We called him Stadium David Wells because one day in practice we were doing something wrong and Wells was coaching us. Wobble got mad and threatened to make us all run the stadium steps and said he was going to make Coach Wells run, too. Mike Robbins was a graduate assistant who worked with the freshmen, but Wobble was the only fulltime assistant who handled the freshmen.

We played a separate schedule against other teams and went three and one. Our first game was with LSU and they beat us 21-0. Wobble was very unhappy. So the next week on Monday we went out to practice and Wobble wasn't out there, just the managers. We got out there and there weren't any footballs on the field. So Archie hollered at one of the managers and said, "When are y'all gonna bring the footballs?" The manager said, "We're not. Coach said y'all aren't going to need them this week." So we practiced all week without a football, just blocking and tackling. It was brutal.

A couple of weeks later we went over to Alabama and beat them handily. The score— 21-2—was not nearly as bad as the beating. After the game we were running off the field, and Bear had come down there. He was about to have a stroke he was so mad. Bear was screaming at the freshman football team and the freshman football coaches, all of them. He wouldn't let them go in the dressing room. He turned around, was cussing and raising hell:

"Y'all sorry SOBs are not going into that dressing room. Turn around, we're going back out there and practice." It tickled Wobble to no end. He got the biggest laugh out of that you ever saw in your life.

Wobble did it all: coached the quarterbacks, the running backs, everyone. We called him the "Man with No Eyes," like the guy in Cool Hand Luke who wore the reflective sun glasses. Wobble could be down on one end of the field doing something and he'd scream at you at the other end. He was amazing. He was all over the place. Wobble could really teach blocking and tackling. If you survived him and did what he wanted you to do, you were ready to go play varsity football when you got through with Wobble or when he got through with you. He ran off more All-Americans than most teams ever even had.

Bob White was from Meridian. He was all-universe in high school and was really good. In the high school all-star game that summer he started in front of Archie and in the first quarter he tore his knee up. They put Archie in and Archie threw five touchdown passes and that was the end of Bob White. Bob hurt his knee again in the fall. He never had it operated on after the all-star game and tried to come up to Ole Miss and play and it got worse. Bob had to have it operated on, then he got hurt again and he never saw the field. The quarterbacks were Freddie Brister from McComb, Don Farrah from Gulfport, Ernie Brown from Biloxi, Shug Chumbler from Alabama, Archie and a couple of more. I played guard and linebacker because freshmen played both ways. So against LSU I played sixty minutes, in the daytime. When I went up to the varsity they tried to slot you one, where they needed help, two where your best skill set was and three they'd ask you what position you wanted to play. I weighed about 210 pounds when I entered and about the same when I went up to the varsity then went up to 228 or so when I got older. We did some weight work, just a hodge podge of training techniques. Some years it would be weight work and the next year it would be speed. They were just all over the board. In the spring we had to be able to run a mile by the start of spring training in a certain time and you had to do it every day during spring training until you got to it. I never could figure out why an offensive lineman needed to be able to run a mile in six minutes or whatever the time was. That was what was in vogue back then. It changed from year to year.

Wobble's practices were brutal: a lot of contact and a lot of running. They were designed to see if you could take it or not, and a lot of them couldn't. Thirty of us survived it. We lost all of the walk-ons and about a third of the scholarship guys. Coach Vaught believed in running. You had to be able to run to play for him. He liked the offensive linemen to be able to run, liked to pull the guards so you had to be able to run to get out in front of the play.

That was one thing I could do. I could run. The offense we ran as freshmen was identical to what the varsity ran: everything, terminology, plays, everything. So the learning curve was pretty short going up to the varsity.

Vaught brought in Bob Tyler my sophomore year to coach wide receivers and quarterbacks. Coach Vaught continued to be the offensive coordinator, but with Coach Tyler, we became more of a spread, tailback-type offense running quarterback options. My sophomore year showed Coach Vaught that Archie really wasn't a classic option quarterback. He was good but his skill set was much better suited for other things. We had become almost a spread offense by my senior year. If you go back and look at some of that film with Bob Tyler, we were running four wide receivers, a split backfield, one back, it looked a lot like the spread offenses now. We didn't have the direct snap, though. Everything was done under center.

As a freshman against Alabama, Archie played safety and intercepted three passes. Shug Chumbler played quarterback that day, and so did Don Farrah. Wobble thought Archie was a hell of a safety. He was such a good athlete, he could have played just about anything. The next game was against Vanderbilt and by that time Archie had moved back to quarterback. We beat Vanderbilt 80-8 and I'm pretty sure that he threw eight or nine touchdown passes. We had them 49-0 at the half and were sitting in the dressing room. Wobble never came in the dressing room and Wells came in and said, "Where's Coach Davidson?" We said we didn't know, we hadn't seen him. So about two minutes before we were to hit the field, Wobble showed up and walked in and looked around, and said, "Good job, men. We got these sono-fabitches down so let's beat the hell out of 'em. Now hit the field." That was all he said. I don't know that he hated Vanderbilt particularly. I think he hated everyone, the best I could tell. Man, he hated Mississippi State. He gave one of the most inspiring speeches before the Mississippi State game I ever heard.

Jake was coming back then to coach quarterbacks but he had to go to spring baseball training so he missed our spring practice. Coach Vaught always said he wanted our spring training early because if anyone got hurt they'd be able to get well by August. We always thought he wanted to go turkey hunting and didn't want spring practice to mess up wild turkey season. In the fall, Jake worked with the quarterbacks on Coach Vaught's rollout offense. Coach Vaught's philosophy was to put pressure on the corners.

My sophomore year we went 6-3-1 and played in the Liberty Bowl in Memphis. It was the coldest day on record in Memphis and it was in December. It was so cold, as the sun came across the field and left a shadow, the field was freezing behind it. We were down 14-0 before we ever touched the ball. They onsides kicked the opening kickoff and recovered it. Then they ran a trick play the first play of the game and scored. Then they onsides kicked it again and recovered, then scored again. The trick play they had half of the guys line up on one side of the field and half on the other. Then one of them went in motion—you'd just have to see it.

In '68 we beat Alabama 10-8 in Jackson. They had two tough-as-nails linebackers. Bob Childs and a guy named Mike something who were as tough as they could be. What I really remember is they blocked a punt toward the end of the game and went down there and scored and went for two and made it, making the score 10-8. Then they tried an onsides kick right at the end of the game. If they had recovered it they would have had a shot at a field goal to beat us but they didn't. What I remember most is how tough those two linebackers were the whole game. Coach Bryant came to our dressing room after the game and congratulated us.

In '69 we went seven and three and lost that tough game 33-32 to Alabama in Birmingham. It's funny that everyone wants to talk about a game that we lost, but we don't really see it that way. The game never should have been in that posture. Ever. We blew three scoring opportunities in the first half, got inside their five yard line twice and inside their ten yard line once more and didn't get any points. If we had scored like we should have in the first half, that game wouldn't have had a chance to be like it was. Instead it was 14-14 at half-time. Then we missed an extra point. That put us behind the curve so when you're swapping touchdowns, you end up having to go for two. Then you go for two and if you don't make it, everything snowballs. We could have put the game away then without it even being close. We never dreamed the way the game was being played, how we were moving the ball, that we'd lose. We moved it up and down the field and were moving it at the end of the game but we ran out of timeouts and time. I can remember it was kind of warm that night and the Alabama defensive guys ran out of gas so they put a couple of offensive linemen at the end of the game to play defense and rush the passer. A guard named Alvin Sample who made all conference with me that year was in there rushing the passer at the end of the game. If you watched Archie that night, it would be understandable. Hell, he ran all over the field all night long. He would have been hell to try to catch. He was hell to try to block for. Up until Manziel came along, Archie held the record for total offense in a single game. Manziel finally broke it but Archie had like 540 yards total offense.

LSU was in Jackson that year. They were undefeated. We beat Georgia and Tennessee. They were both undefeated. We matched up good with LSU. The defense played well and we were able to come back and hang on right there at the end and win that ballgame. We beat them the year before down in Baton Rouge driving 80 yards in the last 2 and 1/2 minutes to win that game. The noise down there was a big factor in the game. You couldn't hear the snap counts so you went on the snaps.

We had lost to Kentucky, which was a joke. Coach Vaught decided we were going to run the option against them. We didn't have an option football team but he was just bound and determined to do that. Sure enough, right out of the chute, Archie broke one for about sixty yards on an option keeper, and then we tried to run that option the rest of the night but they had adjusted to it. Regardless of that, at the end of the game, we got down inside their ten yard line twice and got no points. Leon Felts was going over the goal line with the ball and they had a little linebacker named Wilbur Hackett who was about five-nine. He popped up out of nowhere, his helmet hit the ball and popped it loose and they recovered. The defense held them and they punted from their own end zone and didn't kick it thirty yards If we had just caught it we were in field goal range, but our guy fumbled the punt. We did everything we could possibly do to lose that game. Hackett was one of the first black players we played against.

The week leading up to the 1969 Tennessee game on campus they had pep rallies every night except Monday. It was Kiner who got everyone stirred up with that comment about mules. So we showed up at practice on Monday and Coach Vaught had a mule tied up out there on the practice field. Then, Tuesday, this plane flies over and drops all of these leaflets out on the practice field about a bunch of mules. I know Vaught was doing all of that. The students really got into it and it just turned into one of those perfect storms. The year before we had played up there and Archie threw five interceptions and had two fumbles. That's what started the mule stuff with Kiner, who was a linebacker. They were good. Jack Reynolds was the other linebacker for Tennessee and he was the real player in the box.

We got down to Jackson and had a big pep rally out at Highland Village and another spontaneous pep rally over at the Jacksonian where we were staying. I'll never forget, before the game, an hour and fifteen minutes, the rest of us were lying around in our underwear. I looked over there and Hap Farber was totally dressed, his ankles were taped, his helmet was on and his chin strap was buckled, He was just sitting there. It was one of those deals: everything we did worked and if you could play a perfect half of football, that was it, that first half. Bo Bowen was fullback and Randy Reed was the tailback and I think both of them rushed for over a hundred yards. Archie even fumbled the ball at the goal line and we recovered it in the end zone. It was just one of those days when everything was going our way. They had widened their defense to keep Archie from getting outside so much, so they moved one of the linebackers out. They were basically going to play us a man short on the inside so we were able to take advantage of that. We were using audibles at the line of scrimmage, and Archie was calling most of the plays. They had set up a series of plays that we were going to open with but after that Archie called most of the plays. Coach Vaught would send in Vernon Studdard or Leon Felts if he wanted a particular play run.

We played Houston in the Astrodome and could have played them for a week and we wouldn't have beat them. They had some tremendous black athletes. We didn't play well but like I said, we would have had to play perfect to even have had a chance. We did play perfect the next year—1970—and beat them except Archie broke his arm. They were just loaded. I think they beat Mississippi State 77-0 and Tulsa 100-0.

The Southern game my senior year was a case of a perfect storm in the other direction. We had played three very difficult games in a row. We opened with Memphis State but there wasn't much to that. Then we played Kentucky, Georgia and Alabama. For whatever reason we struggled with Kentucky all three years I was there. We played them in Jackson during the daytime and it was 100 degrees and brutal. Then we played Alabama on national television at night and beat them handily. After that, we had to go to Athens and play Georgia over there. They were really good but we were too. It was hot as hell in Athens and the game was a dog fight all the way. So we got back home and were going to play Southern. Well, we had beat them the year before 69-7. Bear Underwood, their coach, had said then that the turning point of that game was when they turned off of I-55 In Batesville going over to Oxford.

Coach Vaught preached and preached all week long, but it was just not to be. We had some things that mentally we were, for whatever reason, in a bad place. We let ourselves get there. It was no one's fault but ours. Archie was banged up and had a gimpy leg. We came out and scored two quick touchdowns and then they ran a couple of trick plays and scored. We made a mistake or two and they got back in the game. We went out in the second half, and as good as we were, just laid an egg. Just played like dogs. The harder we tried, the worse we got. Archie had over 400 yards total offense but we made a mistake every time we got in the red zone.

There is no truth to the story that everyone was out partying the night before. There may have been one or two, but there are always going to be one or two. They are generally the ones who aren't going to play. There is no truth to that at all.

I had some great teammates. I roomed with Worthy McClure who was the right tackle and I was the right guard. I was suite-mates with Freddy Brister and Buddy Mitchell so I got pretty close to those guys. I was close to Archie, particularly after his father's situation in the summer of 1969. My high school buddies—three in my class and four in the class in front of us—and I were all close. We had a tight knit bunch with good senior leadership.

If you weren't a quarterback, you didn't have a lot of interaction with Coach Vaught. The quarterbacks would go over to his office after lunch until practice time. He spent most of his time with them. Coach Vaught knew my name but we didn't have a lot of interaction with him during practice until we came together for teamwork. He let his assistants coach. Vaught rarely gave much of a pregame pep talk like someone like Lombardi did. He expected you to prepare and get ready and do your job.

Doc Knight did a lot of the motivational, psychological stuff and he was very good at it. He was the guy you went to if you needed anything. Doc was who you talked to. Wobble and Sara weren't living in the dorm by then. Billy Mustin and his wife were in the dorm with us. That was a big change from Wobble.

I went through M Club initiation. It was still tough at that time and lasted a whole week. I thought it was really silly. I wasn't into freshman hazing or any of that kind of stuff. One day of that would have been plenty and I didn't think it was real funny. I wasn't one of the ones who thought M Club initiation ought to be like that.

I joined the Pikes, was initiated and went to a few chapter meetings. I'd go by there and eat two or three times a month and go to the parties. Our time was pretty much taken up with football.

What I think about my time at Ole Miss is how self-contained it was. Ole Miss had only about 5500 students. Everyone lived on campus pretty much, maybe a few seniors lived off, and of course we lived in the athletic dorm, so all of the activities were over on fraternity row and around the Grill. You could walk over to fraternity row to a party, then walk back to the dorm. The student union was small, and classes weren't very big, so you got to know a lot of people. You see an obituary now or run into someone somewhere, and you realize how many people you knew at Ole Miss then. It was really, really special. My best friends are still my teammates. I tell you, if anybody ever had any more fun than we did going to college, then I don't want to know about it. It was really a special time.

What I'm proudest of is that when I packed up as a senior and left campus after graduation, I was driving out Highway 6. I have no idea what possessed me but I pulled into Coach Vaught's house. He'd been sick and I went to the door and Mrs. Vaught came to the door. I said, "Is Coach home?" She said yes, and I went in and there he was. He said, "What can I do for you, son?" And I said, "Well, Coach, you can't do anything for me. I just came by here to thank you for my education." It meant so much to him and it's been a great memory to have and to hold on to.

LYMAN HELLUMS

We beat Tennessee out here (Jackson Memorial Stadium) 38-0 when they were ranked number three in the country in 1969. That Alabama game that year they beat us 33-32 and Manning had over 500 yards of total offense. I was over there and met Kris Schenkel and Bud Wilkinson, who called the game for ABC. It was the first nighttime football game televised. Stan and I did that game. There were a lot of great games when Archie was here—The Georgia game out here (Jackson-1969). In that game, Ole Miss was behind at halftime and Manning got hurt. He came back in the second half and pulled the game out. I remember over there we were the underdog going in and we kicked off to them to start the game. We held and they punted and we got the ball on the 30 or 31 yard line. On the first play Manning just stood up and threw the ball to Jim Poole right across the line of scrimmage and he dropped it, but he was wide open. So the second play the center snapped the ball and Archie faked a throw to Poole. The defenders all converged on Poole and Archie hit Studdard running down the sideline for a touchdown. It was a beautiful thing. Studdard was a heck of a ballplayer. He was from Columbus and Billy Brewer coached him in high school. We were out in Houston to play in the Astrodome for the first time. That was an awe-inspiring place for a bunch of country boys like we were.

Vaught and Bruiser worked close together. That offensive line has got to do certain things to make that spread offense that Vaught ran, work. I remember when we beat Tennessee 38-0 in 1969 Bruiser said they had scouted Tennessee against Clemson the week before. He said Clemson ran one play that was very successful but they never ran it again the whole game. He said the quarterback would sprint to the right and the linebackers would overrun the play and then the quarterback would turn and hand it to a back going up the middle. We had a boy named Randy Reed and he had a heck of a game that day. So did Bo Bowen. Archie had a good day, too, but the big thing was not the passing game but the running game.

Bob Tyler said Vernon could whip anyone on the team except Wimpy Winther. Bob coached receivers and Vaught was the offensive coordinator and coached the quarterbacks. Billy Mustin said that Vaught would sometimes call him at twelve or one o'clock in the morning and tell him about a new play he had thought up. He'd say, "I want to try that. I think it'll work." Vaught and Spook Murphy became good friends after they both quit coaching. Coach Vaught was an avid golfer. He loved to play golf. He tried to talk Coach

Bryant into retiring a little early; told him you retire and we'll be able to get on any golf course in the country. Won't cost us a penny. But Coach Bryant wanted to set a record and I think he did the following year.

The Southern game of 1970 was just a beating. They played well and put it to us. That kid Willie Heidelburg had a great game. We moved the ball all day but couldn't score. I think the heart attack caused Coach Vaught to retire. They were all set to hire Bob Tyler as head coach and Coach Bruiser said, "I'm not exactly opposed to him but I've got a brother who's coached with Green Bay, and Arkansas and several places and has really fine credentials. He coached for Lombardi at Green Bay." And the truth was that when you put their records side-by-side, Billy had a much better record than Tyler did, so they hired him. Billy was a good coach. He didn't know how to handle people, but I think he got along with the players okay. He had his own style and he put together a really fine staff. He had Ken Cooper on the offensive line and a boy named Dick Wood as his offensive coordinator. It was a heck of a staff. Head coaches don't coach that much; it's the assistants who do the coaching. Of course, he tells them what he wants done but to actually get out there on the practice field and coach a boy and teach him the moves he needs to make, that's the job of the assistants.

WANDA ENGLAND POOLE

My favorite bowl game was the LSU rematch game in the Sugar Bowl after the Billy Cannon run. We beat them 21-0. And another one of my favorite games was the Tennessee game when we had the mule running around on the campus and all of that. That was just like whipped cream. It was wonderful.

Doc Knight was our Yankee. He'd say the prayer before every game then he'd say, "Now go beat those sonofabitches." He was just amazing. He took care of each and every boy. Every one. And all of them loved him. And then there was Nub. He was the equipment manager. Poor old Nub Sanders. The players would put him in the garbage can. They loved him. Those two were down at the field house and all the players played with them and loved them. When Ray Jr. was little he worked down there. He was still in diapers I think. I think his job was to pick up the jockey straps. Nub was wonderful. Doc Knight was a big, big piece to the puzzle. He kept them all in order and lined up. He gave them fatherly advice. He was really, really important. He'd straighten them out, too. You know, Wobble would just scream and holler and carry on, and Buster and Bruiser might yell a little, too, but the rest of them didn't do all of that hollering.

The Billy Cannon game was not the worst loss. The worst loss was when Mississippi Southern beat us in 1970 at homecoming. That was not good. We were physically ill. I can still see it. I can remember when Archie broke his arm against Houston. And I can remember when we played LSU later, and poor old Archie had his arm in a cast. And then he still did later in the Gator Bowl. Coach Vaught had a heart attack after the Southern game, but I really never thought he had one. He went to Jackson, then came back and Ray and I went out there to see him. He was just sitting in a chair. I never thought he had a heart attack. I think we all had one. I think his was just like ours. Bruiser was coach the rest of the year.

And then the next year is when the trouble started. You know, Vince Dooley called me the other day. And I asked him, "Why in the world did you send that trashy bunch of coaches over here to ruin the best program that anybody ever had?" And he said, "Who're you talking about?" I said, "Ken Cooper and all that crowd. They fired all the coaches who had been to twenty straight bowls and the new coaches wouldn't even speak to them. They were jealous. I've been wanting to ask you that a long time." And he said, "Well, they did about the same thing to me over here."

Ray coached with Billy Kinard one year. Now, Billy has changed from when he coached here. I think he's mellowed. And I love Kay, his wife. Billy comes back to the M Club now. He's been back three years now. It was the next group that was so trashy and bad.

I feel that for the years I was here in school, and then after Ray and I got married and went to New York and Canada and then came back to coach, it was all perfection. It was nothing but joy and fun. We don't remember any problems for years and years. My children can't remember anything but good about growing up.

PETE BOONE

1968-1971

I entered Ole Miss in the fall of 1968 and graduated in 1971, but I had been redshirt-ed and came back for my senior year in football in 1972, finishing after the first se-mester of the '72-'73 school year. Freshmen played on the freshman team then, and the next year I was redshirted but my redshirt year, I was one of two who traveled with the team but didn't play, which was a great experience—no pressure. That was the year that we went to the Sugar Bowl and played Arkansas. 1970 was Archie's last year and it was Coach Vaught's last year, and then I played two years under Billy Kinard: 1971 and 1972. Wobble had left the year before I came. Mustin was at the dorm at Miller Hall and Eddie Crawford was the freshman coach. That was when he had been promoted from head basketball coach to freshman football coach. His assistant was a guy named S. E. Sullins and we called him Savage Sullins. He was really a tough nut. The interesting thing back then was you could sign eighty players over two years, so you could sign forty one year and forty the next, or fifty one year and thirty the next. We ended up with maybe 38 or so on our freshman team and I think the job of the freshman coach was to run people off. Wobble had done that very well and so everything we did was designed to do that. We only had like four or five games so everything was set up to see who wanted to be there. It was more of the mental intensity or pressure pushing you in every drill, every position, every step, everything. And it was always fast-paced and then at the end you had your wind sprints. I don't know that it was quite much of a teaching period of time, other than teaching you how to survive, as it was when you got into varsity.

I finished in Grenada in the spring of '68. Jake Gibbs is my second cousin on our mothers' side. I didn't know Jake that well growing up. I knew who he was, of course, but I never really followed Ole Miss football very much. The only game I ever remember seeing was the Ole Miss-LSU game that they tied 6-6 in Oxford (1960). I think that was the only game I ever went to. I was not recruited much in high school. As a matter of fact, I was not recruited at all except by Ole Miss, and that was not a recruitment. That was a "You come to a game" type thing. Jake was playing with the Yankees then and he would come in October and coach through spring until he had to go back for spring training. He also recruited for Coach Vaught. I came to one game and went to the locker room. At the time, I was 6'4" and weighed about 180 pounds and I was a lineman, so it never dawned on me that I'd be playing college football. I never really thought about it much. And then one Monday, in November or the first of December, Jake calls up before I went to school, and he said, "Pete, this is Jake," so I said, "Jake how're you doing?" He said, "You want to come up here?" I said, "Yeah, but I got school this week." He said, "Naw. I'm talking about to play ball up here." I said, "Well, yep," and he said, "All right. I'll be there Saturday." So he came Saturday and signed me.

During my freshman year—1968—I got down to 177 pounds. It was just intense and a lot of it was not knowing what's going on. Everything was moving at lightning speed and the varsity was mean as snakes. But at the end of the year I was up to 205 and we really didn't lift weights much at all. If we did, we did it on our own. There was no organized weight lifting until Billy Kinard got there. And I think that's what put us behind a lot of schools. LSU was lifting weights in the early sixties, with an organized strength and conditioning program. We did lift on our own some.

I lived in Miller Hall my freshman year. They had us in a separate wing up on the second floor and the varsity was on the first floor. They'd come through all hours of the night. The bad time was in the spring when there were no games and no curfews. So at one o'clock in the morning they'd be beating on the door: "Get out here freshman." The hazing, I think it toughens you up and makes you know you can get through anything. I remember M Club initiation. It was brutal. I remember Paul Dongieux and Elmer Allen were coming back from New Orleans and the first night of M Club initiation was Sunday and that's when the upperclassmen had a baseball bat. The word "paddle" is not anywhere near the right word to use for what they did. One of them (the initiates) came in about half drunk and said, "All right boys, line up and give me the best you got." He bent over and they were fighting to get that bat because all of them wanted to get a swing at him. One of them took a grand slam swing and it put the initiate to his knees. Everyone else just shut up after that. We went all week doing the things we did, and then the last night was hell night, when they stripped you down, blindfolded you and tied your hands and did all sorts of things. Then they took you out and left you. Blindfolded you and left you in the woods, twenty or thirty miles from town. We had our clothes but had no clue where we were. You had to find your way back. John Gregory, who's a judge now, and I, and I think Don Leathers ended up in New Albany, and that's where John's family lived. His brother, Jack, who played for Cleveland, took us to the highway so we could thumb our way back so we missed practice that afternoon. Coach Mustin came over and said, "Where've you boys been?" I said, "Coach, we couldn't find our way back to town." We didn't want to say anything but he knew what had happened so he said, "All right," and turned around and walked off. It was just one of those unspoken things. But it was helpful in toughening your spirit.

I played under two different coaching staffs. On the Vaught staff, Bruiser Kinard was the offensive line coach. The first thing is that the players were in awe of these coaches. Once you get in and see who they are and what they've done. They've been together for years, it's ultimate respect, so you're going to do whatever you can do to please your coach. Bruiser's style was "Whip that guy in front of you. It's you and him and you've got to win." And that's a way of doing it. I don't think it's probably the most effective way of coaching. When Ken Cooper came on Billy Kinard's staff he showed you techniques: footwork, steps, all sorts of things that turned the light on. Yeah, there's an easier way to do this, because you're not always going to be stronger than the guy in front of you so you have to find leverage—ways to get your job done. I thought that staff was more in line with the day than Coach Vaught's staff toward at the end. An example would be when we were playing LSU in that 17-16—the "long clock"—game in 1972, and they had a nose guard who, the week before when they played Alabama, was the lineman of the game. He was really quick, really quick. He lined up about two or three inches from me, and as soon as one finger on me twitched, he was there and if I went this way, he fought through immediately to keep me from getting an angle on him. I quickly figured that this guy is bigger and stronger and faster than I am, so what

I did was this: he was looking at my hand and I'd go like that (wiggles his finger) and he'd jump offsides. And next series, I'd do it again, and he jumped offsides again. Of course, the officials couldn't see what I was doing. So the nose guard backed up about six or eight inches and he started looking at my face. I'd gotten him offsides about three or four times. Well, he was still bigger and faster and stronger than I was so I'd also figured out that as soon as I went to the left, he was going to fight through to the left, thinking I was trying to cut him off, so I went to the left and then came back around with my butt and my legs to shield him from the right. Those are the kind of things that Ken Cooper would teach you to do. That's not to say that the guy didn't make a lot of tackles, but what you pick up on is that there are a lot of ways to get what you need done and it does not have to be the one that's most obvious and that's in life, too.

In freshman football you only had two coaches and a graduate assistant, Mike Robbins, who later was the president of Delta State and was really a nice guy. He used to call me "Dizzy" because during that freshman year, at 175 or 180 pounds I was going around with my eyes stuck out most of the time. There's always the emphasis to win but the reason we loved to play games was it was a week we didn't work as hard. We only had two coaches and a graduate assistant and with 38 players, the only game we knew we had to win was Mississippi State because we'd get our hair cut again if we lost, just about the time you were getting where you could part your hair. The funny thing about that game is we were ahead of them the most of the game and then they scored with about a minute and a half to go. They kicked off and we took the ball on the twenty, and Frank McKeller, our quarterback, hit Bill Young with an eighty yard touchdown pass. Other than that last one, I don't remember there being a big emphasis on winning those freshman games. With only two coaches and one graduate assistant there wasn't a lot of instruction.

We had 38 freshmen on our team, with maybe two or three walk-ons. We ended up with 28 or 29 who played on the first or second team at some point in their careers. It was an amazingly high percentage. Paul Dongeaux, Elmer Allen, Preston Carpenter, Crowell Armstrong; we had some good players. We had Sentell O'Marry and Roy Alexander. They were killed on the highway between Batesville and Oxford. Someone was passing over a hill and hit them head-on.

I went to Birmingham with the 1969 team for the Alabama game. It was a festive, sort of a carnival atmosphere: a night ball game, ABC's first night game, and of course you had Alabama on the other side with Bear Bryant and then Coach Vaught here. It was one of those things where I was glad to be redshirted so I could watch the game. It was purely a game of when the clock ran out and whoever was ahead when the clock ran out. It was not necessarily one team being better than the other. Scott Hunter wasn't bad but Archie did it all: he passed and ran and his statistics were amazing. Archie was quality. I mean, he had it all. I remember probably more than anything else how devastated our team was that we lost. It was like, "Wait a minute, let's play some more. This can't end like this." Coach Vaught was really good in the locker room after the game. He let our team know that we were winners and that he was extremely proud of us for what we did. I think we missed an extra point and that put us behind the eight ball trying to catch up.

Archie had a big game against Georgia in Jackson. He got hurt before the half and we went in at halftime and they had him either in another room or over in the corner of the dressing room. He didn't come back out with the team and it was still a battle but there was a little bit of air that had left us. Then you heard the crowd start roaring and you didn't know what it was for. Archie came walking out of the dressing room with Dr. Hopkins or one of the team doctors. He and the team doctor were walking back on the field and it was just like walking on water. The crowd got excited and the players did, too, and Archie had that leadership instinct about him without even trying.

We also played LSU in Jackson. I recall that they were driving toward the end of the game and I don't know whether we intercepted the ball or not but those were games that you just stood up and watched and appreciated the level of play. I would look at those teams and their guys were so much bigger than we were: stocky and well-built offensive linemen. I remember watching Georgia and LSU both and you wonder when you're watching them and then looking at our players—and that happened for years—they were just bigger and stronger players than we were. That says a lot about the Bruiser Kinard-Coach Vaught mentality and also, the game plans. While I said earlier that our coaches may not have been that good at techniques as newer coaches were, they knew how to prepare for and coach a game. I remember when we played Tennessee, we'd take their defense and run it against them. He changed up the offense and the defense to almost run their plays. In one week's period of time, he'd change up your whole offense. It would be the same type of rollouts and stuff and a lot of stuff in the middle on both offense and defense.

The 1969 game with Tennessee—the mule game—the week of the game was unlike any other week I remember at Ole Miss. They had Steve Kiner and Jack Reynolds, two great linebackers, and Kiner was a big mouth. Somebody put a junk car right in front of the old union and they had a sledge hammer so everyone who came by hit the car with the sledge hammer. It was painted orange with UT on it and Kiner's name or something on it. We had pep rallies every Thursday but you could tell this was on a different plane. And the practices were total focus, total intensity. No one talked very much. Unlike Southern Mississippi a year later, it was total focus. I think someone dropped some fliers out of a plane, so you could tell the team was going to be ready. I remember Jim Poole, the tight end, caught a bunch of balls early, and I don't think they were ready for that. Jim had the greatest catching hands of any tight end I've ever seen. It seemed like every play that needed to happen, happened the way we wanted it to happen on offense. I think the defense was zeroed in, too. We ran Bo Bowen a lot inside. Coach Vaught would do things we hadn't done and he did it that day. I don't think we had used the tight end as much even though I thought Poole was a great tight end catching the ball but I don't think we had been tremendously successful running the ball up to that game. So I think it was a well-designed offense and defense but I also think our players were zeroed in.

The pep rallies were in front of Miller Hall and we usually went out there but I don't remember it as any sort of emotional advantage. Strangely enough, I never really heard the crowd and part of it was because what I started out doing was snapping for punts, extra points and field goals and I had to really focus on what I was doing. I had to not let anything get in my mind other than my technique and things I was going to do.

I don't know who the defensive coordinator was but we were constantly changing what we did from week to week. Buster coached defensive line and Junie Hovius coached defensive backs. I think Roland Dale coached linebackers. Johnny Cain coached offensive backs, Ray Poole coached ends, Bruiser was offensive line, and Coach Vaught had the quarterbacks. Eddie Crawford did a lot of scouting. You don't need to do that now because they swap tapes but back then you could go watch the game and Eddie Crawford was that person for us. He'd bring back what he thought their tendencies were and the type offense and defenses they would run and maybe Roland Dale would put in the kind of defense we needed to run. We had the sixteen millimeter, reel tapes, and Sunday night we would look at our game by groups—line, backs and so forth—and then we would have maybe two games of the opposing teams and what you would do is look at it together. Then, they would take the film to Miller Hall in the film rooms down below in the basement and you could go in there any time you wanted to and look at the film. I remember time and time again going in there and there would usually be a group in there on their own looking at the film and just talking to each other. So there was a sincere interest in being the best you could.

When Scottye and I decided to get married, we knew that Coach Vaught didn't like his players getting married. We also knew a couple of players on the team—Steve Hindman and maybe one other—were married. Steve Hindman would slip out every night after bed check and go to his house or apartment. The coaches knew he was doing that. And I think it was one of those things that if it had been a lesser player, maybe they would have stopped it, but Steve was a pretty good player. It reminded me of the old saying about Alabama: if they get caught cheating, then Vanderbilt gets fined. So there were a couple of other folks who I knew were going to get married that summer. I went and told Bruiser and all he did was look at me and say, "I'll get back to you," but he never did. So there were about four or five of us who got married that summer and Coach Vaught at the first meeting—we had walked into that basement in Miller Hall where we were all together—and he said, "I got one final thing I need to talk to you about. It's my understanding that some of you are married now and you know, I've never liked that. I don't think you can be married and your mind not drift from football. I don't think you can keep your mind on football but I see that it's happening and I see that it's not going to stop so I'm going to allow it." That's exactly what he said: "I'm going to allow it." And then he said, "Now the rest of y'all, I feel I need to do something for you, too, so I'm going to let you next time you get a chance to go home—Thanksgiving or Christmas or whenever—y'all can bring your cars back. You can have your cars on campus." Well the next day the whole Miller parking lot was full. The cars had been off campus.

Coach Vaught was one of those guys whom you didn't want to disappoint. You never knew if he even knew who you were other than if you were a quarterback because he spent a lot of time with them. I remember the first day he called me by name and I don't remember anything else that happened that day because I didn't believe he knew who I was. And the fact that he did was just that sort of respect that you had for the guy and so everyone wanted him to think well of them. The biggest disappointment when I felt like we really let him down was that Southern Mississippi game in 1970. They were ahead of us at the half and he came in. We did all of the regular things and then he said, "Boys, let's don't leave this field without winning that game today. Y'all got to win this game." That's the only time I ever heard him tap on us emotionally. Of course, we didn't and I think we were all just devastated by that, as much for disappointing him as for losing the game, because he asked us to step it up and we didn't. I think that game was just lack of focus. There could have been some players out the night before and there probably were, but there were players out before every other game, the same players, and just one or two. But that was not it. You've got to focus on every game and you've got to know your position, you've got to know when the other team does this, then you do that. You have got to be prepared. As you go through the week, they talk about that, and if you're not prepared during the week then you're not going to be prepared Saturday. A lot of the time you can get by with that, because you're a lot better than the other team, but if the other team is focused and they've got something that's pushing them and they're in there every day absorbing as much as they can, then you have trouble—a lot of trouble.

Southern just out-maneuvered us position by position. I remember them going around end with Willie Heidelberg. They had a quick toss and they hooked our end every time the whole game and we never adjusted. We just weren't focused enough to play them. The sideline was like you kept thinking it was going to turn but you kept worrying that it wouldn't because every time there was a chance to do something, we didn't do it. That was the year we were supposed to have a really good team and I think we did. I also think this: I think the coaches let up on us during fall practice. I don't think they practiced us as hard. I think they were worried about injuries. We had all of our offensive line back, had almost everyone back, but we didn't have the intense practices—two-a-days and all of that—that we had had before. To a certain extent the Southern game was the culmination of us not being Ole Miss, of not practicing like Ole Miss had always practiced. That's the way a lot of us felt. They had let the first team practice some, and then it'd be the second or third team. And that's just not the way Coach Vaught normally had done it, so I think some of it was that. I never mentioned that to anybody, never talked to anyone about it, but I do think there was a little pullback.

I was watching when Archie got hurt in the Houston game. That was a brutal game anyway. The two times we played them—Houston out there where they ran all over us and when I was a senior in high school Houston played here and there was blood everywhere—I mean those were big strong men and they were older guys. They didn't let age and number of years in college deter them from playing. As a matter of fact, one year we played them and the defensive backs who were going to play against us weren't even on the roster at the first of the year. The year that Archie got hurt we had that new artificial turf on the field. You knew it was bad because Archie had learned to take a beating over the years but he was in big time pain coming off the field. Then State that year was a heartbreaker. It was here, and Frank Dowsing intercepted that pass in the end zone to end the game. I remember distinctly that not one flag went our way that day. They won 19-14.

That was an up-and-down year with Archie leaving and coming back and Coach Vaught having that heart attack. I don't think we heard much about it—certainly no details—but it was after the Southern game and then we played Vanderbilt next. We just thought he would be in the hospital a day or two but Coach Bruiser Kinard took over and there was a torrential rain. They had an artificial turf and when we went out there to practice there was a hump and only the hump was out of water. We were standing on the sidelines in six inches of water and I went in to snap the ball for a punt. The way it worked back then is only two people could go in on any one play. If Wimpy Winther snapped low—he was the first team guy—then Coach Vaught would put me in on third down because he had the punter and a wide receiver who went in on the fourth down. So I think Wimpy had a low snap or something and long snaps were something I could do fairly well. I went in and the ball was heavy so I said, "I'm going to put a little more mustard on this thing because I want to make sure it gets back there to him." I snapped the ball and started going downfield and the crowd was yelling and I knew it was something bad. I thought they had blocked it because it was Vanderbilt's home crowd cheering. So I turned around and we had recovered the ball in the end zone or knocked it out of the back of the end zone, something like that. I had snapped the ball and the punter had taken two steps to his right and jumped and still couldn't touch it. I remember Coach Bruiser—we ended up winning like 26-16 or something like that—when I came off the sideline, I was stunned because I could snap the ball long. There was never a question in my mind about doing that. He said, "What did you do that for?" And I just stared at him. I didn't know what to say but it was just one of those things. I thought the headlines in the paper the next day would be "Boone Screws Up Snap," but it got lost in the footnotes. I think, strangely enough, we ended up having to punt to them and we somehow got a safety on the next series. I also think that was the only time I did that. There is a timing sequence that goes on with punts. From the time the ball moves to the time it hits the punter's hand and then how fast he gets it out so from the very first movement of the ball to the punt is supposed to be like 2.7 seconds. If it gets over three seconds there's a good chance it will be blocked. And it's like 1.7 seconds for extra points and field goals. You let the guy on the outside go—you make him go a little around, but you're not trying to block him—so if you do it right he's going to be a tenth of a second too late. For that reason, when I went out there, I really had to focus to get the ball back there on time.

The last game that season was the LSU game down there when Archie came back and played with a cast on his arm. We were hoping it would be sooner than that. The LSU game was delayed so they could run it on national TV until after the State game. If they had played it when it was originally scheduled, Archie would have been ready. It would have been the week before the Houston game but they postponed it and tacked it onto the end of the season. We thought it was just going to be a matter of Archie being Archie. There was a lot of time spent getting him physically ready, but I don't remember that he was out there practicing and doing all those things just like normal. Two things happen in real time: one is the speed picks up. You can practice all you want and I'm sure he was running and trying to stay in shape, but there's nothing like the game atmosphere where your adrenaline is going and everybody else's is flowing because the adrenaline can wear you down, too. I think Archie started out well but he had to do a lot of running and he was running around on the fly trying to make things happen. I think that they were just a lot better team than us that day. There is no question that Archie was giving it 110 percent. I think all of the energy that it took to make things happen took a toll on him. They had like three punt returns for touchdowns. Tommy Casanova had some and so did some other guy and once LSU starts going downhill, they are hard to handle.

Doc Knight was old school and he had certain treatments that you got no matter what the ailment was. You got in a tub of ice and then there was some kind of electric stimulation of your nerves and that was about it. You taped up but I never did tape my ankles. I never had an ankle problem. If you weren't bleeding, you weren't hurt. I say that with a lot of respect for him. He really did obviously know what he was talking about because we didn't have that many injuries. We didn't have a lot of pulled hamstrings and we didn't have a lot of twisted, high ankle sprains. I don't know why. It could be this: the strength and conditioning programs are so advanced now and it's 365 days a year, almost, so I think our kids are in lot better condition than we were. We never wore braces on our knees or any of that. But we weren't as big and strong as the kids are now. The speed is a lot faster now, and you get that size going that speed and you can get people hurt. I've been on the sidelines during a game and it's scary how fast things can happen in front of you with the speed and size of those guys. It's almost like when I was a senior in high school coming to watch an Ole Miss game: I couldn't believe the speed and size and velocity and intensity of the players and I can't believe it now.

Even though a lot of folks carried on with him, I think everyone respected Nub. You're dealing with some outlaws in football who are always looking for jerseys to sell, anything you could do to augment your $20 a month laundry money and Nub had to fight all of that. He was pretty good at it and even though he was small and had his physical limitations, he'd get in your face and you'd back down. He knew everything and he was really smart. He would sell our football tickets. You got four if you were traveling and two if you were not and they were worth six or seven dollars face value. What you tried to do is get someone to buy your tickets at six or seven or ten or twenty. There were times when you hadn't sold them at game time and you'd give them Nub. He'd go out and sell them and bring you back the cash. So he did those kind of things for you. He'd say, "I cudden get you but d-sixteen dollars." You just thanked him. One time Nub ran out of practice jerseys that had "UMAA" across the front. People would stuff them down their pants and go to Guess Hall and sell them for five dollars apiece. It was spring and Nub went up to Coach Vaught and said, "We ain't got anymore derseys." Coach Vaught said, "What's happening to them?" Nub said, "Dey stealing 'em." And Coach Vaught said, "What are they doing with them?" Nub said, "They selling 'em." Coach Vaught said, "Well what're they getting for them? And Nub said, "They gettin' five dollars for 'em." So Coach Vaught said, "Well go buy 'em back. That's cheaper than we can buy 'em new for."

I was a business major and had plenty of time for academics. We didn't have tutors. You took the catalog in there and went up to the Coliseum and scheduled your classes. We got to go in first so you could get all of your classes in the morning. If we were going to take a class, we would find an athlete who had taken it before and would find out which professor they had and whether the professor was accommodating. We did our own homework, our own scheduling, our own planning, all of it. We didn't have all of the things they have now, but we didn't have all of the off-season drill work that they have now either.

I think in so many ways at so many different levels Ole Miss prepared me very well for life, especially the athletic part of it. The things that you go through—the ups and downs, the pressure, the never give up, the getting in shape and doing things you didn't think you could do but did, I go through those things all of the time. Just get through the day, take the next step. There're so many different things you learn in athletics that apply to life. I'm sure I would have learned those things somewhere but that was a great way to learn them and Ole Miss was a great place to have that experience.

COOLIDGE BALL

1970-1974

I grew up in Indianola, Mississippi, and went to Indianola Gentry High School. We integrated in 1969 and 1970 but we didn't have any students from the white school come over to Indianola Gentry, so my class—1970—was the last minority class at Gentry. I had several scholarship offers and New Mexico State was one of my top choices at the time because my home boy, Sam Lacey, had been a freshman there in 1968. I also had offers from Jackson State and Alcorn and others, but Kenneth Robbins came down to see me play a couple of times and liked what he saw. The first time he came, I didn't really have a good scoring game but I played okay. The next time he came I had a super game: about thirty points and 17 or 18 rebounds.

New Mexico State had just finished third in the nation and had two players on that team, Sam Lacey and Jimmy Collins, who got drafted. There were people who wanted me to go there and I thought that was where I wanted to go at first. I think in February of 1970 I took a visit out there. My high school coach went with me. One visit doesn't give you a good feel of what is going on. You get to see a game and you move around the campus some. I never had signed a letter of intent with them. Then, I went out there and worked that summer and after a month, I decided "This is not where I want to be," so I called the recruiter at Ole Miss, Kenneth Robbins, and said, "I'm not going to New Mexico State. Would you have a scholarship available?"

At that time he was concerned about whether I had signed a national letter of intent but I told him I had not signed anything. So he checked to see and I called him back after the 4th of July. He said they didn't have any record of me signing anything. He asked, "When are you coming home?" I said, "I'm going to stay out here the month of July and I'll be home the first of August." They had six scholarships that year and five freshmen, so there was one scholarship left. I told him I wanted to come to Ole Miss and he said, "Call me when you get back and we'll come down and sign you." So I got home around the 1st of August and he came down to Indianola and signed me for Ole Miss and the rest is history.

Freshmen were still playing freshman ball when I entered. My freshman team went 22-2. We played the varsity at different locations throughout north Mississippi and we beat them four out of seven. That was the Johnny Neumann team and it kind of teed them off that the freshmen could beat the varsity. My class was the best class Ole Miss had ever gotten up to that point. The 1969-70 class with Johnny Neumann was good and we had another good class after me.

Some people in my hometown, because of the past with James Meredith, didn't know anything positive about Ole Miss but I came up here in 1970 in February for a recruiting visit and Ole Miss was playing Kentucky. Dan Issel was playing and of course, nobody could hold Dan Issel. At that time they could introduce players at halftime. There was a white kid there from Alexandria, Louisiana, named Steve Khoury. He was a 6'7" kid, president of his class, so they introduced him and he got a great ovation. Then they introduced me: "Coolidge Ball from the Magnolia State," and I got a great ovation and the bigger applause I guess because I was from Mississippi. When I decided to come to Ole Miss some people said, "I can't believe you are going to Ole Miss of all the schools you can go to." I told them, "Have you been to Ole Miss?" They would say, "No," and they would talk about things they had heard in the past. I knew that a lot of what they were talking about was in the past, because that was eight years after James Meredith and things had changed a lot since then, from 1962 to 1970. I was treated like any other eighteen-year-old on campus. It was a good fit for me and I just loved it.

Johnny Neumann was a sophomore when I was a freshman and led the nation in scoring with a 40.1 points per game scoring average, then he went pro. Cob Jarvis was the head coach at that time. Ken Turner was one of the assistants and Kenneth Robbins was the top assistant. On my freshman team we had Keith Michael from Georgia, Chuck Hedde from Illinois, and Tom Jordan from Bell, Tennessee. Tom scored from the outside and we called him the blond bomber. The others in that class were Doug Kenny from Illinois, Fred Cox from Bainbridge, Indiana, and Tommy Sykes, who was from Philadelphia, Mississippi.

They had cut out most of the hazing when I came along. There was still a little of it in football. When you go through M Club there was also a little of that but after my first year on the varsity I told them, "I'm not for all of this hazing." I lettered but I told Danny Hooker, "If I've got to go through hazing, then I just won't get a letter." I think Cob Jarvis knew I was serious about it and he told the varsity players, "Now y'all take it easy on all the basketball players." I wasn't going to be tolerating all of this stuff and I didn't believe in it anyway so they were very lenient with us. This was just a different era and our teammates respected me and anything they ever wanted from the coaches they always came to me and said, "Coolidge, would you go talk to Cob Jarvis and the coaches?" And I'm looking at them thinking, "You're white and I'm black." So I'd say, "They'll probably listen to you better," but they'd say, "No they'll listen to you, Coolidge," so I was the spokesperson for the team.

There were about 100 minority students on campus when I was here. Now it's up to about 14 percent. My sophomore year Omega Phi Psi was the first black fraternity to come on campus. I think the guys were initiated my sophomore year. I lived in Guess Hall right on the hill. The football players lived in Miller where the cafeteria was and we lived up on the hill in Guess with all of the baseball and basketball players on the third floor. We ate at the cafeteria at Miller Hall, which was very special, because we had the top meals you could get. At that time I think they were spending about $15,000 a month, which was a lot of money. Now that wouldn't get you through a whole week.

Games that stood out: we played Texas, which had about 34,000 students in 1972 and we had 7500 or 8000. I remember going to class on campus and if you drove to class you didn't have any problem getting a parking place. We played a home-and-home with Texas, and I had good games against them. I rebounded well whether I scored well or not. I think I had double-doubles in both of those games.

I always rebounded well because I had a sense for the ball. I knew where the ball was coming off the board and I made myself available to get there. Texas was a good team. We played Long Beach State, which was coached by Jerry Tarkanian before he went to UNLV, where he coached so many years. Adolph Rupp was coaching at Kentucky—he was a legendary coach—and he gave me a great compliment when they asked him who was the best freshman he had seen that year. He said, "Coolidge Ball is the best freshman I've seen this year." He retired after my freshman year and Joe B. Hall took over so I never got to play against Coach Rupp. We didn't beat them until my junior year. I scored like twelve points and had a dozen rebounds. It wasn't a high-scoring game.

When I went on the road I always got respect from the other coaches, players and fans. One thing about athletics, people respect good athletes. They are just drawn to the athletes. I tried to carry myself a certain way—I didn't try to be smart or get in any fights—but I was aggressive and played hard. I would knock your socks off to get rebounds, but it was all in the game. I didn't play dirty or anything like that. It's the way you carry yourself, so I got respect on the road.

I didn't have any problems on the road or at home. I don't remember ever being called a name or hearing any negative words or anything like that. I'm not going to be naive; there were probably some negative words or insults said, but I didn't hear it. That's just part of it. My roommate for a year was Fred Cox. Barry Jacobs, who was writing a book on the first blacks in the ACC and the SEC, interviewed Fred Cox. Fred said that they couldn't have picked a better person to represent the University as a minority than Coolidge Ball so that really made me feel good coming from one of my teammates. I was co-captain of the team my junior year and captain my senior year. I got the respect of my teammates, which is what you get when you are a good, polished ballplayer. That's why they wanted me to be their representative and to go talk to the coaches.

I was unanimous All-SEC freshman team and made the All-SEC team all four years, although I don't think I was ever first team. I was the school's most valuable player my three varsity years, which was really special, because my teammates voted me that.

When I look back and think about my time at Ole Miss it's just a great feeling: that red and blue and all the great memories. I met beautiful people here and I talked to people who had never really had a conversation with a minority person. I remember this guy came up to Guess Hall and like I said, people are always drawn to athletes, and I didn't have any problem talking to anybody. If they were respectful and wanted to talk, then I talked to them. This gentleman came up and we talked about different things, He was just so impressed and after it was over, he said, "Coolidge, I'm impressed. I had no idea that you could talk about anything besides basketball. To be honest, in my family, we didn't talk to minority students or people that much. That's just how my family was." I said, "I don't hold that against you." I met a lot of beautiful people and I didn't have to talk basketball. Most of the time I didn't want to talk basketball anyway.

ARCHIE MANNING

1967-1971

I was recruited by a graduate assistant named Roy Stinnett. Coach Wobble Davidson usually recruited that area and he came by but they kind of turned me over to Coach Stinnett. He had been a high school coach at Clarksdale High School and had gone up to Ole Miss to work on a masters. He went on to become a long time administrator at the University of Chattanooga. Roy was a really good fellow, a good coach. He was a little older than the typical graduate assistant who were usually some 22 or 23 year old. Roy was probably in his thirties and wasn't like a kid. I hit it off with Coach Stinnett. He was recruiting me and some boys from Clarksdale and Bubber Tollison from Ruleville. Jim Carmody from State recruited me. Coach Paul Davis was over there at the time and they recruited me hard. Tulane came in late and offered me, so those were the only three offers I had: Ole Miss, State and Tulane. State really recruited me hard because Ole Miss had already locked up seven other quarterbacks. Coach Vaught always recruited a lot of quarterbacks and fullbacks. He thought that in Mississippi high school football, it seemed like a lot of times the players you wanted played those two positions. Of course, a lot of players changed positions. Fullbacks became linebackers and even defensive ends and quarterbacks were moved to a lot of different positions. All of us stayed in the quarterback position.

Bob White was one of those eight quarterbacks who signed my year. He was from Meridian, where Bob Tyler was the head coach. They had a really good team and really threw the ball around and Bob was named All-American quarterback. I was fortunate to get to play in the Mississippi High School All-Star game and in that game, Bob Tyler was the coach of the north team. Of course, Bob White was his quarterback and started the game. He hurt his knee in the early part of that game. I went in and had a good game. We beat the South that night something like 55-33. I threw four touchdown passes and ran for one. Bob never really recovered from that knee injury. We went on up to Ole Miss and he rehabbed his freshman year. He played a little bit in one freshman game and he never played again. It was a pretty serious injury.

When we went up there and played freshman football under Wobble Davidson they had a chart up every day of where you stand. So there were eight quarterbacks on that list the first day. The first team wore red and the second wore blue and the third wore white, right on down the line. We had green and every kind of color. That's really for just one day. So the first day I wore red and was on the first team but I don't think I would have been there if it hadn't been for that All Star game. Really, most of those quarterbacks were from the Big Eight Conference, which were the bigger schools around the state. I was from Drew in the Delta Valley Conference and Brent Chumbler was from Centerpoint, Alabama.

That freshman year was a tough year. In those days you could sign forty players and then we had probably 25 or thirty that walked on. So you had a lot of players out there and I think really part of Coach Wobble's job as freshman coach was to run some people off or to see who really wanted to be there. You didn't play but four games so it was three weeks between every game. That's a lot of practice time but they were evaluating us with a lot of hitting to find out who wanted to stay. It was a tough year, and Coach Wobble's policy was that in those first two games, you played both ways. So if I was first team quarterback, I was also the free safety. If Skipper was starting at left guard, then he was the starting inside linebacker. So he just walked across the line of scrimmage and played a comparable position. That's what we did against LSU and Alabama. LSU beat us and I didn't play very well at quarterback. I did intercept a pass but I remember getting beat for a touchdown from my safety position.

The next game was at Alabama and I didn't play that well at quarterback. I kind of got my bell rung a little bit but I intercepted three passes that day and I was a little worried when we went back to Oxford. I knew that the last two games we would only play one way and I was afraid I was going to be Wobble's safety rather than his quarterback. But fortunately I kept my red jersey at quarterback all that year. I never did lose my red jersey and then I had a really good game against Vanderbilt and Mississippi State. When we played Vanderbilt, it was a wet day. It rained and they came into Oxford with the best freshman record they had ever had. They had just tied Tennessee up in Knoxville so they were 2-0-1 and had a real good freshman team. That was when we converted and played one way. We came out throwing and beat them 80-8. Wobble had no mercy. At halftime, we had them 35-8 and I thought Coach Wobble would say, "We're going to back off a little bit," but he told us, he said, "Men. I've always had a theory: if you get somebody down you just kick the shit out of them." He said, "I'll worry about the coach after the game."

Wobble was hands on with the quarterbacks. He was hands on with everything. He had Eddie Crawford who was an assistant and happened to be head basketball coach at the time. He had some graduate assistants like David Wells, who went on and spent years at Ole Miss in the Athletic Department. There was a guy named Rocky Fleming who had been a receiver at Ole Miss and was from Laurel. But Wobble had his hands on everything, believe me. He wore these sunglasses and when Cool Hand Luke came out I think all of us thought he was like that guy who wore sunglasses in the movie. Wobble had a job as a freshman coach: to evaluate and kind of weed out. He was a very intelligent man with a great vocabulary. He felt that the way to communicate with 18-year-old college freshman is to kind of get down and dirty. His language had a purpose and I don't think most of the time around other people he was a bad language guy. He just felt like with 18-year-old freshmen, he wanted to get our attention. And believe me, he did.

I didn't play freshman baseball. I wanted to play baseball. Actually, I was supposed to play basketball and baseball but by the time we got through with that freshman football season, we had to weigh in every day, and I was writing on the weight chart, 163, 164 but I was lying. I was under 160 so I really needed to gain some weight. I knew I wanted to play first team quarterbck the next year. Bruce Newell was graduating. They had a backup quarterback named Terry Collier—a good guy—but I felt like I needed to gain some weight when I finished freshman football so I didn't need to play basketball.

Coach Vaught didn't let me play baseball that spring. We had an early spring training. He said I needed to get bigger and put on some weight. That spring, I earned the number one quarterback job. He didn't announce that until the summer but I came out of spring training running first team. I played my sophomore year and then he let me play baseball my sophomore and junior years. The 1969 baseball team—my sophomore year—won the SEC, won our regional and went to the College World Series. I didn't have a great year. It was a big transition for me coming from kind of small town baseball but I was the shortstop and was a contributor and we had a good team. The next year I led the SEC in batting average most of the year. I had a better year but we didn't win the conference and didn't advance. I didn't play my senior year because I had broken my arm and had a plate in my arm and had already been drafted by the Saints. I played two years for Tom Swayze and thoroughly enjoyed it. Coach Swayze was a disciplinarian and a really good baseball coach. You know, it was kind of unique. Here was Coach Vaught's recruiter all of those years. He had to sign off on every quarterback, even though Roy Stinnett might have been recruiting, or Wobble, or whatever assistant coach, Tom Swayze had to sign off on every quarterback. So he came and signed off on me. I wanted to play baseball for him. The baseball players were really good to me. I got a lot of attention on the road. It wasn't always good attention. It was harassment from the fans and the students sometimes. I got recognized on the road. The baseball players were good-natured about it and had fun with it but they did accuse me of being Coach Swayze's pet and reflecting now on it, I probably was his pet a little bit, but he'd jump my ass just like he'd jump anybody's ass. I think he did it a few times because he knew everyone else thought I was his pet. He was a fun guy to play for.

I was drafted out of high school by the Atlanta Braves and of course I didn't go. Then, you couldn't get drafted again until you were 21 years old, so I turned 21 at the end of my junior year and I got drafted by the White Sox. To go with them I would have had to pass up my senior year of football and I wasn't going to do that so I didn't go. Once you get eligible for the draft and don't go, you're eligible for the next draft six months later. So that January of 1971 at the same time I was drafted by the Saints, I got drafted by the Kansas City Royals and six months later, got drafted again by the White Sox. So I got drafted four times. I never really considered playing professional baseball. I was going to college. I wasn't going to sign out of high school. My dad wasn't going to let me do that—not go to college. And then by the time I got drafted again my junior year I had my eyes on pro football and thought I had a better chance of getting to the big leagues in football. You can rot in those baseball minor leagues.

My sophomore year we beat Alabama 10-8 in Jackson. Anytime you beat Alabama it's a big win. That was a defensive game. I thought we were better than they were. They were a good defensive team and we were really glad to come away from that game with a win. I think I got banged up a little bit. Coach Bryant came to the dressing room after the game. Coach Vaught called him "Paul," and they were good friends. I had never known anything but "Bear Bryant." Coach Bryant was good about that. He was good about coming to your dressing room and shaking hands with some people, always saying good things. At the end of the season we tied State 17-17. State had a good passing game. The SEC in those days was still a run-the-football conference. State had a good passing game, had a quarterback named Tommy Pharr. He had a couple of good receivers. Sammy Milner, who I think we lost a year or two ago, was one of them. We weren't doing much on offense. They were really getting after us. We drove the length of the field late in the game, scored a touchdown and kicked the extra point to tie them. I'm not sure that people look on a tie game as being good, but I've always had pride in that drive because we were fixing to get beat. It was late when we scored, and people questioned Coach Vaught a little bit for not going for two right there but I thought he did the right thing. We were really about to get beat and we didn't need to lose that game. It was hard driving down there and scoring, so I think he did the right thing. That put us 6-3-1 with two quality wins right there: Alabama and LSU. We had an embarrassing loss to Tennessee (31-0), the worst game I ever played in my life. Houston beat us and Georgia, the SEC champions, beat us. We had a good team and we lost to some pretty good teams there. We went to Memphis for the Liberty Bowl and beat a good Virginia Tech team. It was the coldest game I ever played in, colder than Buffalo, Green Bay, or Minneapolis when I was playing professional ball. Virginia Tech had us 17-0 and we came back and whipped them. That was a good win and a good way to finish. They scored on two trick plays. Jerry Claiborne was their coach and he was a really fine football coach for years there and at Kentucky. They were a tough bunch. Their strong safety was Frank Beamer, who coaches there now. We settled in after they got us down. Steve Hindman was one of the toughest guys I ever played with. I was a sophomore and he was a real boost to me. In a way I took a little of his thunder. He had led the SEC in rushing the year before and carries but we didn't run him that much my sophomore year. But he never fretted, never complained; he kind of had it figured out. He wasn't trying to go to pro ball; he was going to med school. I remember one day we were in the huddle in spring training and a manager came running there and said, "Steve, there're two scouts up there: one from the Eagles and one from the Cardinals, and they want to know if they can talk to you after practice. Steve said, "They don't need to talk to me. I'm going to med school." He's a good guy and boy he was a tough, tough guy.

My junior year we lost to Kentucky 10-9. I can say in my three years playing for Coach Vaught, that was the only game that I felt like we had a bad plan. I never asked him about it. We had a pretty good balanced team and we went into Kentucky and it was hostile there and they had a new coach. We ran a power running game that night. The game we were going to have the next week against Alabama was going to be one of the biggest games ever because it was going to be a national TV night game, which they had never done before. So Alabama on TV in Birmingham all over the country. I'm pretty sure Coach Vaught thought we could beat Kentucky so let's save some stuff for Bear Bryant. We went in there and could have beat them with that power game and we fumbled and missed a kick, but that's football. One of the great coaches I played for in pro ball was Bud Grant and Bud always said, "It's all between the ears." You can't just roll your helmet out there and beat Kentucky. You got to go whip 'em. They beat us and I think because of that the next week in that memorable Alabama game, we let it all hang out. We moved it up and down the field, but that fumble right before the half was a killer. It was a freak game in 1969 to have a game like that, because Alabama went up and down the field, too. Teams do that now, throw for four touchdowns and 500 yards, but back then that was amazing. Floyd Franks caught 13 or 14 passes and back then that was unheard of.

I got my bell rung in the Georgia game in Jackson that year. I had a doctor call me the other day. He was a Georgia fan and his daddy was a Methodist minister. They were at that game. He said, "All these years, our family has had a little saying. When anything comes up, we say, "Uh, Oh!" They kept me in at halftime and Doc Knight was working on me a little bit so when I came out it was kind of funny there. Our dressing room was on the other side of the stadium from our bench, so I had to come out and walk across the end zone. Georgia had the ball and the Ole Miss fans cheered pretty big and he told me his daddy looked at him and said, "Uh, Oh!" They've been saying it ever since. He wanted to tell me that. It's been forty-something years ago.

Coach Dooley has always talked about that, too. He's coaching and hears this roar from the Ole Miss fans and Georgia has the ball. He can't figure it out. Fortunately we did come back and beat a good Georgia team, I mean a really good Georgia team. We had been picked to win the SEC but had lost two one-point games—Alabama and Kentucky—and we still had Georgia, who had won the SEC, LSU—the best defense Charlie Mac ever had—Tennessee, who was rolling and looking at a national championship and Houston, who was just loaded. The score against Houston (25-11) was not even close to being indicative of how bad they beat us over there in the Astrodome. They were like a pro team.

Looking back on the Tennessee game in 1969, it was so much fun to see the campus that riled up for a game. Of course, Coach Vaught had a lot to do with it. He was good at stirring things up with what they had said the year before. They just beat us really badly the year before in Knoxville. When Peyton—he's kind of a historian; he was always more interested than the other boys in my career—went to Tennessee he dug out the film of that game and he converted it from 16 millimeter to VHS and he sent it to me and on the outside of the tape, he said, "Dad, you were bad." And I was. It was just awful, so it was so much that went into the game the next year. The biggest thing was, we were playing good. We had two SEC losses and even though we had lost to Houston, we had beat LSU, which had a heck of a team, and of course, we had beat Georgia. So we were just playing good. It just built up on campus. I don't think I've ever been a part of anything like that where we were so excited and ready to play. Just really, really ready. Tennessee was good. They might have been headed for a national championship. They were undefeated and probably one win away from going to the Orange Bowl. So it wasn't so much that we beat them. It was that we beat them so bad. We jumped them. It wasn't indicative of the difference in talent; it was just our day and we beat them physically. We never let them get going. I know right before the half, we had them 21-0 and lined up for a long field goal and the kicker didn't hit it good, just knuckled it down there. It hit the cross bar and went in, so it was just our day.

I think Coach Vaught wanted to be careful with me. I had played so bad the year before and I wanted to have a big day. He wanted to tame me down a little bit and make me remember that we could run the ball and be a good balanced team and didn't have to throw, throw, throw, so he let me call the plays but he didn't want me to get carried away with payback. We had a great plan: Bo Bowen had a great day. Randy Reed ran hard. Man he ran hard. You know, Tennessee calls it "The Massacre in Jackson." When Peyton went to Tennessee and I went to games up there for four years, it was unbelievable how many people talked about that game. They are pretty nice people: they never said anything about the game with us the year before. Of course they've won a lot of big games, but I remember the year before. I really stunk up there in Knoxville but they were pretty nice. No one mentioned that; they just talked about the massacre in Jackson. It was a 69 point swing in 1969. That conference has some strong teams: Florida, we didn't play, but they had a good team. Tennessee was good. Auburn had Pat Sullivan and was coming on. Lot of good teams there. Our 7-3 record got us in the Sugar Bowl so that kind of tells you what kind of year it was. I think Coach Vaught's influence and our late season play got us that bid. Of course, we still had to play State but we weren't going to screw that up. We had to go to Starkville and play them in the rain but we got after them, too.

Bob Tyler came up to Ole Miss either my freshman year when Bob White came or he may have come my sophomore year. Coach Vaught hired him to coach receivers and he was really a good coach and a good guy. After my junior year, I had had a good year and I got invited to all of these award banquets. Coach Vaught didn't let me go alone. I wasn't a bad boy, but it was just protection. There were some agents out there at that time. It wasn't like it is now, but he always sent a coach along. I went a lot of places where no one else had a coach with them but Bob Tyler went a lot. He was a good coach and a good guy. I thought he made some really good contributions. He had been a high school coach and had a good passing game. I really liked what he did at Ole Miss with Riley Myers and Floyd Franks and Buddy Jones, our wide receivers, the way he developed them. They really got better. But the plan was always Coach Vaught's. He was the offensive coordinator, but I felt that Coach Tyler made some fine contributions.

Jake Gibbs also coached me. He was playing with the Yankees so his baseball season didn't end until almost October but he lived in Grenada and would drive up every day. Jake would be at the meetings and would work with the quarterbacks. He'd be a little late getting there but he worked with us. I treasure those years of being with Jake and him coaching us. He was my hero growing up in Drew and following those great Ole Miss teams. Number 12 was my hero and so it was great to be able to play for him and have him coach me and become a good friend. To this day, I love Jake Gibbs.

I pulled a groin muscle against either Kentucky or Alabama because I had it when we went to Georgia. That was the worst thing I could have because our game was sprint-out. I was a sprint-out passer and it's hard to sprint-out when you've got a pulled groin. We were able to go over to Georgia and that was a tough place to play. We beat Memphis, we beat Kentucky in Jackson. It was really hot so we were going to wear white. Coach Vaught was always going to wear white when it was hot. So Kentucky showed up with white and the night before, Coach Vaught said we're wearing white, so they got in touch with Hale and Jones, a sporting goods store, and asked if they had any blue jerseys and they did, kind of Kentucky's color. So we fixed them up with some nice wool ones. We beat Kentucky, which was always a struggle, then beat Alabama in kind of a rematch there in Jackson and after that, had to go to Georgia. That was a huge win. For us to be 4-0 I thought we might be rocking and rolling, but you just never know in football.

The Southern game was the next week. It is a great example of what Bud Grant said about football. We had beat them the year before 69-7. We should have known. Southern would be tough. They have tough kids. They just hit us in the mouth. We had some opportunities and couldn't score and they built momentum. It was a lifetime win for them to beat Ole Miss. You have to give them credit. They came in there and beat us. I know it hurt. Coach Vaught didn't recover from it. We were up fourteen zip right off the bat. We had beat them 69-7 the year before and go out there and score two quick ones early and then it's back between the ears, you think you are fixing to cruise and you start thinking, "Hell, I'm probably not going to play but a half." Something like that. It was a happy time in Hattiesburg but it was a heartbreaker for us.

We learned about Coach Vaught's heart attack the first part of the week. So a week earlier we were 4-0 and had already beaten Alabama and Georgia and were looking forward to the rest of the season. You don't think you are going to be tripped up by Southern Mississippi and lose your coach.

Houston had really dominated us the previous two years and we needed to beat them. They had talented, talented kids. You know, we didn't play many games on campus but this one was homecoming. Olivia was homecoming queen and we were playing good and getting after Houston. It was just one of those deals. I called a straight drop-back pass. We didn't do many of those and then I just got knocked down. It's not smart to put your arm out on that artificial turf when someone can come down on top of you. My arm went pop and that was it.

I met Olivia at a pledge swap. I had pledged Sigma Nu and she was a Delta Gamma and we had a little freshman swap over at the Sigma Nu house, just pledges on a week night social. I knew who she was and she knew who I was. I had played in a North Mississippi basketball tournament in Philadelphia my senior year. We played Philadelphia in the opening game. They were really good, had a good basketball program. We were excited just to go and we beat them in double overtime. She saw that game. She always went to basketball games with her daddy. Her brother Tommy was up at Ole Miss. He was a scholarship player in basketball so she followed basketball. She says I was cocky and shot a lot. That's what she remembers. She's probably right. But we met that night at the swap. I was not very active in the fraternity. You couldn't be, playing ball, living in Miller Hall. Those guys in the fraternity were so good to me. Every now and then you needed a little break and it was fun to go over and sit down with some other guys. They always made sure we were welcome. They were a good bunch of guys.

When I got recruited we all went in to see Coach Vaught. He was already a legend. I was kind of like a puppet bobbing my head and grinning. He offered you a scholarship and you said, "Yes, sir. Yes, sir. Yes, sir." And then I started playing for him and we had meetings at noon, all the coaches would come over to Miller and have lunch and then there would be little meetings after lunch by position. We would plan for practice that day. The quarterbacks always got in the car with Coach Vaught and went back over to the athletic office. We were the only ones who didn't meet in the dorm. So you'd ride back across the campus and go in and meet with him for thirty minutes or an hour. And then, when I lost my dad after my sophomore year—I had had a good year and was clearly the starter—that coaching staff was special. I have memories of situations where every one of them wanted to do what they could for me to fill that void. But I was around coach Vaught more than I was any other coach. He gave me good help during that period of time. He told me how to handle things. I didn't have a dad to go ask, "How am I supposed to deal with this?" We spent good quality time together and he was a great influence on me. He gave me good advice. Coach Vaught was a smart man and a real gentleman. I treasure that time with him. After I went to New Orleans and started playing pro ball, all those years I stayed up with Coach Vaught. We played golf together four or five times every year. When I was on campus I'd go by to see him. He'd get down to New Orleans so I always stayed up with Coach Vaught. I tell players today: "If you have a good relationship with a coach, don't let it go. Stay close to your coach." Those are good relationships. You know, a lot of people talk about the relationship that Peyton and Eli have with David Cutcliffe, so I think that's very healthy if you have that relationship. Even a high school coach, I think it's important. You know, the high school coaches don't do it for the money. The influence that high school coaches have on our young people is probably not recognized enough throughout our society.

When I was negotiating with the Saints, I had asked Frank Crosthwait, an attorney from Drew, to help me. The draft in those days was early—in January—so the Saints drafted me. The Saints called and wanted to negotiate a contract. I was talking to some agents and in the meantime, I had asked Frank to help with the agents. But the Saints wanted to meet before I had an agent, so Frank said, "For the first meeting, I think y'all ought to come to Oxford." They said okay, and Frank then said, "I think we ought to meet out at Coach Vaught's house, out at his ranch." So they came into town—a general manager and a lawyer—and we took them to lunch at the old Holiday Inn. We then went out to Coach Vaught's house. It was going back and forth about everything and it finally got down to them wanting us to make an offer. Frank wouldn't do it. He said, "Let's hear what y'all got to say." So they threw an offer out there and we thought it was a low ball kind of thing. Coach Vaught really hadn't said much said, "Damn, son, he made more than that playing here at Ole Miss!"

When I look back and think about my time at Ole Miss—all I did, all I accomplished, all the good and bad things that happened to me—my experiences at Ole Miss are one of the greatest things of my life. I really didn't share this publicly for a lot of years: when I reflect back on everything that happened to me in sports—me, my children and what they've done—I'm very proud of them and it's been some really special times. But personally, the greatest thing that ever happened to me and the greatest accomplishment I ever had was when I was named the quarterback at Ole Miss—when I became the quarterback at Ole Miss—because that was my childhood dream. And I think I was just one of thousands of kids in Mississippi who wanted to be quarterback at Ole Miss. When I was growing up eighty miles away and there were all of those good teams that Coach Vaught had, whoever was playing quarterback was my guy: there was Jake Gibbs, there was Glynn Griffing, there was Doug Elmore and Jimmy Weatherly and before Jake, Ray Brown and Bobby Ray Franklin. Those were my guys. So that's what I wanted to be and at the end of the day, that's the greatest thing that ever happened to me.